GREEK AND ROMAN SLAVERY

THOMAS WIEDEMANN

THE JOHNS HOPKINS UNIVERSITY PRESS
BALTIMORE AND LONDON

First published in the United States of America, 1981, by
The Johns Hopkins University Press, Baltimore, Maryland 21218

First published in Great Britain, 1981, by
Croom Helm Ltd, 2-10 St John's Road, London SW11

Library of Congress Cataloging in Publication Data

Main entry under title:

Greek and Roman Slavery.
    Bibliography: p. 252
    Includes index
    1. Slavery in Greece — History — Sources. 2. Slavery
in Rome — History — Sources. I. Wiedemann, Thomas E. J.
HT863.G73   1981   306'.3   80-25432
ISBN 0-8018-2515-6
ISBN 0-8018-2514-8 (pbk.)

Printed and bound in the United States of America

CONTENTS

Contents

Contents

9 THE TREATMENT OF SLAVES: CRUELTY,
EXPLOITATION AND PROTECTION

Contents

PREFACE

In recent years, the study of slavery amongst the Greeks and Romans has increased considerably. Students, and their teachers, have become generally more interested in social and economic questions than in political and military history of the traditional kind. In North America, comparisons and contrasts between the roles and conditions of slaves in the ancient Mediterranean world and in the West Indies and United States have underlain many studies of ancient slavery since the nineteenth century. Another intellectual tradition going back to nineteenth-century presuppositions has also directed attention towards ancient slavery: Marx's analysis of slave-holding as one of the characteristic types of organising an economy (or, in the debased 'vulgar-Marxist' form, one of the economic stages through which all human societies inevitably have to pass). Many of the studies on ancient slavery undertaken in Europe since the war have been initiated either by Marxist scholars, or in response to the questions posed by them. Scholars are agreed that many particular historical problems associated with slavery have yet to be solved before a comprehensive 'account' of Greek and Roman slavery can be written – and that such an analysis will effectively have to be an account of ancient social and economic patterns as a whole.

Simply because slavery was something which affected virtually every aspect of society, ancient references to it are unsystematic and occur in a wide range of sources of different kinds, epigraphical as well as literary. No selection of such sources has hitherto been published, even in the original languages; and it is not always easy for readers interested in social and economic history who do not know Latin and Greek to locate the texts and inscriptions to which books and articles about slavery appeal as their evidence. This selection is intended primarily to assist such readers. It is not intended as a substitute for a systematic treatment of the subject – something altogether more ambitious – and it is assumed that readers will be using it in combination with other books on the subject, or within the framework provided by a school or university course. Hence only a minimal attempt is made to introduce the reader to even the most basic theories about how ancient social and economic institutions functioned, or to explain different interpretations of why slavery was so widespread in Greece and Rome and what roles slavery meant — many of them naturally shared by other societies which practised slavery. It is hoped that readers who prefer historical narratives to be in chronological sequence, and believe that enough evidence exists for a diachronic picture of slavery in the ancient world, will nevertheless be able to make some use of this selection with the help of the indices.

A word of explanation may also be needed regarding the English transliteration of Greek personal names and place names. The problem is well known: in the English cultural tradition, ancient Greek names have been rendered in the form of transliterations made by the Romans. There seems to be no reason why these distortions have to be maintained in modern English — after all, transliterations of contemporary Greek names are not made via Latin; and the French and German conventions for classical names are quite different. On the other hand, Latinised versions of Greek names have become so familiar that many of them are accepted as English: this is particularly so for place names. I have there-fore refrained from spelling Socrates, Plato and Aristotle as Sokrates, Platon and Aristoteles, but have given most Greek names in a form approximating to the Greek alphabet. (Where names which are clearly Roman occur in a Greek literary text, I have generally given them in a Latinised form.) With place names I have been even less consistent; in order to avoid confusion, all but the least significant places are given in the forms in which they are most frequently referred to in English (at least by historians); most of these are Latinised, and many are given in modern (French, Italian etc.) forms. The objective has been to preserve the 'flavour' of the Greek, but not at the expense of confusing the reader.

A similar principle lies behind the rendering of certain Greek words like *doulos* and *oiketēs*; generally both have been translated 'slave'. In passages where the author may conceivably have intended an important distinction (principally in Athenaeus, No. **80**), *oiketēs* is given as 'house-slave' or some similar phrase, or in the last resort transliterated, in order to make the distinction plain.

The translations are all my own; to assist readers who wish to look up the wider context of these passages, an Index of Passages Cited is provided, with references to where the original text may be found, and to the most accessible modern English or French translations (which may be rather more readable than the literal versions here offered). It is to be hoped that there will not be too many occasions on which readers will find that a particular reference has to be checked against its context for the full significance to become clear, but sometimes this will be inevitable — Aristotle's analysis, for instance (No. **2**), can only be fully understood in the context of his ethics as a whole.

It would be impossible for me to mention by name all the friends and teachers in London, Oxford and Bristol as well as other parts of it performed. Some users would no doubt have preferred more detailed introductions to the passages selected; but on consideration it was thought better that a non-classicist reader should have to turn to a separate reference book (such as the *Oxford Classical Dictionary*) for explanations of names and events with which he might be unfamiliar, than that the amount of original material here presented should have had to be restricted yet more. The selection is limited enough as it is, and many readers will inevitably feel disappointed that some passages which they would consider crucial are omitted. Limitations of space have been keenly felt: perhaps epigraphical and papyrus evidence has suffered proportionately more than it should. But it is in the nature of a selection that a great deal of material has to be left out. References are made to parallel passages in Lewis and Reinhold's useful source book, *Roman Civilization*, and in Austin and Vidal-Naquet's stimulating *Economic and Social History of Ancient Greece*. Except where absolutely necessary, I have avoided duplicating material provided in these selections.

The omission of many illuminating passages from drama and poetry is less easy to defend. Rather than take passages out of their dramatic context (which would generally have required a detailed commentary), I have thought it better to omit such ambiguous material altogether; the hope is that when readers find a reference to such passages in any of the books or articles they are using, they will wish to look up the whole of the poem or play in question. This particularly applies to comedy, both Greek (especially Menander) and Roman (Plautus and Terence) — full of allusions to the behaviour and treatment of slaves which can be considered only in their context. Homer, too, will be conspicuous by his absence; here the defence is that, however we understand the system of slavery in the *Iliad* and the *Odyssey*, this is not the chattel slavery of classical Athens. The assumption has been that most users will be interested primarily in slavery as it appears in the classical periods of fifth and fourth century Athens and of Rome in the first centuries BC and AD. As with other institutions, there were very different forms of slavery in other times and places in antiquity; and not just the Homeric period, but Graeco-Roman Egypt and the late Roman colonate are not dealt with here.

Of course even in the two 'classical' periods there will have been major differences in the way slavery was practised in each particular Greek *polis* and Italian municipality — indeed, no doubt each individual household was unique. But a social institution like slavery does not consist merely of a series of individual cases occurring over historical time: it is a set of ideas in men's minds. The arrangement of material by themes is intended to bring out the ways in which Greeks and Romans had similar (and occasionally different) perceptions of what

Europe, who over recent years have been prepared to discuss social and cultural history with me, and who have encouraged me in the preparation of this book. Nevertheless, I must make explicit my gratitude to Professor Dr Joseph Vogt — not just for his advice and assistance but also for the kindness and hospitality he has shown to me in Tübingen. Professor Peter Brunt of Oxford and Professor Sir Moses Finley of Cambridge have given helpful advice at various stages in the preparation of this selection. Dr Peter Parsons was kind enough to answer some questions regarding papyrus evidence. I must thank Dr Oswyn Murray for first arousing my interest in this subject. Jean Bees kindly prepared the maps, Hilary Betts helped with the typing, and Mary Sheahan with proof-reading. Richard Sheahan gave constant help and encouragement.

T.E.J.W.
Bristol

ABBREVIATIONS

AVN	M.M. Austin and P. Vidal-Naquet, *Economic and Social History of Ancient Greece: An Introduction* (London, 1977); passages are cited by number.
Bruns	C.G. Bruns, *Fontes iuris Romani antiqui*, 7th edn (Gradenwitz, 1909); passages cited by number.
CIL	T. Mommsen *et al.* (eds.), *Corpus Inscriptionum Latinarum* (Berlin, 1863 -).
CTh.	*Code of Theodosius.*
IG	*Inscriptiones Graecae* (Berlin, 1873 -).
ILS	H. Dessau, *Inscriptiones Latinae Selectae* (Berlin, 1892-1916).
L&R	N. Lewis and M. Reinhold, *Roman Civilization* (two vols., New York, 1966); passages cited by number.
PG	Migne, *Patrologia, series Graeca* (Paris, 1857 -).
PL	Migne, *Patrologia, series Latina* (Paris, 1844 -).
Schwyzer	E. Schwyzer, *Dialectorum Graecarum Exempla Epigraphica Potiora* (Leipzig, 1923).
ZPE	*Zeitschrift für Papyrologie und Epigraphik* (Cologne).

Square brackets [ ] represent an editorial comment, or a restoration of a lacuna in the text.

A crux † represents that the original Greek or Latin text is corrupt or uncertain at this point.

Numbers in **bold type** refer to excerpts included in this book.

WEIGHTS, MEASURES AND CURRENCY

Attic measures:

talent (*talanton*)	= 60 minae	26.196 kg or 57.8 lb
mina (*mna*)	= 100 drachmae	436.6 gr (just under 1 lb)
statèr	= 2 drachmae	8.73 gr
drachma (*drakhme*)	= 6 obols	4.36 gr
obol (*obolos*)		0.73 gr

The stade (*stadion*) is equivalent to 178.6 m (approx. $\frac{1}{9}$ mile)

Roman measures:

libra (pound) = 12 *unciae* 327.5 gr (11.5 oz)

uncia (ounce) = 6 *denarii* 27.3 gr (0.963 oz)

denarius ('ten-As-piece') = 4 Sesterces originally 4.55 gr; during period from *c*. 200 BC to AD 64, $\frac{1}{84}$ lb or 3.98 gr; by the late 2nd century AD, it had fallen to 2.3 gr

sestertius ('HS', *ie.* two-and-a-half Asses)

As originally 10, later 16, to the *denarius*

Gold coins:

aureus = 25 *denarii*; from time of Caesar, $\frac{1}{40}$ lb (8.19 gr)

solidus from the time of Constantine, $\frac{1}{72}$ lb (4.55 gr)

The *modius* is equivalent to 8.74 litres (approx. 2 gallons or 6.5 kg wheat).

The *iugerum* is equivalent to 0.25 hectares ($2{,}523.3\text{m}^2$, $\frac{5}{8}$ acres).

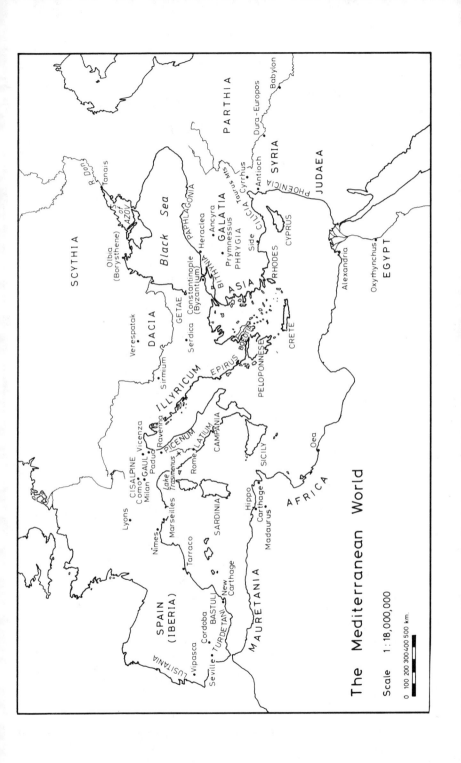

The Mediterranean World

Scale   1 : 18,000,000

0 100 200 300 400 500 km.

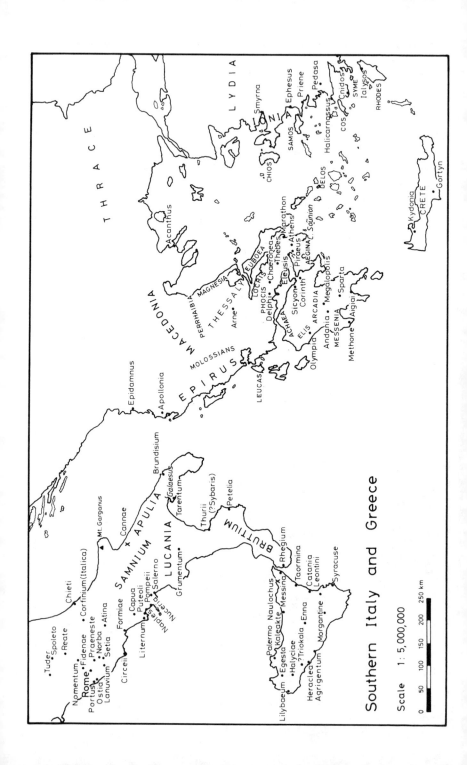

Southern Italy and Greece

Scale 1 : 5,000,000

0   50   100   150   200   250 km

INTRODUCTORY OUTLINE

Societies which formally recognise the differences between their powerful and their weaker members have a variety of institutions which try to regulate and control the ways in which the good things in life are abstracted from the latter and allocated to the former to consume or in turn redistribute as they please: forced labour, indentures, apprenticeship, rent, taxes, gifts, the 'free' market — not to mention the relationships between husband and wife and parents and children. Slavery is an accepted institution in many (but by no means all) pre-industrial societies, and may fulfil a wide variety of different social and economic roles. But wherever it occurs, it is conceived of as being at the extreme end of this spectrum of unequal relationships. A slave, like a son, may normally be called a 'boy' (*pais*, *puer*), but he does not have certain, defined obligations balanced by reciprocal rights, as a son or apprentice has, or expects in due course to obtain. Instead his whole person is absolutely under the control of another; he is another's property, part of the household unit to which his owner belongs (the owner may not be the head of that household, but a wife, son or even another slave).

Enormous emphasis is placed on slavery as the key principle of social organisation in Rome (1) and Greece — by which is primarily meant Athens, not only because much of the literary and epigraphical evidence relates to Attica, but also because that was where intellectuals codified a set of ideas which influenced educated Greek-speakers everywhere. Greek philosophers (2), because of their tendency to organise ideas in terms of pairs of mutually exclusive polar opposites, and Greek (3) and Roman (4–11) legal texts, leave us with the impression that slavery was an essential division of the household (*oikos*, *domus*), and that other bonds (excepting perhaps those of citizenship and kinship) and forms of dependence and economic exploitation were comparatively insignificant, at least in the classical period. At Rome in particular — because of the extent to which professional jurists felt it necessary to define and demarcate the rights and obligations of each status group — slavery is clearly presented as a state of absolute subjection. The slave has no kin, he cannot assume the rights and obligations of marriage; his very identity is imposed by the owner who gives him his name (12,13). And conversely Roman law guaranteed the citizen's status to such an extent (14) that that status could be forfeited only by legally recognised processes:

1

capture in war, or when a free man sold himself as a slave in order to defraud an unsuspecting buyer (*CTh*. 4, 8.6).

The uniformity of rightlessness ascribed to all slaves by legal codes of course masks the wide range of different social and economic roles slaves played, and the fact that most functions performed by slaves could also be undertaken by persons of free status. This impression that slaves and free men are totally separate components of society is not just due to the polarities of philosophers and definitions of lawyers. What Athens and Rome had in common was the absence of a dependent class of serfs as in other states — including many parts of the Greek world (80,263d). The Laconian Helots are the purest example (15): not slaves, since their relationship was not one of personal dependence upon a citizen household, but one of a community with its own internal bonds of kinship being dependent upon a conquering state (in the case of Helots, this relationship was perceived as one of permanent war). Since Greek social philosophers lacked a clear concept of serfdom, they tended to assimilate Helots and similar groups to slaves — as do modern Marxists, keen to demonstrate that 'slavery' was the typical method of abstracting surplus wealth in all Greek states.

Because Athens and Rome in the classical period developed very clear notions of the privileged status of citizens, neither society could accept extreme degrees of exploitation of one 'insider' by another. In the circumstances of peasant agriculture, smallholders are continually in danger of becoming indebted to their land-lords or to more fortunate or powerful neighbours (17,146). At Rome, they continued to be liable to forced labour and imprisonment until the debt had been paid (*addictio*); in the course of centuries, the superior power of the land-lord naturally tended to force free as well as slave tenants down to the dependent status of late Roman *coloni*. Yet Solon's attempt to prevent political discontent in Attica (16), and the pressure which Roman peasant-soldiers were able to exert upon an elite which needed them to wage war (18–19), meant that for particular (and quite separate) reasons neither Athenians nor Romans accepted that a citizen who fell into debt should formally lose his independence to another. Hence the enslaving of outsiders (already attested by our earliest sources, Homer and Hesiod) became much more economically significant than it had earlier been and continued to be in those other areas of the Greek and Roman world which continued to recognise semi-servile statuses. The failure to understand how widespread were forms of dependence outside the household (e.g. landlord and tenant) meant that Greeks and Romans found it simplest to describe semi-servile relationships (including the colonate) as though they corresponded to those of slave (or freed slave) status, since these were the concepts with which they were most familiar (20–1).

The division of mankind into the extremes of free and slave also obscures the extent to which slavery can be interpreted as a process rather than a permanent condition — a temporary phase by which an outsider is allocated a place within a society which has no natural obligations of kinship or guest-friendship towards him. In some societies in Africa and elsewhere, slavery can be seen as a 'mode of integration' through which outsiders pass prior to adoption as full members of existing kin-groups. This model has little applicability to Greece; Athenian slaves, when freed, acquired the status of Metics (resident foreigners) and continued to be subject to a wide range of legal disabilities. They could not buy land, and had to be represented at law by a citizen registered as their official patron (27). Some Greeks asserted that freedmen continued to be 'natural' slaves (80,267b). An Athenian who married such an outsider would come in for much criticism (22). Documents from the Greek world show that on some occasions freedom would be granted on condition of continuing service, so that during the years subsequent to manumission, the freed person's actual condition was little better than it had been as a slave (23–6). The evidence for Greeks taking it for granted that loyal household slaves would be set free at the owner's death appears to date only from the Roman period (94,95).

When a Roman manumitted his slave, he would (if the correct formalities had been observed) attain restricted citizen status (5,28,29). extending even to the right to inherit his patron's estate (47,92). There is evidence (30,31) that the feeling that a loyal domestic servant ought automatically to be granted freedom and civic rights after a number of years was so widespread that the 'model' of slavery as a process of integration may be useful here. This is borne out by the fact that Roman liberality surprised the Greeks (69), and is not contradicted by the new regulations introduced after the disorder of the Roman civil wars (5,6,71). Roman jurists recognised a slave's right to use his *peculium* to buy himself free from his owner (32). On the other hand the *familia rustica*, those slaves working on agricultural estates (126), received very different treatment and had virtually no opportunities to benefit from this ideal.

The ex-slave continued to be in a special relationship of dependence towards the person who had owned him or her — even when this was her husband (33). Such dependence would entail *obsequium*, deference and obedience similar to that which sons owed their father (34–6); from time to time the State intervened to reassert the inferior status of freedmen and their dependence upon their patrons in the sharpest terms (37). The position of freedmen as dependent members of their patron's household is symbolised by their right to share the family tomb (39), and the patron's right to exclude them if they were disloyal (39). But there were also economic obligations, *operae* (40–5), which show that when an owner freed a slave, he retained the right to extract economic advantage from him.

Once they had been formally accepted into Roman society, some freedmen felt the compulsion to reinforce their position by striving harder for success than most of those who were free-born would have felt necessary. Since freedmen were barred from political activity (though their sons were not, and are frequently found holding municipal office), such success had to come from attaining wealth (this does not imply that freedmen should be seen as an 'entrepreneurial class'); to bestow respectability, wealth had to come from agriculture (46). There was of course a danger that such success would be perceived as uncanny (47) and cause resentment (48). One substitute for the full social integration which could really only come from landownership was an ostentatious tomb (49). Inscriptions show the extent to which the Roman *domus* could act as a framework for the emotional as well as merely economic support and integration of rightless outsiders (50, 171–5).

Whatever the proportion of slaves who might win their freedom or be transferred to *paramone*-status in Greece, and the degree to which ex-slaves would be integrated into Roman society, this did not alter the universal prejudice felt against slaves by those who were free. The evidence is equally strong for Greece and Rome, at all periods (51–5). One area in which it was felt particularly important to keep free men and slaves separate was warfare (56). Only when the citizen community felt itself desperately threatened would slaves be called upon to fight side by side with their masters (57,58); and even then the fiction that only free men should be involved in the organised violence of warfare was normally maintained by manumitting the slaves in question first. A warlord who used slaves for fighting – even for such arduous labour as rowing in the fleet – was labelled as no better than a pirate (59–61). This attitude remained to the end of antiquity (62–3). Although the fact that slaves had the same religious needs as free man could not be denied, another respect in which their inferiority could be symbolised was their exclusion from some religious cults particularly associated with citizen status (64).

It was considered by some a paradox that slaves were not distinguished from free men by their dress (65), and the feeling that slave and free ought to be clearly separated led some Romans to question the ease with which freedmen could become totally integrated into the Roman upper class (66). There are many examples of how the barrier between slavery and freedom might be spectacularly breached in practice – as when a fugitive slave was elected to a Roman magistracy before being detected (67); such cases were particularly prone to occur in times of political instability (68), and will have been among the reasons which led Augustus to reassert the distinctions between different status groups and impose tighter regulations upon manumission **(5,6,69–71)**.

The fact that within their own household, citizens might depend upon slaves to perform certain essential services, was seen as an affront to the principle that slaves were morally worthless **(72–3)**. In a Greek law court, one way of calling into question evidence given by a slave was to play on the jury's prejudices **(74)**; and one way of blackening the reputation of a Roman emperor was to accuse him of having used the evidence of slaves to bring about the condemnation of citizens **(75)**. Even where the result was to their advantage, Romans had ambivalent feelings about relying on slaves against enemies who were citizens **(76,77)**.

There are only a few indications of how an ex-slave might come to terms with his status and career to balance this universal condemnation of slaves by those ancient writers who belonged to the citizen class **(78,79)**.

Precisely because slaves as a class were denied any moral worth of their own, they could be seen as things, the possession of which conferred status upon their owners, like other objects of material value. Although Athenaeus' list of recondite information relating to slavery is quite unsystematic **(80)**, it does illustrate that owning slaves was seen primarily as a means of showing off one's wealth, as well as a means of controlling labour. This attitude is universal in all periods of Greek and Roman (and many other) societies **(81,82)**, and paradoxically leads to criticisms of owning large numbers of slaves in the context of attacks on luxury **(83,84)**: in the ancient community, luxury – too much conspicuous consumption – defied the principle that all members of a status group ought to be equal.

Of course slavery fulfilled other functions apart from being a demonstration of wealth. It clearly did provide the head of a household with additional economic resources **(85–7)** – just as he would have a right to profit by the labour of his wife or sons. But perhaps more significantly, it was a mechanism for ensuring that services would be guaranteed to the primary economic unit, the household: a household would not have to rely upon kin, friends or contract labour if it was rich enough to afford slaves to provide services **(88)** which might only occasionally be needed, but were essential for its proper functioning.

While some suggestions can be made about how slavery fitted into the household economy, it is unprofitable to try to quantify this **(80,89–96)**. Some unsurprising general trends may be deduced, such as the existence of (some) slave-holdings in the Roman Empire which were much larger than (most) at classical Athens; but such evidence does not permit us to draw conclusions about changes in the proportion of slaves in the total population. The development of an autonomous science of economics in the eighteenth century led to an enormous emphasis on statistics, and to attempts to apply statistical methods to the ancient world (it is no coincidence that the first such undertaking was by David Hume, Adam Smith's associate in the 'Edinburgh Enlightenment'). But where both production and consumption largely occur within the confines of the household, there is only a very limited need for statistical information about the way an economy is functioning as a whole: governments need figures of manpower and taxation resources in order to plan for warfare (the Roman census: **104**), and of course accounts have to be kept for each particular household (**82**). But even if the evidence were sufficient to allow us to deduce global figures for the size and productivity of the slave population at different periods of antiquity, such figures would be much less illuminating than in a society in which economic activity is regulated by a centralised 'market' or by redistribution from a single centre.

Since it was the person, not the labour, of a slave that was bought, attempts to compare the efficiency of slave and free labour on the basis of ancient evidence for prices (**97–100**) are fruitless. There is insufficient evidence to assess the extent to which prices reflect the greater or lesser availability of slave labour at different periods and in different areas in terms of a 'free market' model.

Slavery was universal in Greece and Rome, even if its role cannot be quantified; so it is surprising that we are told so little about slave-traders, except that they were disliked (**101,102**). There is some evidence about the ports-of-trade through which slaves entered the Greco-Roman world from outside (**103**). At all times in antiquity Greek and Roman cities had laws regulating slave sales: the increasing complexity of such regulations does not reflect increasing difficulties in obtaining slaves (**104,105**).

As regards the sources of slaves, there is plenty of evidence for the role of piracy, especially during the second century BC, when the political insecurity of the Eastern Mediterranean resulted in the deracination of particularly large numbers of human beings (**106,107**). These persons were transferred to Rome, as the centre of wealth (**108**); Roman writers knew how traumatic the experience of enslavement was (**109**), and the slave rebellions of 134–70 BC show that household slavery was totally unable to integrate such great numbers of newcomers into Italian and Sicilian society (Chapter 11). Despite the greater security provided by the emperors, illegal kidnapping continued as a source of slaves, even in Italy (**110–12**). Even more important was capture in warfare – not always to be distinguished from piracy; again, the insecurity of the second century BC greatly increased the number of rightless persons who had somehow to be fitted into the society of their conquerors (113–19). The increase in the number of available slaves was surely a result and not a cause of these wars; although booty was clearly always an incentive to wage war, we are not justified in assuming that Greeks or Romans waged war because they needed slave labour.

Another group of human beings towards whom no one felt any obligations were babies exposed to die by parents who did not want them. If anyone wished to raise such a foundling, he could treat him as a slave (120). Under Roman law, if the child had inherited freedom from its parents, nothing could prejudice that status (121,123), although in late antiquity the foundling's right to have his freedom vindicated tended to be circumscribed by the requirement that he pay back the cost of his upkeep over the years (122–3).

The extent to which the slave population was maintained by home-born slaves rather than continually replenished by imported outsiders is controversial. Certainly home-born slaves (*oikogeneis, vernae*) were more highly regarded than slaves bought from outside the household; but it does not follow that female slaves were bought primarily as potential mothers (124).

Enslavement to the state as the result of condemnation in a court of law was a major source of forced labour in the Roman Empire, but it should not be treated as chattel slavery in the strict sense (125).

Roman sources recognised a division between 'urban' slaves, employed to provide services at the owner's residence (whether at Rome or elsewhere), and those he kept primarily as a labour force on his 'rural' estates (126), but this was a distinction of status as much as of economic function. Slaves cannot be seen as a homogeneous economic class — while the jobs allocated to them tended to be the most unpleasant and dangerous, there were no jobs which slaves performed perforce which might not also be done by freedmen or the free-born, if poverty reduced them to the level of having to seek employment (this was as true of domestic jobs like nursing as of handicrafts or agriculture). Then as now men could be found to undertake the most dangerous and demeaning activities if they were paid enough (for free men as gladiators, see *CTh*. 15, 12.2). So it was not because no other source of domestic or skilled craft labour could be found that Greeks and Romans kept slaves; the words *oiketēs* and *famulus* apply to free as well as slave household servants. Rather, the existence of slaves gave the powerful additional opportunities to display their wealth by keeping more dependants, and giving them more specialised functions (127–34). Unproductive jobs could be found to enable an old slave to be displayed to visitors (doorkeepers, 135); and ideally the relationship of personal dependence on the head of the household guaranteed freed slaves their maintenance when they reached old age (136).

Apart from services within the household, slaves and freedmen would be found performing those services perceived as 'marginal' in terms of the ancient economy. The status of craftsmen varied in different Greek and Roman societies; everywhere it was considered inferior to that of the producers of 'natural' wealth through agriculture. The same applied to trade and financial dealings: the status of these activities was lower in proportion as they were more dangerous and risky, and a high proportion of those involved in them were slaves or freedmen, often working with capital advanced by the head of their household (64,137, 139). The high proportion of slaves and freedmen attested in industry and commerce does not imply that Greek and Roman chattel slavery expanded in order to provide labour in periods of hypothetical 'industrialisation' in seventh and sixth century BC Greece, or second century BC Italy.

As in virtually all societies before the early nineteenth century, agriculture was of far greater importance than industry, commerce and mining combined, and any assessment of the importance of slaves as producers (rather than as symbols of wealth or providers of specialised services) must concentrate on agriculture. Even though the evidence for the use of slaves in agriculture in classical Athens is sparse, it was clearly taken for granted that wealthy farmers would have slaves to assist them (139); philosophers advocated a systematic division of the ideal society into citizen landowners and slave labourers (140). The massive influx of slaves into Italy in the second century BC greatly strained the traditional patriarchal relationship between master and slave (83); whether or not slaves actually constituted a majority of agricultural workers, they were clearly a major source of labour for the rich (141), and enabled them to own and work *latifundia* (not so much large single estates as conglomerations of adjacent holdings) and go in for large-scale ranching. The danger this constituted to the survival of the peasantry was widely recognised (142,143). There were some suggestions that slave labour was less productive than free (144); certainly the low level of technology in antiquity and the need for constant direct supervision meant that the use of slave gangs could not result in appreciable economies of scale (145,146). Roman agricultural handbooks include detailed discussion of slaves as labourers and herdsmen (147–50); the crucial role played by the estate-manager and his wife comes through clearly (149,151–7).

Greek and Roman communities as well as individuals would use slaves to perform those services considered difficult or inferior (158–61). Because the slave was an outsider not involved in controversies between citizens, he could be entrusted with supervisory functions such as responsibility for the city accounts or weights and measures (162–4). On the other hand the principle of the rapid circulation of office-holding in ancient communities meant that supervision of state slaves was often ineffective (165); in practice such slaves had considerable freedom. At Rome, they might in time be manumitted, like other slaves (166).

In imperial Rome, responsibility for public works was shared between slaves belonging to the state and those belonging to the imperial household, the *domus Caesaris* (167) — one household for which the evidence is relatively detailed. The unique status of the emperor gave his slaves and freedmen a privileged position — such slaves were allowed to marry citizen-women (168), and their status was such that people might enrol themselves in this household voluntarily (169). Evidence from literature and inscriptions throws light on the specialised household and administrative tasks of these slaves and freedmen (170–5). Especially under the Julio-Claudian emperors, individual freedmen held positions of enormous influence and responsibility — the imperial administration was still regarded primarily as the emperor's private concern, and free Roman citizens were not at first willing to sacrifice their independence by serving in another's household. It was only after the imperial system had existed for a century that members of the upper classes accepted appointment to permanent administrative posts; by the fourth century, citizens had come to replace slaves throughout the administration, but not of course as domestics and craftsmen. Emperors continued to turn for objective advice to persons in their immediate entourage who as outsiders had no personal links with the citizen group (typically, eunuchs). Not surprisingly, this provoked enormous resentment on the part of the citizen elite (176).

The influence and wealth which some slaves could attain as members of the *domus Caesaris* only underline the total powerlessness normally associated with slave status. A particularly vivid symbol of this was the use of torture to extract evidence from slave witnesses in courts of law, both in Greece (177) and Rome (178); the limitation was that torture could only be applied if the owner had offered the slave as a witness — though at Rome the general rule that a slave (or freedman) could not testify against his master or patron did not apply in cases of treason (75,179). The lack of concern for the physical integrity of slaves is exemplified by the *SC Silanianum*, requiring the interrogation under torture and execution of all slaves who happened to be present and had offered no help when their owner was murdered (180).

The tension between the slave's total rightlessness in law and the fact that he was a human being meant that there had to be limits to the brutality which society would tolerate in practice — but these rules had to be phrased in such a way as not to challenge the absoluteness of the owner's theoretical rights. It is not clear whether at Athens the killing of a slave by his owner was forbidden by law (181) rather than by religious (182) or social (183) sanction. At any rate an Athenian slave-owner was free to use violence to force his slave to do what he pleased (184). At Rome, the rights of heads of households to punish their slaves, like their sons, as they saw fit, had been absolute in the early republic. The general tendency for these powers to be restricted by legislation applied also to the right to execute children and slaves, which was transferred to ordinary state judges (185–7). A more effective form of protection for a slave was the principle that as a piece of property, anyone who harmed him attacked his owner's rights — even though at Rome (as at Gortyn, 3) damage to a slave cost less than the same damage inflicted upon a free man (188,189).

Such principles could not effectively protect slaves against their own masters; the typical example of extreme sadism was that of Vedius Pollio and his lampreys (190). It is difficult to assess how widespread or 'normal' such degrading treatment was; slaves certainly had to do unpleasant work in horrifying conditions, but it should be remembered that work in the treadmill (191) or imprisonment in *ergastula* (not referred to by Cato and Varro) were considered punishments. The conditions of slave miners (192) were frequently shared by free workers (87); the *servi poenae* used as miners in the Roman Empire were condemned criminals (125).

There is widespread evidence for the sexual abuse of slaves. The absolute power of owners entailed the right to prevent slaves from entering into family relationships (193): neither Greek nor Roman law normally recognised the unions of slaves as regular marriages before the Christian period. Where Roman imperial legislation gave slaves some protection against prostitution, this was an incidental effect of asserting the rights of former owners to impose binding conditions upon anyone to whom they sold their slaves (194). In late antiquity, Christians were very much preoccupied with the deleterious effects that slavery continued to have on sexual morality (195).

The ill treatment of slaves by their owners should be seen in the context of the general level of brutality and violence in the ancient world. Of course whipping served to symbolise the absoluteness of the owner's power (196); but then in the ancient world (as in other pre-industrial societies, whether or not slavery was widespread) children were quite normally punished by beating (the Latin phrase 'to submit one's hand to the cane', *ferulae subducere manum*, is equivalent to 'going to school'). Perhaps we should see brutality towards slaves less as systematic or intentional than as the effect of outbursts of rage on the part of persons in authority, analogous to violence against wives or children in our own society (197–9).

At all times heads of households must have been tempted to fulfil their responsibilities towards their dependants only if this was in their own interests; the treatment of sick slaves is a case in point (200). The attitude of Cato the Elder (201,202) is no evidence that owners were particularly inhumane in the second century BC; nor is Claudius' legislation in favour of sick slaves (203,204) evidence for the theory that Roman emperors systematically attempted to improve the treatment slaves received, under the influence either of powerful *liberti* or of Stoic humanitarianism. The advice on how to make the most of slaves in earlier Greek philosophical handbooks discussing practical ethics (205,206) may strike us as cynical, but there are no grounds for believing that in the Roman world humanitarian ideals of Jewish (207) or Stoic (208) provenance led to restrictions upon an owner's rights in law.

The extent to which an owner would apply these theoretically absolute powers was of course controlled by social convention and by his own religious or moral feelings. There was also control from below, by the ways slaves themselves reacted to the treatment they received. This is again analogous to the treatment of inferiors by superiors within any family: since it is difficult for society to control such behaviour, the only way dependants can often express their dissatisfaction at the way they are treated is the extreme one of breaking up the family unit – either by murdering the superior, or by physically removing themselves from his authority. Although murder of masters by slaves certainly occurred (209,180), we should not assume that it was so frequent that all masters went in continuous dread of being killed by their slaves – the permanent state of war between Spartans and Helots was exceptional, and again suggests that Helots should not be seen as slaves. Violent death was widespread and expected in the ancient world as in most societies, but lawyers assumed that men expected it to come at the hands of external enemies or brigands, or the supporters of a powerful rival, and not of slaves, any more than spouses (see *Digest* 39, 6.3).

Another mechanism by means of which inferiors could express their sense of grievance against superiors was sorcery (210); throughout antiquity persons of high as well as low status believed in magic and would use it when they felt powerless to do anything more effective to resist their opponents.

If a slave could not control the ill treatment he received, the only practical solution was to flee. The evidence shows that this was widespread both in Greece (211) and Rome (212), where there are clear regulations for the return of runaways; Christians accepted the obligation to return a slave to his owner (213). A master might offer a reward to retrieve his property (214), and could count on the support of the state, though in practice this might need some prompting (215). When all else failed, masters might use magic to prevent slaves running away (216), or even insure themselves against such occurrences (217). If a slave was thought prone to leaving the household, he would be punished by being branded on the face (218); in late antiquity this practice was replaced for religious reasons by forcing the slave to wear a metal collar so that he would be recognised as a fugitive (**219–21**).

Society recognised that as the only effective way in which slaves could protest against ill treatment, flight could never be stamped out; it thus had to be regulated. Religion provided a mechanism through which flight could be accepted as legitimate without directly challenging the absoluteness of an owner's power over his property: the decision of a priest (or at Rome a magistrate) as to whether a fugitive's complaints against his master were justified or not, was perceived in terms of accepting the superior power of a god or of the imperial *numen* to which the slave had appealed for help, not as surrender to the wishes of the slave. The slave could not become free simply by running away, but exchanged a new master for the one who had treated him intolerably; this might be the god himself, or (following a compulsory sale) another citizen. I.M. Lewis' *Ecstatic Religion* illustrates the role of religion in regulating conflict between husband and wife in analogous cases in some contemporary societies. Evidence for regulations regarding asylum survives for all periods of Greek and Roman antiquity (**222–6**).

The dividing line between running away, brigandage and open rebellion is not always clear (see Drimakos of Chios, **80**,**265d**). Like flight, slave rebellions should be seen as the effect of dissatisfaction against ill treatment by particular masters rather than opposition to the institution of slavery as such. Wherever slaves were properly integrated members of the masters' households, rebellion could not make sense; and the ancient sources show that in fact slave rebellions only occurred precisely where the ideal that slaves were a recognised group within the household ceased to be effective – because as recently enslaved prisoners of war they were still loyal to leaders from the society they came from (**227**), or because they were physically distant from the control of their owners as the result of their work (**228**,**233**), or because their owners failed to maintain them (**234**).

Both the general causes and the particular events triggering off the two great slave wars in Sicily (**229**,**230**) and Spartacus' rebellion (**231**,**232**) can be traced to the failure of the recognised ideal that the head of the household was responsible for his dependants to cope with the influx of outsiders into Sicily and Italy in the late Republic. Yet antiquity was unable to develop any more effective social institution than household slavery for the integration of war-captives who, unlike guest-friends or kin, were rightless and rootless. It may be interesting to speculate whether these revolts would in time have developed new social forms (for example, whether the whole of Sicily might have developed into a unified palace economy directed by the King), but we have no reason to suppose that the insurgents would have abolished slavery. Eunous' prisoners were certainly forced to work in chains. It did not occur to slaves any more than to anyone else in antiquity that social equality might be a viable political programme; whether or not the Stoic ideal of the just king may have influenced Aristonikos' rebellion in Asia Minor in 133–129 BC, this war should not be seen so much as a slave rebellion than as an instance of slaves being promised their freedom in return for fighting on behalf of someone who saw himself as a legitimate ruler threatened by a foreign power (see 57,58, 63,243). There is no evidence that Aristonikos envisaged the permanent abolition of slavery as an institution.

While Stoic philosophy, and later Christianity, cannot be considered to have had any noticeable effect on improving the conditions of slaves, let alone leading to its 'abolition', the attitudes of intellectuals towards slavery did have some interesting consequences. By making the slave/free polarity analogous to that between Greeks and barbarians, philosophers provided the basis for later racial justifications of slavery. Such racialism was quite inappropriate in the circumstances of Rome, where slavery served precisely as a method of integrating outsiders (and hence the Romans had no qualms about enslaving racially kin groups like Italians).

By developing the metaphor of 'moral' slavery to vice, philosophers made real slavery more acceptable by suggesting that it was not important (235,236). The metaphor of 'slavery' to Chance or Fortune (237,238) or the Christian God may have helped the Greco-Roman elite to come to terms with the contradiction between the ideal that a citizen was absolutely independent and the reality of government by autocrats. Although the prejudice that slaves had to be moral inferiors was unassailable, both pagan and Christian writers stressed that persons of slave status could, and had, attained virtue (239,240,243).

But this in no sense implied criticism of slavery as an institution (242,242). The semi-servile tenancy arrangements which the jurists labelled the 'colonate' replaced chattel slavery on the farms as the typical form of dependence in late antiquity, and slave-owning was less widespread in the early middle ages than in Rome of the late Republic (although there is continuing evidence for its importance in the households of Byzantine potentates as well as barbarian nobles and western Senators). But although the restraints which social convention had exercised over an owner's power were being replaced by the more identifiable but equally ineffective ones of imperial and ecclesiastical legislation, slavery continued to be accepted as the extreme case of one man's personal dependence upon another.

CHAPTER 1

'ALL HUMAN BEINGS ARE EITHER FREE OR SLAVE': THE SLAVE AS PROPERTY

1. *Digest* **1, 5: 'On the Status of Persons'; 4: Florentinus, from** *Institutes*, **book 9**

Both Greeks and Romans assigned their slaves a legal position which clearly separated them from other, 'free', members of the community. Although chattel slaves were human beings, and thus had certain moral rights (see Chapters 9 and 12), legally they were property in the absolute control of an owner — even to the extent that the owner could transfer his rights to someone else by gift or sale. All slaves were alike in being denied any legal claims on society; this masks the different social and economic roles that slaves played, for instance as either producers or consumers, as well as the fact that free citizens often performed identical economic functions to slaves.

Definitions and explanations of some of the most common terms associated with slavery are to be found in a passage from Justinian's *Digest* of Roman law, excerpted from an earlier textbook for law students.

Being free (*libertas*) is the natural ability to do whatever anyone pleases, unless one is prevented from doing it either by force or by law.
(1) Slavery is an institution of the common law of peoples (*ius gentium*) by which a person is put into the ownership (*dominium*) of somebody else, contrary to the natural order.
(2) Slaves (*servi*) are so called because commanders generally sell the people they capture and thereby save (*servare*) them instead of killing them.
(3) The word for property in slaves (*mancipia*) is derived from the fact that they are captured from the enemy by force of arms (*manu capiantur*).

2. Aristotle, *Politics*, 1, 2

In the ancient Greek and Roman world, the polarity between 'slave' and 'free' seemed as natural a way of dividing up the human race as those between men and women or young and old. But Greek philosophers soon recognised that these pairs of words were not all alike. That human beings were *either* male *or* female was clear; but in the case of the opposites 'young and old' or 'rich and poor', the reason for classifying certain intermediate examples as one *or* the other could be relative, or simply arbitrary. Although the 'slave/free' polarity was deeply rooted in Greek thought, it raised a number of problems. Was it analogous to that between the magistrates who ruled Greek communities and the people over whom they exercised authority? After all, every citizen had to be either subject or ruler. Or was it like the division of functions between parents and children who cannot look after themselves? And was there a natural correlation between master and slave, and superior and inferior – either in power or in moral virtue (we still use the word 'liberality' to denote a moral virtue)?

Aristotle begins the *Politics* with an analysis of what it is that differentiates a political relationship from analogous ones like those between husband and wife, masters and slaves, Greeks and barbarians. Since the city community consists of a number of separate (and, ideally, self-sufficient) households, Aristotle first analyses the distribution of authority within the household. He explains his own interpretation of slaves as 'tools to assist activity', rather than merely economic 'productivity' (4–7); goes on to discuss the problems raised by fifth-century Sophists' opinions that slavery had to be *either* natural *or* merely a conventional institution of some human societies (7–21: *physis* (nature) and *nomos* (convention) was another favourite, and misleading, Greek polarity); and finally considers whether there is a skill involved in the ownership of slaves (21–23). These questions continued to exercise philosophers, some of whom concluded that the institution was unjust or morally irrelevant (see Nos. 235–9 below).

(1) We must first discuss household units, since the city as a whole consists of households. The subject can be subdivided into the parts of which a household is made up: a complete household consists of slaves and free persons. Since one ought to examine everything in its smallest part first, and the primary and smallest constituents of a household are master and slave, husband and wife, and father and children, we ought to examine what each of these three relationships is and ought to be – (2) the institution of 'being the master', 'marriage' (there is no current word in Greek for the relationship between husband and wife) and 'having children' (again there is no specific word for this in Greek). Let these be the three basic relationships. There is another subdivision which many people think is actually equivalent to household management, or the most important part of it, and we shall have to consider that too – I mean what is called dealing with money.

Let us first consider the relationship between master and slave, in order to see what needs it fulfils; perhaps we shall be able to understand it better if we approach it in terms of the ideas that are commonly held.

(3) Some thinkers believe that there is a 'science' of how to be a master, and that (as I said earlier on) running a household and controlling slaves and being a politician and being a king are all the same. Then there are others who hold that controlling another human being is contrary to nature, since it is only by convention that one man can be a slave and another free; there is no natural difference, and therefore it cannot be just, since it is based on the use of force.

Aristotle's View: Slaves as 'tools'

Property is a part of the household, and the art of acquiring property a part of household management (since no kind of life, and certainly not a fulfilled life, is possible without the basic necessities); (4) and so, just as in particular crafts the relevant tools are needed if a job is to be done, exactly the same applies to managing a household. Tools can be divided into animate and inanimate (for instance, for the helmsman of a ship, the rudder is inanimate while the look-out man is animate: since an assistant can be categorised as a 'tool' as regards that particular craft). So a piece of property is, similarly, a tool needed to live; 'property' is a collection of such tools, and a slave is an animate piece of property. (5) Every assistant is a tool taking the place of several tools — for if every tool were able to perform its particular function when it was given the order or realised that something had to be done (as in the story of Daedalus' statues or Hephaestus' tripods which Homer describes as 'entering the assembly of the gods of their own accord'), so that shuttles would weave cloth or harps play music automatically, then master craftsmen wouldn't need assistants, nor masters slaves. The tools I have mentioned are tools used to make something else, and must be distinguished from property which is useful in itself: a shuttle, for instance, is good for something other than the activity of using it, while clothes or a bed are simply used themselves. (6) Now, since we must distinguish 'being productive' (*poiēsis*) from 'being active' (*praxis*), and both of these need tools, there must also be some difference between the two kinds of tools. But living is a matter of 'being active', not of 'being productive'; so the slave can be classified as a tool assisting activity.

The word 'property' is used in the same way as the word 'part': a part is not simply a section of something else, but belongs to it completely, and the same is true of a piece of property. Therefore a master is simply the master of a slave, but does not belong to the slave, while the slave isn't just the slave of a master, but belongs to him completely.

(7) It will be clear from these facts what the nature and the functions of a slave are.

A: A human being who by nature does not belong to himself but to another person — such a one is by nature a slave.

B: A human being belongs to another when he is a piece of property as well as being human.

C: A piece of property is a tool which is used to assist some activity, and which has a separate existence of its own.

'Nature' or 'Convention'?

The next thing to consider is whether by nature there is in fact any such person or not, or whether all slavery isn't rather contrary to nature. (8) There are no difficulties here either as regards theoretical analysis or empirical observation. Ruling and being ruled are not only among the things that are inevitable, but also among things that are beneficial, and some creatures are marked out to rule or to be ruled right from the moment they come into existence. There are many types both of rulers and of subjects, and rule over a better type of subject is a better type of rule — ruling a man is better than ruling a wild beast; similarly, something produced from better materials is a better piece of work. (9) Everything that consists of several parts which become one common whole, whether the parts are continuous or discrete, always has an element that rules and an element that obeys, and this is true for living things as a consequence of their whole nature (there is also a ruling element in things that have no life, such as harmony in music, but that isn't relevant to this investigation). (10) But animals primarily consist of soul and body, of which by nature the former rules, and the latter obeys. We must look for what is natural in things that are in their natural state and not in things that have degenerated; thus we must consider a human being whose mental and physical condition is in the best possible state, in whom this will be obvious — for in bad specimens, or specimens in a bad condition, it may appear that the body often rules the soul because of its evil and unnatural condition. (11) But as I was saying, it is in living creatures that it is particularly possible to see rulership both of the master/slave variety and of the political variety: for the soul rules the body as a master rules a slave, while the intellect rules the desires as a politician or king does. In these cases it is clear that it is natural and advantageous for the body to be ruled by the soul and the emotions by the intellect (which is the part that possesses reason); it would be harmful if the components were on an equal level or if the situation were reversed. (12) The same is true of the relationship between man and the other animals: tame animals are naturally better than wild animals, yet for all tame animals there is an advantage in being under human control, as this secures their survival. And as regards the relationship between male and female, the former is naturally superior, the latter inferior, the former rules and the latter is subject.

By analogy, the same must necessarily apply to mankind as a whole. (13) Therefore all men who differ from one another by as much as the soul differs from the body or man from a wild beast (and that is the state of those who work by using their bodies, and for whom that is the best they can do) — these people are slaves by nature, and it is better for them to be subject to this kind of control, as it is better for the other creatures I have mentioned. For a man who is able to belong to another person is by nature a slave (for that is why he belongs to someone else), as is a man who participates in reason only so far as to realise that it exists, but not so far as to have it himself — other animals do not recognise reason, but follow their passions. (14) The way we use slaves isn't very different; assistance regarding the necessities of life is provided by both groups, by slaves and by domestic animals. Nature must therefore have intended to make the bodies of free men and of slaves different also; slaves' bodies strong for the services they have to do, those of free men upright and not much use for that kind of work, but instead useful for community life (and this category can itself be subdivided into appropriateness for peaceful activities and for military ones). Of course the opposite often happens — slaves can have the bodies of free men, free men only the souls and not the bodies of free men. (15) After all, it is clear that if they were born with bodies as admirable as the statues of the gods, everyone would say that those who were inferior would deserve to be the slaves of these men. And if that is true of the body, it would be far more correct to apply this rule with regard to the soul. But then it isn't as easy to see the beauty of the soul as that of the body. To conclude: it is clear that there are certain people who are free and certain who are slaves by nature, and it is both to their advantage, and just, for them to be slaves.

(16) Yet it is not difficult to see that those who assert the opposite are also right in some respects. For there are two senses of the words 'to be enslaved' and 'slave'; there is such a thing as a person who is enslaved as the result of legal convention. This legal convention is an agreement that whatever is captured in the course of warfare is said to belong to the conqueror. Many of the people who discuss legality treat this principle just like a politican who makes an unconstitutional proposal — they say that it is horrible that someone who is less powerful should be the slave and subject of someone who is able to use violence and can apply superior force. Even among theorists there are some who accept this point of view, and some who accept the other.

(17) The cause of this controversy and of the confusion in the arguments is that when something which is good has managed to obtain the necessary means, it is also able to exercise power, and there is always some good quality of which the winning side has more, so that it looks as though the powerful are never without some good quality, and that

this dispute is purely about justice — since there are some who think that legitimate authority requires goodwill towards the subject, while others think that it is sufficient justification for the ruler to be more powerful. If the two issues were separated, there would be no basis or validity for any other arguments, since the implication would be that someone superior in goodness ought not to rule and govern.

(18) Some philosophers who can't abandon the notion that right and wrong must be relevant to this problem (since legal enactments are in some way based on ideas of right and wrong) suppose that enslaving people in the course of warfare is just, but at the same time deny this, since it is possible that the reasons for going to war may not be just; and they conclude that one cannot say that someone who became a slave undeservedly was a real slave. (If this were false, we would be forced to conclude that people of the most respected family suddenly turned into slaves just like slaves by birth, simply because they happened to be captured and sold.) So they don't mean to say that people of that kind become slaves; those who do become slaves are non-Greek foreigners. Of course when they say this, they are only looking for a definition of natural slavery such as I gave at the beginning — we have to recognise that some people are slaves under any circumstances, and others under none. (19) The same is true of the concept of 'nobility'; Greeks think that they themselves are noble not just here but anywhere, while barbarians are only noble in their own communities, so that absolute nobility and freedom is one thing, relative nobility something else, as Theodektes' Helen says:

> I am the child of two divine parents —
> to whom would it occur to talk to me as though I were a servant?

When they say this, they distinguish slavery and freedom and high and low social status purely in terms of goodness and badness. They think that just as a man is descended from another man and a beast from beasts, so a good man comes from good parents. This may be what Nature generally intends to do, but she doesn't always succeed.

It has become clear that there is some basis for this controversy, and that there are some slaves and free men who are not 'naturally' so. (20) But in some cases there is such a distinction, and it is advantageous for some to be slaves and others masters, and just and proper for some to be ruled and others to exercise the sort of rule which corresponds to their natures. Furthermore, bad rule would be disadvantageous for both of them (since the same thing is good for a part as is good for the whole of both body and soul, and the slave is part of his owner — like a distinct part of the body having a soul of its own). (21) Thus slave and master have a certain common interest and friendship, if their statuses are deserved by their respective natures; but the opposite is true if the relationship is not of this kind but purely based on convention and superior force.

What emerges from all this is that the power of a slave-owner is not the same as that of a political leader, and that all forms of government are not, as some assert, identical. The one concerns men who are free by nature, the other slaves, and control over a household is a form of monarchy (since each household is ruled by a single person), while political leadership is the government of free men who are equals. (22) The word 'master' is not therefore applied to someone with a particular skill, but to someone who is in the position of a master, and so are the words 'slave' and 'free man'. Of course there might be a skill involved in owning slaves or being a slave; this was what the man in Syracuse used to teach who made a living by instructing youngsters in the ordinary duties of slaves. There could even be a more detailed science than this, such as cookery, and the various other types of domestic service — since different slaves have different jobs, some of them more honourable and some more restricting: in the words of the proverb,

One slave comes before another, and one master comes before another.

(23) All these kinds of things are the skills with which slaves are particularly associated; a master's skill consists in being able to make the best use of his slaves (the function of a master consists not in buying slaves, but in using them). But this skill has no importance or status attached to it — it is simply that whatever the slave has to know how to do, the master will have to know how to order him to do. So anyone who is rich enough to avoid this troublesome business has a manager to exercise this office, and they themselves go off and become politicans or philosophers. The skill or science of obtaining slaves justly is quite separate from both of these; it is more analogous to warfare, or hunting. That, then, is my analysis of the master/slave relationship.

3. The Gortyn Code, 1, 1–49

In the middle of the fifth century BC, the city of Gortyn in Crete set up an inscription containing a revision of its ancestral laws. From the very first line we are made aware of the way in which men were classified as either free or slave; as in other parts of the Greek world, and in other societies, this status distinction is expressed in terms of the money value of fines prescribed (see AVN 62).

The Code begins with regulations against those who try to imprison someone who has not, or not yet, been condemned by a court; it may be noted that the possibility is envisaged that a slave may be unwilling to return to his legitimate owner (see Nos. **211–26** below).

The Gods

Anyone who initiates proceedings concerning a free man or a slave is not to lead the person off before the trial. If he does lead him off, let him fine him for leading off: for a free man ten staters, for a slave five; and order him to release the person within three days. If he does not release him, let him condemn him to a fine: for a free man one stater, for a slave one drachma, per day, until he release him: and the judge, having sworn an oath, shall make a ruling as to the time. If he denies that he led him off, and there is no witness to testify, the judge, having sworn an oath, shall make a ruling. If one side claims that a man is free, the other that he is a slave, the benefit of the doubt is to be given to those who claim that he is free. If both sides argue that a slave belongs to them, then if there is a witness, he is to declare judgement according to his testimony, but if there are witnesses on both sides, or on neither side, the judge, having sworn an oath, shall make a ruling. If the court decides against the person who is holding a man, he must release the man within five days, if he is a free man; and he must hand him over in good faith if he is a slave. If he does not release or hand over the man, let him declare that the complainant is being awarded compensation: for a free man, fifty staters, plus one stater per day until he releases him, for a slave ten staters, plus one drachma per day until he hands him over in good faith. If one year elapses after the judge has pronounced judgement, three times the original compensation may be exacted, or less, but not more; and the judge, having sworn an oath, shall make a ruling as to the time. If the slave who has been ordered to be returned to his owner flees to a temple, the defendant shall summon the complainant and with two free adults as witnesses he shall show him the slave at the temple at which he has taken refuge; he may do this in person, or someone else may do it on his behalf; but if he does not summon the complainant and show him the slave, he is to pay the compensation specified above. If he has still not handed over the slave after a whole year, he is to pay the simple fines as well.

4. *Digest* 1, 5: 'On the Status of Persons'; 5: Marcianus, from *Institutes*, book 1

Roman jurists codified clear and strict rules about the conditions under which a person was legitimately a slave:

The status of all slaves is the same, but free men are divided into the free-born (*ingenui*) and freedmen (*libertini*).

(1) Slaves come into our ownership either by civil law or the common law of peoples (*ius gentium*) – by the civil law, if anyone over twenty allows himself to be sold in order to benefit by retaining a share of the purchase price; and by the common law of peoples, those who have been captured in war and those who are the children of our slave women are our slaves.

(2) The free-born are those who are born of a free mother; it is sufficient for her to be free at the time when the child is born, even if she was a slave when she conceived, and conversely, if she conceived as a free woman, but later gave birth as a slave, we recognise the child that is born as free. (It does not matter whether the mother conceived the child within or without a recognised marriage.) The reason for this is that the mother's adversity ought not to prejudice a child in the womb.

(3) This raises the question of whether the child of a slave woman who was set free when pregnant, but was again reduced to slave status or sent into exile before giving birth, should be slave or free. But it has rightly been accepted that the child is in fact born free, and it is sufficient for an unborn child that its mother was free at any time in between.

5. Gaius, *Institutes*, book 1, 1; 8–55

In the second century AD, an otherwise unknown jurist called Gaius wrote a textbook of Roman law for students. He sets out clearly the different legal statuses of slaves, citizens and different categories of freedmen, and mentions the various pieces of legislation which affected slaves, particularly the *Lex Aelia Sentia* of 4 AD; we may note the similarity in Roman law between the dependence of a slave and that of a son on the master of the household (*c*. 55).

(1) Every community that is governed by laws and customs uses partly its own particular law and partly the law common to all mankind. For whatever system of justice each community establishes for itself, that is its own particular law and is called 'civil law' as the law particular to that community (*civitas*), while that which natural reason has established among all human beings is observed equally by all peoples, and is called 'law of nations' (*ius gentium*) since it is the standard of justice which all mankind observes. Thus the Roman People in part follows its own particular system of justice and in part the common law of all mankind. We shall note what this distinction implies in particular instances at the relevant point.

(8) The system of justice which we use can be divided according to how it relates to persons, to things and to actions. Let us first see how it relates to persons.

(9) The principal distinction made by the law of persons is this, that all human beings are either free men or slaves.

(10) Next, some free men are free-born (*ingenui*), others freedmen (*libertini*).

(11) The free-born are those who were free when they were born; freedmen are those who have been released from a state of slavery.

(12) Freedmen belong to one of three status groups: they are either Roman citizens, or Latins, or subjects (*dediticii*). Let us examine each status group separately, beginning with subjects.

Dediticii

(13) The *Lex Aelia Sentia* requires that any slaves who had been put in chains as a punishment by their masters or had been branded or inter-rogated under torture about some crime of which they were found to be guilty; and any who had been handed over to fight as gladiators or with wild beasts, or had belonged to a troupe of gladiators or had been imprisoned; should, if the same owner or any subsequent owner manumits them, become free men of the same status as subject foreigners (*peregrini dediticii*).

(14) 'Subject foreigners' is the name given to those who had once fought a regular war against the Roman People, were defeated, and gave them-selves up.

(15) We will never accept that slaves who have suffered a disgrace of this kind can become either Roman citizens or Latins (whatever the procedure of manumission and whatever their age at the time, even if they were in their masters' full ownership); we consider that they should always be held to have the status of subjects.

Citizens

(16) But if a slave has suffered no such disgrace, he sometimes becomes a Roman citizen when he is manumitted, and sometimes a Latin.

(17) A slave becomes a Roman citizen if he fulfils the following three conditions. He must be over thirty years of age; his master must own him by Quiritary right; and he must be set free by a just and legitimate manumission, i.e. by the rod (*vindicta*) or by census or by Will. If any of these conditions is not met, he will become a Latin.

(18) The condition about the age of the slave first appeared in the *Lex Aelia Sentia*. That law does not allow slaves below thirty to become Roman citizens on manumission unless they have been freed by the rod after a council (*consilium*) accepted there was just reason for the manumission.

(19) A just reason for manumission exists when, for example, a man manumits in the presence of a council a natural son, daughter, brother or sister; or a child he has brought up [*alumnus* = foundling], or his *paedagogus* [the slave whose job it had been to look after him as a child], or a slave whom he wants to employ as his manager (*procurator*), or a slave girl whom he intends to marry.

(20) In the city of Rome, the council comprises five Roman senators and five equestrians; in the provinces it consists of twenty local justices (*recuperatores*) who must be Roman citizens, and meets on the last day of the provincial assizes; at Rome there are certain fixed days for manumissions before a council. Slaves over thirty can in fact be manumitted at any time; so that manumissions can even take place when the Praetor or Proconsul is passing by on his way to the baths or theatre, for instance.

(21) Furthermore, a slave under thirty can become a Roman citizen by manumission if he has been declared free in the Will of an insolvent master and appointed as his heir [i.e. to take over the liabilities: the *heres necessarius*], provided that he is not excluded by another heir.

Junian Latins

(22) ... [persons who do not fulfil the conditions for full citizenship] are called 'Junian Latins': Latins because they are assimilated to the status of those Latins who lived in the ancient colonies; Junian because they received their freedom through the *Lex Junia*, since they were previously considered to have the status of slaves.

(23) But the *Lex Junia* does not give them the right to make a Will themselves, or to inherit or be appointed as guardians under someone else's Will.

(24) When we said that they cannot inherit under a Will, we meant that they cannot receive anything directly as an inheritance or legacy; but they can receive things by way of a trust (*fideicommissum*).

Digression – Dediticii

(25) But those who have the status of subjects cannot receive anything at all by Will, no more than any foreigner can, and according to the general opinion, they cannot make a Will themselves.

(26) The lowest kind of freedom is therefore that of those whose status is that of subjects; and no statute, Senate Recommendation or Imperial Constitution gives them access to Roman citizenship.

(27) They are even banned from the city of Rome or anywhere within the hundredth milestone from Rome, and any who break this law have to be sold publicly together with their property, subject to the condition that they must never serve as slaves in the city of Rome or within a hundred miles of Rome, and that they must never be manumitted; if

they are manumitted, the law stipulates that they become slaves of the Roman People. All these provisions are laid down by the *Lex Aelia Sentia*.

(28) But there are many ways in which Latins can become Roman citizens.

(29) First of all there are the regulations laid down by the *Lex Aelia Sentia*. Anyone under thirty who has been manumitted and has become a Latin; if he marries a wife who is either a Roman citizen or a colonial Latin or a woman of the same status as himself, and this marriage was witnessed by not less than seven adult Roman citizens, and he has a son; then, when that son becomes one year old, he has the right under this law to go to the Praetor (or in a province the governor) and prove that he has married in accordance with the *Lex Aelia Sentia* and has a year-old son.

And if the magistrate to whom the case is taken declares that the facts are as stated, then both the Latin himself and his wife (if she is of the same status) and son (if he is of the same status too) must be recognised as Roman citizens.

(30) (I added the phrase 'if he is of the same status too' with respect to the son because if the wife of a Latin is a Roman citizen, then her son is born as a Roman citizen, in accordance with a recent Senate Recommendation proposed by the Divine Emperor Hadrian.)

(31) Although the *Lex Aelia Sentia* only gives this right to acquire Roman citizenship to those who were less than thirty years old on manumission and thus became Latins, this was later extended to persons who were over thirty on manumission and became Latins, by a Senate Recommendation passed in the consulship of Pegasus and Pusio [early in the reign of Vespasian].

(32) But even if the Latin dies before he has been able to establish that he has a year-old son, the mother can prove it, and if she was previously a Latin she will thus become a Roman citizen herself.[. . .] Even if the son is a Roman citizen already, because he is the child of a mother who is a Roman citizen, she still ought to prove his case; for then he can become the natural heir (*suus heres*) of his father.

(32a) What was said regarding a year-old son applies equally to a year-old daughter.

(32b) Furthermore, under the *Lex Visellia*, anyone who has become a Latin through manumission, whether he is over or under thirty, acquires the full rights of a Roman citizen if he has completed six years' service in the *vigiles* (police) at Rome. It is asserted that a Senate Recommendation was later passed granting citizenship on completion of three years' service.

(32c) By an edict of Claudius, Latins also obtain full citizen rights if they have built a sea-going ship with a capacity of not less than 10,000 *modii* of corn, and that ship, or its replacement, has been used to bring corn to Rome over a period of six years.

(33) Furthermore, it was enacted by Nero that a Latin who owned property worth 200,000 Sesterces or more and built a house in the city of Rome on which he spent not less than half his property, could obtain full citizen rights.

(34) Finally, Trajan enacted that if a Latin kept a mill going in the city over a period of three years, grinding not less than 100 *modii* of corn daily, he could acquire full citizen rights.

(35) Persons who are over thirty when manumitted and have become Latins can obtain full citizen rights by having the ceremony of manumission repeated; so can those manumitted below thirty, when they reach that age. In every case a Junian Latin over thirty, whose manumission is formally repeated by the man who has Quiritary ownership over him by the ceremony of the rod, the census or Will, becomes a Roman citizen and the freedman of the man who performed the second manumission. Consequently: if you hold the right to use a slave (*possessio*), but he belongs to me according to Quiritary law, then he can be made a Latin by you, acting alone; but the second manumission can be performed only by me, and not by you as well, and as a result he becomes my freedman. Even if he attains the full status of a Roman citizen by any of the other procedures, he still becomes my freedman. On the other hand you are given possession of any property he leaves behind when he dies, whatever the way in which he had obtained full citizen status. But if he belongs to the same owner both by possession and according to Quiritary law, he can become both a Latin and a full Roman citizen by a single act of manumission.

Restrictions on Manumission

(36) Not everyone who wishes to manumit is legally permitted to do so.

(37) A manumission made with a view to defraud creditors or a patron is void; the liberation is prevented by the *Lex Aelia Sentia*.

(38) The same *Lex* also prevents an owner under twenty from manumitting, except by the rod and after a council has accepted that there is a just reason.

(39) Just reasons for manumission exist where, for instance, someone manumits his father or mother, or his *paedagogus*, or someone who has been brought up with him. But the reasons instanced above for the case of slaves manumitted when under thirty can be put forward here too; and conversely, those mentioned in the case of an owner under twenty may also apply for a slave under thirty.

(40) The result of this restriction on the freeing of slaves by owners aged under twenty imposed by the *Lex Aelia Sentia* is that, although an owner who has reached the age of fourteen can make a Will and

institute an heir and leave legacies, if he is still under twenty he cannot give a slave his freedom.

(41) And even if an owner under twenty wants to make his slave a Latin, he still has to prove before a council that there is a just reason, and only afterwards may he manumit the slave informally in the presence of his friends.

(42) The *Lex Fufia Caninia* [2 BC] set an additional restriction on the manumission of slaves by Will.

(43) Those who own more than two and not more than ten slaves are allowed to manumit up to half the number; those who own more than ten and not more than thirty are allowed to manumit up to a third; but those who own more than thirty and not more than a hundred have the right to manumit up to a quarter; and finally, those who own more than a hundred and not more than five hundred are allowed to manumit not more than a fifth; those who own more than five hundred are not given the right to manumit any more — the law forbids anyone to manumit more than a hundred. But if you only own one or two slaves, you are not covered by this law, and there are no restrictions upon your freedom to manumit.

(44) Nor does this law apply to those who free their slaves by some other procedure than by Will. Thus a master manumitting by the rod or by census or informally in the presence of his friends, may set free his whole household, so long as there is no other impediment to giving them their freedom.

(45) What we have said regarding the number of slaves who may be manumitted by Will is to be interpreted in such a way that in a situation where only half, a quarter or a fifth may be freed, there is no requirement to manumit fewer than could have been manumitted under the preceding proportion. This is provided for in the law itself, for it would have been absurd if the owner of ten slaves should be allowed to manumit five (because he may free up to half that number), while the owner of twelve should not be allowed to manumit more than four.

(46) [When a Will manumits more slaves than permitted by the law:] If a Will requests freedom to be given to slaves whose names are written in a circle, then because it is impossible to establish any ranking by which some have a greater right to manumission than others, none of them may be set free. This is because the *Lex Fufia Caninia* makes void any act intended to cheat the objectives of that law. There are also a number of particular Senate Recommendations which make void tricks contrived to evade the law.

(47) In conclusion, it should be noted that the *Lex Aelia Sentia* forbids manumissions made in order to defraud creditors, and this was extended to foreigners as well, by a decision of the Senate proposed by Hadrian; but the other provisions of this law do not apply to foreigners.

Types of Dependence

(48) We now come to a second distinction made by the law of persons. Some persons are independent agents (*sui iuris*) and some are dependent on the rights of another (*alieni iuris*).

(49) Furthermore, some of those who are in a condition of dependence are in another's power (*potestas*), some in their hands (*manus*) and some in their ownership (*mancipium*).

(50) Let us now look at persons who are in a position of dependence; for when we have established what sort of people these are, we shall be able to see who are independent agents.

(51) And first let us consider those who are in another's power.

(52) Slaves are in the power of their owners. This power is derived from the common law of nations, for we can see that among all nations alike owners have the power of life and death over their slaves, and whatever is acquired by a slave is acquired on behalf of his owner.

(53) But nowadays neither Roman citizens nor any other people who are subject to the sovereignty of the Roman People have the right to treat their slaves with excessive and unreasonable brutality. For a Constitution of the Divine Emperor Antoninus orders anyone who kills his own slave without due reason to be brought to justice in exactly the same way as one who kills another's slave. Excessively harsh treatment on the part of owners is also limited by a Constitution of the same Emperor; for when certain provincial governors asked him for a ruling regarding slaves who had taken refuge at the temples of gods or statues of emperors, he declared that owners were to be forced to sell their slaves if the cruelty of their behaviour appeared to be unbearable. In both cases he ruled justly, for we ought not to misuse our rights — that is the ground for interdicting those who waste their own property from administering it.

(54) Now since there are two kinds of ownership among Roman citizens — slaves may belong to their owners by possession or by Quiritary right, or both — we say that a slave is in the power of an owner who has possession over him, even though he may not belong to the same man by Quiritary right. For someone who simply has the title to Quiritary ownership of a slave cannot be said to have power over him.

(55) Similarly in our power are those of our children who are begotten in a recognised marriage; this is a custom peculiar to Roman citizens.

6. Suetonius, *Augustus*, 40

The background to the *Lex Aelia Sentia* of 4 AD, which introduced the regulations for certain kinds of manumission recorded by Gaius, is described by historians like Dio Cassius (No. 71 below), and the pressures

on the Roman government to maintain clear boundaries between slavery
and freedom are mentioned elsewhere (Nos. **68–70** below).

(3) He also thought it very important that the people should be kept
pure and uncorrupted by any taint of foreign or slave blood; so he was
very sparing in granting Roman citizenship, and set limits to the number
of slaves that might be manumitted ... (4) He was not satisfied with
imposing all sorts of difficulties to prevent slaves from being given their
freedom, and many more difficulties preventing them from being given
full freedom (for he introduced detailed conditions regarding the
number, status and types of those who could be manumitted); he ruled
in addition that no one who had ever been chained or tortured should
attain citizenship through any form of manumission.

7. *Digest* **48, 19.10: Macer, from** *Public Courts*, **book 2**

One of the effects of this status distinction was that any legal judgement
had to demonstrate the slave's inferiority publicly, either by assessing
damage to a slave as less costly than to a free man (see the fines in the
Gortyn Code, No. **3** above, or the compensation in the *Twelve Tables*,
No. **188** below), or by inflicting a more degrading punishment (for
sentencing to hard labour, normally in the mines, see No. **125** below).

(1) Slaves should be sentenced according to the rules applying to the
punishment of the lower orders. For those crimes for which a free man
[of the lower orders] is thrashed with rods, a slave must be sentenced
to be whipped and returned to his owner; for those crimes for which
a free man is first thrashed and then condemned to hard labour, a slave
must be sentenced to be whipped and then to be returned to his owner
to be kept in chains for the same period of time. If a slave who has
been sentenced to be returned to his owner to be kept in chains is not
in fact taken back by him, he is to be sold; and if he can find no one
who is prepared to buy him, he should be sentenced to hard labour for
life.

8. Caius, *Institutes*, book 2, 86–91 (= *Digest* **41, 1.10: 'Acquiring Property Rights')**

A consequence of the owner's absolute right of property over his slave
was that the slave could not be entitled to own property himself;
everything he had or acquired through inheritance or business dealings
legally belonged to the head of his household. Conversely, the master

was liable for any damage that a slave he owned might have caused (hence outstanding liabilities had to be announced at sales of slaves: No. **104**). At Rome, the head of a household had the right to choose to surrender such a dependant (*noxus*) to the claimant rather than pay damages.

On the other hand, Roman law had at an early date recognised that a son who had not been formally emancipated by his father nevertheless had full use of and responsibility over whatever property his father, as head of the household, had decided to entrust to him (his 'flock' or *peculium*); and it was accepted that slaves too had a right to their *peculium* (No. **32**).

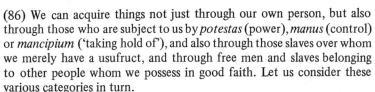

(86) We can acquire things not just through our own person, but also through those who are subject to us by *potestas* (power), *manus* (control) or *mancipium* ('taking hold of'), and also through those slaves over whom we merely have a usufruct, and through free men and slaves belonging to other people whom we possess in good faith. Let us consider these various categories in turn.

(87) Anything that those children who are in our *potestas*, or our slaves, receive by mancipation or obtain by handing over or by stipulation or by any other legal procedure, that thing is acquired for us. This is because anyone in our *potestas* is unable to have anything of his own. Thus if he is named anyone's heir, he cannot take over the inheritance except on our orders, and if he does take it over on our orders, that inheritance belongs to us exactly as though we ourselves had been named as heirs; similarly of course any legacy left to them belongs to us.

(88) It is worth stressing that if a slave is in the possession of one man (*in bonis*), but belongs to someone else by full legal title (*ex iure Quiritium*), the things he acquires by any legal process whatsoever all belong only to the man in whose possession he is.

(91) The rule regarding those slaves in whom we only have a usufruct, is that anything they acquire by using our property or as a result of their own activities, that is acquired for us. But anything they acquire on any other account belongs to the person who has the ownership of the slaves.

9. *Codex* 7, 8.6; 10.6

The only person entitled to decide whether a slave should be manumitted was the person with legal ownership — and if he were a minor, neither his guardian or even his father could exercise that right on his behalf.

A. The Emperor Alexander Severus, to Auctor.

If your guardian manumitted some slaves who had been bought with your money, then they did not become free: since slaves of this kind, like other property bought with a ward's money, are pledged on the ward's behalf.

B. The Emperors Diocletian and Maximianus, to Midas (Ad 294).

If your father manumitted your slave, even though you were less than twenty years old at the time and agreed to the manumission, he was nevertheless not in a position to give them their freedom.

10. *Codex* 7, 12.2

If an owner's right was absolute, then he could impose conditions affecting a slave on subsequent owners – either when he sold the slave (see Gaius 27, No. **5** above; Nos. **119** and **194** below) or when he died and left him to an heir; as third-century emperors reminded petitioners:

The August Emperors Valerian and Gallienus, to Theodorus.

A slave who was expressly forbidden to be manumitted in his owner's Will cannot be given his freedom.

1. But it is relevant to this case whether the testator forbade those slaves whom he described as having been brought up together with his son to be sold or freed because their service as slaves was needed for the good of his children, or whether he was rather imposing a penalty because they had served him badly.
2. For if the first is the case, then freedom can be gained when the requirement for service comes to an end with the death of the person whose interests were intended.

   But if the second is the case, then the decision taken against the slaves as a punishment must remain in force, since our Sacred predecessors as Emperors decided that such provisions in Wills could impose perpetual slavery on slaves who had behaved badly, so that they could not even be given their freedom if someone bought them as a legal fiction.

11. *Digest* 11, 3: 'Corrupting a Slave'; 1: Ulpian, from *On the Edict*, book 23; 2: Paulus, from *On the Edict*, book 19

Any action which reduced the value of a slave to his owner was an infringement of his property rights. This applied to violence and some-times insults against a slave (see Nos. **188**–**9** below), and also to corrupting him in other ways.

(4) Is a man only liable under the Edict if he has incited a slave of previously good character to do something wrong, or also when he has incited a bad slave to do something, or shown a bad slave how to go about doing it? It is more correct to hold that he is liable even when he has merely shown a bad slave how he could do something wrong. In fact he is even liable if the slave was going to run away or steal something anyway, and he merely praised his intention — for one shouldn't make a bad slave even worse by praising him. Thus a man is held to be guilty of corrupting a slave whether he is making a good slave bad, or a bad slave worse.

(5) And a person also makes a slave worse if he persuades him to commit wrongful damage or theft or to run away or to incite someone else's slave [to do these things] or to falsify his *peculium* or to indulge in sex or become a vagrant or interest himself in sorcery or spend too much time at public shows or be involved in sedition; or if he uses words or bribes to persuade his owner's agent to destroy or falsify the master's accounts, or just to alter an account that has been entrusted to him; or

2. [Paulus] else causes a slave to live in ostentatious luxury or to be disobedient or persuades him to submit to homosexual acts.

12. Strabo, 7, 3.12

The slave was an outsider who brought no rights with him from the society he came from, and had no claims on the host society which maintained him. The extent of this deracination is symbolised by the fact that he had to accept the religion of his new owner's household (Roman slaves would swear by the *genius*, life spirit, of their master: Nos. 82,135), and had no name apart from that which his owner chose to give him.

The Getai are the people living in the area reaching eastwards to the Black Sea, while the Dacians live in the area towards Germany and the sources of the Danube. I think that these people were originally called 'Dai'; and it was because of them that the names 'Geta' and 'Daos' were so common with the Athenians — at least, this is a more likely explanation than that they were named after the Scythian tribe called the 'Daai', since they live far away in Central Asia and it is most unlikely that any slaves were ever brought to Attica from there. The Athenians would either name their slaves after the peoples from whom they were imported, like 'Lydos' or 'Syros', or give them names which were common in those countries, like 'Manes' or 'Midas' for a Phrygian, or 'Tibios' for a Paphlagonian.

13. Varro, *The Latin Language*, 8, 9

At Rome too, a master gave his slave whatever name he decided; in early Rome, slaves were apparently called by their master's name, plus the suffix -*por* ('boy'): e.g. Marcipor (No. 83). Later there was a much wider range of personal names.

The fact that a slave has a name associated with a particular ethnic group is thus no proof that he belonged to that race — which undermines attempts to calculate the ethnic make-up of the slave and freedman population of Italy on the basis of names found in inscriptions.

Latin inscriptions formally identify slaves with reference to their owners, e.g. as *GAI S.*, while freedmen automatically took the personal and family names of their patron. Thus Marcus Tullius Cicero first chose the name *TIRO* ('new recruit') for his slave secretary; on manumission, that became his *cognomen* and he became *MARCUS TULLIUS M.L. TIRO* (Marcus Tullius, Marcus' freedman, called Tiro). Consequently we can date inscriptions of members of the imperial household (Nos. 171–5 below), because freedmen took the family names of whatever emperors presided over their manumission.

(21) There are two ways in which names can be derived; one is arbitrary and the other natural. It is arbitrary to impose whatever name anyone wishes — for instance, when three men buy one slave at Ephesus, often one of them will derive the name from that of the trader, e.g. Artemidorus, and call him Artemas, while another will call him Ion after Ionia, the district where he bought him, a third Ephesius because he was bought at Ephesus; so everyone calls his slave something different after different things, just as he likes.

14. *Code of Theodosius*, 4, 8.5 (Interpretation)

The corollary to the principle that a man who was a slave was a slave for ever unless his owner manumitted him in accordance with the recognised procedure, was that a free man too was free for ever, unless he became a slave in a legally recognised way. Thus Greek law codes lay down heavy penalties for anyone who kidnaps a free man (see No. 3 above; freedmen need particular protection: see No. 25 below, or a fifth-century law from Gortyn, Hainsworth *Tituli Dorici et Ionici* (Leyden 1972), No. 64 = Schwyzer 175). Under Roman law, any person who was forced to serve as a slave illegally — not just a Roman citizen — could appeal to a Roman magistrate to be restored to free status (see Nos. **121** and **230**, ch. 3.1 below). In a Constitution dated Sirmium, 20 July 322 AD, Constantine reminds the Prefect of the City of Rome, Maximus:

If anyone tries to reduce to slavery someone who is free, [the Emperor] commands that, on the order of a judge, he is to be led past the populace and through public places in order to find a man to defend his status; and if he finds such a sponsor, he is to petition the judge in writing, so that his free-born status should not be lost as a result of silence. If the person who is claimed as a slave cannot assist himself or fails to find a sponsor, he is to be handed over as a slave to the master who claims him back, but is not to suffer any legal penalty. But he is not to lose utterly any hope of freedom as a result of being handed back in this way, and if he does later find an opportunity and a sponsor, he is to claim free status and must be heard by the law. If the suit is renewed in this way and those who are claimed as slaves prove that they are free-born, then he who had unjustly imperilled their free-born status is to be required to pay the same number of slaves of the same age and sex to those whom he tried to reduce to slavery. In the assessment of this fine, those slaves are not to be included who are shown to have been born while the case was pendent.

CHAPTER 2

DEBT-BONDAGE AND SERFDOM

15. Pausanias, 4, 14

Greeks saw all around them persons whose legal status gave them an intermediate position between the full citizens of self-governing democratic communities and chattel slaves in the absolute ownership of their masters — 'between free men and slaves', as they were called by the second century AD lexicographer Pollux (3, 83). But their tendency to classify everything in terms of exclusive and exhaustive polarities led them to ignore the separate existence of such groups. (Cf. the tendency in the New World to assimilate black freedmen or Free Coloureds to slaves.) Democracies in particular asserted the independence of tenants and wage-labourers, non-citizen residents (Metics) and the women and children of citizens, and classified them all as 'free' despite their social, economic or juridical dependence upon others. On the other hand, various groups of serfs or tenants who had no political rights but lived in family communities of their own, working inherited plots of land, like the Spartan Helots, were considered slaves. Athenaeus lists various serf-like groups which he fails to distinguish from chattel slaves (No. **80**, 263d and 271 below); for the Spartan Helots (whom Plato too assimilated to chattel slaves: Athenaeus 264f) see AVN 58—60; Varro mentions similar dependent workers in Asia, Illyricum and Egypt (No. **148** below). But the words of the seventh century BC poet Tyrtaios make it clear that the obligations and social position of these serfs were quite unlike those of chattel slaves.

(4) The Spartans imposed the following conditions on the Messenians: first, an oath not to rebel against Sparta and not to make any constitutional changes of any kind; secondly, instead of imposing a fixed sum of tribute, the Messenians had to bring half of all their harvest produce to Sparta; and at the funerals of Spartan kings or rulers, Messenian mourners had to attend, with the women wearing black. (5) There was a penalty for non-compliance. Tyrtaios mentions these impositions in his poetry:

> They were like asses, exhausted beneath their burdens:
> they were forced to bring their masters one half of the produce of
> their lands.

And the following lines show that they had to participate at Spartan funerals:

Men and women both lamented their masters
when the day of death came upon them.

16. Aristotle, *Constitution of Athens*, 2; 6; 12.4

In classical Athens, everyone who was not an immigrant or descended from immigrants (i.e. Metics and slaves), had full legal and even political rights; however deeply they got into debt, they knew that they could never be sold abroad as slaves.

But Athenians remembered that, once upon a time, they too had had a class of bondsmen; and it was the abolition of this status category (rather than any hypothetical political reforms) which made Athenians claim the lawgiver Solon as the man responsible for their democracy. Even in agricultural societies with a much more advanced technology than that of Athens, debt is an endemic problem, since a series of bad harvests leaves poor peasants with no resources of their own, and forces them into dependence upon wealthier or luckier neighbours – as can be seen from Pliny's reference to tenants in northern Italy (No. 146 below). The legal codes of the ancient Near East contained provisions limiting the extent to which such debt-slaves could be exploited: Hammurabi of Babylon decreed that they should be released after three years; in ancient Israel, they had to be released when the seventh, 'Sabbatical', year came round.

It would seem that in the eighth and seventh centuries BC a rapid increase in the total population, together with the greater availability of luxury goods from the Orient and elsewhere, sharpened the competition among Greek aristocrats to possess and display wealth; there were consequently increasing pressures on them to exploit their dependants, and incentives to enslave and sell abroad those who were unable to meet their demands. By limiting the possibilities the rich had of exploiting the poor, Solon's reforms may well have stimulated the demand for imported slaves at Athens; and this contributed to the development of the slave/free polarity, since henceforth *no* citizen could be made a slave, and every slave would have to be an imported foreigner (or his descendant).

Athenian peasants were well aware that they were exceptional in being protected from enslavement by their creditors (Solon's abolition of enslavement for debt was so exceptional that Athenians thought he had got the idea from Egypt, notoriously the country where all normal habits were inverted: see Diodorus Siculus 1, 79, 3–5).

It is not clear whether in fact the *hektēmoroi* Solon set free were originally free peasants who had become the debtors of the rich, or a pre-existing class of dependent serfs who could be sold as slaves if they failed to pay their dues.

(2) After these events [the conspiracy of Kylon], there was a long period of conflict between the notables and the mass of the people. This was because their constitution was oligarchical in every respect, and in particular in that the poor were the slaves of the rich, both themselves and their children and wives. They were called *Pelatai* and *hektēmoroi* (sixth-sharers); for that was the proportion of rent for which they worked the fields of the rich (the whole country belonged to a very small number of persons); and if they didn't pay their rent, they themselves were liable to be carried off [i.e. sold abroad] together with their children. All money-lending was on the security of the borrower's own person up to the time of Solon; he was the first to become a champion of the people. It was the matter of slavery which was the hardest and most unacceptable aspect of the political system for the majority of people.

(6) When Solon became master of Athenian affairs, he set the people free both for the present and for all time to come, by forbidding the lending of money on the security of the borrower's person; and he enacted laws and decreed the cancellation of debts, both those owed to individuals and those owed to the community; they call this the 'shaking-off of burdens' (*Seisakhtheia*), because they shook off their misery in this way.

(12.4) Solon in his poetry also has the following things to say about his cancellation of debts and about the people who had previously been slaves but had been set free as the result of the *Seisakhtheia*:

Of all the aims for which I called together the people,
which did I abandon before achieving it?
The great mother of the Olympian spirits, black Earth,
will be my best witness, in Khronos' court-of-judgement;
I removed the boundary-stones planted everywhere upon her
when she was once enslaved; and now she is free.
I brought back to Athens, their god-given homeland,
many who had been sold, one unjustly, the other justly;
and those who fled because of the burden of debts, no longer
able to speak Attic Greek because they had wandered so far.
And those who suffered the disgrace of slavery here at home,
trembling at their masters' whims, I set them free.
I did these things with the power of the Law, establishing
harmony between Force and Right.

17. Aulus Gellius, *Attic Nights*, 20, 1

From the fourth century BC on, Rome, like Athens, was exceptional in not allowing its citizens to be sold as slaves if they were unable to pay their debts. But such ultimate sanctions had existed in the earliest Roman law code, the *Twelve Tables*, and its provisions were remembered as quite sensible. It is interesting that the enslaved had to be sold 'across the Tiber', i.e. outside Roman territory: not for fear that slaves would rebel, but rather because the idea of owning a slave who had once been a full Roman citizen gave rise to feelings of unease – just as Islamic law does not allow one Moslem to be enslaved by another.

(41) Our ancestors insisted on the strict maintenance of trust not just in official matters, but also in business contracts, and in particular in the use and exchange of money for loans; for they thought that this form of assistance for short-term problems, which is essential for all of us, would disappear if debtors could evade their obligations without risking serious punishment. (42) So those who admitted that they owed money were allowed thirty days to try and raise the required sum; (43) these were called 'legal' days, as if they were a suspension of the execution of the sentence ... (44) and if they hadn't paid back the loan within this period, they would be called before the Praetor and assigned by him to the people in whose debt they had been declared to be; and they would be bound with ropes or fetters. (45) For I think that that is what the law states:

> Let there be thirty legal days if a debt has been admitted and the case has been decided in accordance with the law. Then let there be an arrest, and let him be brought to court. If he does not satisfy the judgement and no one intervenes on his behalf before the court, let him take him away with him, let him bind him with rope or fetters. Let him bind him with a weight of not less than fifteen pounds, or more if he so wishes. If he wishes, let him live at his own expense; if he does not, the man who holds him bound is to give him a pound of porridge each day. If he wishes, let him give him more.

(46) In the intervening period, the parties could reach a compromise, and if they didn't, they were kept chained up for sixty days. (47) During this period they would be brought before the Praetor at a popular assembly on three market-days in succession, and the amount of money involved in the case would be announced. But on the third of these market-days, they would be punished with execution or sent abroad for sale on the other side of the Tiber.

18. Livy, 6, 27

According to the traditions preserved by the historians of the Roman Republic, popular discontent about debt-bondage came to a head in the years after the sack of Rome by the Gauls (traditionally 390 BC), when peasant farmers were faced with a combination of economic difficulties associated with reconstruction, and the need to defend themselves against their hostile Latin neighbours (see Livy, 6, 14.2–20.5). But the Republic needed the support of every available citizen to fight in the campaigns waged year after year — first to establish Roman hegemony over the Latins, then to expand into Campania, and ultimately to conquer the whole of Italy. Roman commanders could not win wars with discontented soldiers; at the same time the vast booty they obtained from plundering Italians served as an alternative to exploiting and enslaving their own citizens. The connection between the peasant farmer's desire for protection against debt-bondage and the elite's need for soldiers is explicitly drawn in this speech by a popular leader, criticising the Senate for refusing to appoint Censors to look into the status of debtors (dated to 380 BC):

(8) But if the plebeians had the courage to remember the freedom that their fathers had enjoyed, they would not tolerate the enslavement of any Roman citizen because he owed money, and they would not allow any military levies to be held until the question of debt had been examined and a scheme to diminish the problem had been put into effect, and everyone knew what was his own property and what belonged to someone else, and whether his body was still free or whether that too was going to be put in chains.

19. Livy, 8, 28

With the increasing importance of militarism in Roman life, the peasant soldier finally became powerful enough to force the abolition of debt-bondage (according to Livy, in 326 BC; Valerius Maximus (6, 1.9) and Dionysius of Halicarnassus (16, 5) put this development in the aftermath of the disastrous defeat at the Caudine Forks in 321 BC). Smallholders who fell into debt remained liable to forced labour and imprisonment until their debts had been paid off (*addictio*); the position of tenants (*coloni*) *vis-à-vis* their landlords was so weak that by late antiquity the question of whether their legal status was that of citizens or of slaves effectively ceased to matter. But at least citizen-debtors could no longer become their creditors' property, liable to be sold abroad. For wealthy Romans, economic exploitation would increasingly have to be directed towards outsiders; through conquest, and through the ownership of foreign slaves.

It is interesting that Livy describes the events leading to the abolition of debt-bondage at Rome in terms reminiscent of the overthrow of tyranny at Athens: political and economic factors are ignored in favour of a good story clearly based on that of Harmodios and Aristogeiton (Thucydides 6, 54; Aristotle, *Ath.Pol.* 18).

In that year something happened to the Roman people which was like a new birth of freedom, since debt-bondage ceased. The reason for this change in the law was the extraordinary lust and concomitant cruelty of one particular money-lender. This was Lucius Papirius; Caius Publilius had given himself in bondage to him because of a debt he had inherited from his father. His youth and appearance should have aroused sympathy, but instead provoked sexual passion and insolence. The creditor considered his youthful attractiveness an additional bonus for the debt he was owed, and at first tried to solicit the young man with seductive talk; but then, since he wouldn't listen to these immoral propositions, he used threats and reminded him of his position of dependence − and in the end, when he realised that he was more mindful of his free birth than of his present status, he ordered him to be stripped and given a beating. After the thrashing the young man rushed into the street complaining about the money-lender's immorality and brutality, and a great crowd of people gathered, who commiserated with him because he was so young and had been so shamefully wronged and also because they were concerned about the condition of dependence that they themselves and their children were in; so they rushed down to the Forum, and then in a solid column on to the Senate House. The Consuls were forced by this sudden disturbance to convene a meeting of the Senate. As the Senators entered the Chamber, demonstrators fell down at each man's feet, and showed them the young man's mangled back. Because of the unrestrained brutality of a single man, the powerful chains of debt were broken on that day; the Consuls were ordered to propose to the popular assembly that no one should be held in chains or imprisoned (except those who had committed a crime, until they had paid compensation); and that the borrower's property, but not his body, should be subject to distraint for loans. So debt-bondsmen were set free, and it was forbidden for anyone to be made a bondsman in future.

20. Tacitus, *Germania*, 24.3−25.3

For quite different reasons, neither Athens nor Rome happened to have a legally distinct class of dependent serfs: this led to a tendency for Greeks and Romans when they were describing other societies to classify as a chattel slave anyone who did not fit the description of a citizen. Tacitus' account of the early Germans shows that the persons Romans categorised as slaves were in many respects more like free tenants (*coloni*): Tacitus has to point out that they weren't used for personal household service, as chattel slaves were. His account also shows that he shared the Roman prejudice that slaves and freedmen ought to accept a visibly inferior role; and that it was unnatural that, at Rome, some freedmen should have more power than citizens. We may also note that the Germans, like the early Romans, felt that they had to sell abroad a man who had lost his freedom.

It may surprise you that one of their serious pursuits when they are sober is to play dice. They are so keen to risk anything in order to win or lose that when they have lost everything else, they stake their own body and freedom on one last final throw. The loser accepts slavery of his own free will; he may be younger and stronger, but he allows himself to be bound and led away. That is the extent of their unnatural obstinacy when it comes to dicing; they themselves say that their honour is at stake. The winners trade slaves of this sort abroad, so that they may free themselves of the shame involved in having won.

(25) The other slaves are not appointed to particular duties within the household as they are with us; they all live separately and have their own homes. The owner imposes a fixed quantity of corn or cattle or clothing, as one would on a tenant farmer (*colonus*). That is the limit of the slave's obligations; the other duties about the house are carried out by the man's wife and children. It is unusual for a slave to be beaten or punished with chains or extra work; but they are often killed, not as a result of some harsh punishment but rather of impulsive anger, as though they were personal enemies, except that there is no penalty for this. Freedmen are not much higher in status than slaves, and rarely of any importance in the household, and never in public life — except of course among those tribes which are ruled by kings. There they rise even higher than free-born men, even higher than the nobles; in other communities the lower status of freedmen is a symbol of real liberty.

21. Dura-Europos: An Antichretic Loan, 121 AD

Greeks always found it difficult to express the hierarchy of dependence in oriental kingdoms (cf. the use of the word *doulos* for any official belonging to the Persian King's household). In documents from a Greek-speaking community in Mesopotamia, the relationship of dependence between Phraates, a Parthian notable, and his retainer (possibly a soldier) Barlaas, is expressed in terms of the Greek *paramone*-agreement stipulating the obligations of freed slaves towards their master (see Nos. 23–6 below). Barlaas' services are interpreted as payment for a loan of 400 drachmae, for which his property and his person are mortgaged; the form is that of a Greek antichretic loan. But the loan may in fact be a legal fiction — the nearest Greek procedure which could express a Near Eastern 'feudal' relationship.

During the reign of Arsakes, the King of Kings, the Benefactor, the Just, the God made Manifest, the Friend of Greeks, in the 368th year according to the era of the King of Kings but 432nd according to the previous [Seleucid] system, on 29 June, in the village of Paliga in the territory of Iardas, in the presence of the garrison commander Metolbaissas, son of Men [. . .] and grandson of Menarnaios, of the first and most honoured rank of the King's Friends and Bodyguards, in the presence of the undersigned witnesses:
Phraates the eunuch, one of the retainers of Manesos the son of Phraates, a member of the class of the [. . .] and a free man, tax-collector and governor of Mesopotamia and Parapotamia and administrator of the Arabs, has made a loan to Barlaas the son of Thathaios and grandson of Ablaios, one of the people of [. . .] of the sum of 400 drachmae of silver of the standard coined at Tyre, on the security of the whole of his property which will continue to remain with its owner. Instead of paying interest on the above-specified silver, Barlaas is to stay with Phraates until the time of repayment, and shall serve him as a slave and carry out anything he is ordered to do. He is not to stay away either for a day or for a night without the consent of Phraates. He shall pay a fine of [. . .] if he does stay away for a day or for a night, and if he is ill for more than seven days, Barlaas shall pay one drachma for each day he doesn't work. If he runs away to a temple, he shall be ejected from the temple and Phraates shall [punish him?], but shall still continue to provide him with his food and clothing allowance. Flight, death, injury and other risks shall not affect the lender's rights. The above-mentioned sum of silver and any additional amount owing as a result of idleness shall be repaid by Barlaas to Phraates in the month Daisios [June] 433 [122 AD] of the previous [Seleucid] system; if he doesn't repay it within the prescribed time, Barlaas shall nevertheless continue to furnish to Phraates the same services on the existing conditions until the silver is given back. But if when the time has passed Phraates wishes to get back his money but Barlaas when asked is unable to pay, the right of total and valid ownership both over Barlaas and over his mortgaged

possessions and over anything else he may subsequently have acquired shall pass to Phraates or to anyone who presents this document. Barlaas has agreed that whenever he is summoned to do so by Phraates, he will renew this contract through the record office in Europos within five days; if he fails to do so he is to pay Phraates a penalty of 400 drachmae of silver, and the same amount to the Royal Treasury, and this contract is to be considered valid notwithstanding.

Witnesses: Nikanor son of Omaianos;
              Phrani . . . son of Pha . . .;
              Diogenes son of . . .

CHAPTER 3

MANUMISSION

22. Demosthenes 59: *Against Neaira*

The clear definitions of lawyers and intellectuals not only mask the importance of groups of inferiors who were not personally owned, such as serfs and tenants; they also obscure the extent to which slavery can be seen as a process by means of which 'outsiders' become integrated into the host society. In some societies (especially in pre-colonial Africa), slavery is a transitional period leading to the newcomer's full acceptance as a member of a kin-group. At Athens, however, slavery was a 'closed' rather than an 'open' system; citizen status was not conferred by manumission — on the rare occasions when freed slaves were granted citizenship, this was a separate political act (e.g. when they were called upon to fight in times of crisis: **89,235**). The Athenians' exclusiveness can be seen partially as the result of the high privileges of citizens in a democracy, which they were most unwilling to share (Aristotle, *Ath.Pol.*26.3); perhaps more important was the tendency towards endogamy, associated with the need to ensure that an estate remained within the kin-group — a consequence of the shortage of fertile land in Greece.

This did not mean that Greek slaves could not win their freedom if they found the means to pay for their release, although we have no way of assessing what the proportion may have been (**27**). But an Athenian who married such a person laid himself open to the charge of disgracing his citizenship: one of Demosthenes' supporters wrote a speech attacking Stephanos, the husband of an alleged freedwoman and ex-prostitute called Neaira:

(29) Later on she [Neaira] had two lovers, the Corinthian Timanoridas and Eukrates from Leucas; when Nikarete's bills became too demanding for them — for she claimed that all the expenses of the house had to be met by them — they paid Nikarete the sum of thirty minae for her body [i.e. as a slave] and bought her from her outright according to the law of that city to be their own slave. They had possession and use of her for as long as they wished.

(30) When they were about to get married, they told her that they

45

did not want to see a woman who had been their own concubine having to work again at Corinth under the control of a pimp; instead they would be delighted to get back less money than they had spent for her, and see that she herself got some benefit out of the deal. So they said that they would remit one thousand drachmae from the sum she needed for her freedom, five hundred each, and suggested that she pay them back the remaining twenty minae when she had earned it. When she had heard this proposal of Eukrates and Timanoridas, she invited some of the men who had been her lovers to come to Corinth. One of them was Phrynion from Paianeia [an Athenian deme], the son of Demon and brother of Demokhores; as the older ones among you will remember, he lived an outrageous and wasteful life.

(31) When Phrynion arrived, she told him what Eukrates and Timanoridas had suggested to her, and took all the money she had been given gratuitously by her lovers to go towards buying her freedom and gave it to him, together with anything else that she had to spare, and asked him to provide what was still needed to make it up to twenty minae and pay it all to Eukrates and Timanoridas so that she would become free. (32) He readily accepted this proposal of hers, took the money which she had been given by her lovers, made up the balance himself and paid Eukrates and Timanoridas the total of twenty minae as the price for her freedom so that she should not have to work at Corinth.

23. *Fouilles de Delphes*, 3, 6, No. 36

Liberating a slave did not entail that he was immediately free to do as he pleased. When a Greek slave paid his master to become free, a contract was often drawn up which was guaranteed by a god; and many of these contracts survive, inscribed on the walls of public buildings at Delphi and similar religious centres. They are called '*paramone*-agreements', because they usually stipulate that the ex-slave must remain with (*paramenein*) his or her master for a number of years before the contract becomes valid; during that period, the 'freedman' is little better off than a slave (for details, see Hopkins, Ch. 3; see No. 21 above). He can be punished; if a woman, she may be required to give her patron one of her children to take her place as a slave; and occasionally the period of service stipulated is the rest of the patron's life, as in this inscription from Delphi, dating to the first half of the first century AD.

In the magistracy of Pason son of Damon, in the month of Herakleos, when Habromakhos son of Xenagoras and Markos son of Markos were serving as councillors.

Written in the hand of Sosikles son of Philleas on behalf of Sophrona daughter of Straton, who was present and ordered him to write on her behalf.

On the following conditions Sophrona, acting with the consent of her son Sosandros, hands over to the Pythian Apollo to be free the female house-born slave [literally, 'body'] named Onasiphoron, priced at three silver minae, and has received the whole price; Onasiphoron has entrusted the sale to the god, with the aim of becoming free and not to be claimed by anybody at any future time, and to have no obligations of any kind whatever to anyone. The guarantor required by law is Eukleidas son of Aiakidas. And if anyone touches Onasiphoron in order to enslave her, then she who has sold her and the guarantor together are to ensure that the sale to the god is valid; and similarly anyone at all is to have the legal right to take Onasiphoron away so that she may be free, without incurring any penalty or being subject to any legal action or punishment.

Onasiphoron is to remain with Sophrona for the whole period of the latter's life, doing whatever she is ordered to do without giving cause for complaint. If she does not do so, then Sophrona is to have the power to punish her in whatever way she wishes to. And Onasiphoron is to give Sosandros a child.

This sale is to be deposited as required by law: one copy engraved on the Temple of Apollo, the other taken to the public archives of the city by the Secretary Lysimakhos son of Nikanor.

Witnesses: Signature of Eukleidas son of Aiakidas: I have become guarantor of the above-stated sale, appointed by Sophrona with the agreement of her son Sosandros.

There are five more witnesses, two priests of Apollo and three private persons.

24. Schwyzer, No. 341

This *paramone*-agreement from Delphi can be dated to 157 BC:

In the year when Patreas was magistrate at Delphi, in the month Poitropios, Dorema, acting with the agreement of her daughter Hedyle, gave the god Apollo a slave girl called Melissa, worth one mina of silver, to be freed. The guarantor required by law is Teiseas. Melissa is to stay with Dorema for as long as Dorema lives, doing what she asks. If she doesn't stay with her or do what she asks, the contract is to be void.

Witnesses: Andronikos the priest, Nikomakhos, Ariston, Astylos,

Timokritos, Astyokhos.

25. Contract from Chaeronea: *ZPE* 29 (1978), 126f.

At Chaeronea in Boeotia, slaves were granted their freedom by means
of a sale to a god (Sarapis, Isis, the Mother of the Gods, Artemis); during
the period before the contract became valid, the slave was required to
continue to serve his patron, normally (in 32 out of 35 cases) for the
rest of the patron's life; but these obligations might be transferred to
one of the patron's heirs. The following is one of nine cases involving
the same family, dating to about 200 BC:

The god
Good Fortune

In the magistracy of Mnasigeneis, in the month of Hermaios, Menekleis
son of Dionousodoros and Biottis daughter of Mnason brought forward
their own foundling [slave] Parthena to be consecrated to Artemis
Elitheia, with the full consent of their son Mnason; to remain with
them for ten years before the consecration becomes valid. If anything
happens to Menekleis and Biottis before the completion of the stated
period of time while Parthena remains with them, Parthena is to remain
for the remaining years with Menekleis' daughter Telia, who is to complete the consecration through the Council, in accordance with the law.

26. *Fouilles de Delphes*, 3, 3, No. 333

On exceptional occasions, the terms of the *paramone*-agreement were
remitted; this had to be inscribed publicly in the same way as the
original contract. At about the beginning of the Christian era, one
owner at Delphi had stipulated that:

> Eisias is to remain with Kleomantis for the rest of his life and do
> everything that she is ordered as if she were a slave (*hōs doula*). And
> if Eisias does not remain or does not do what she is ordered,
> Kleomantis is to have the right to punish her in whatever way he
> wishes − by beating her or imprisoning her or selling her. (*Fouilles
> de Delphes*, 3, 3, No. 329, lines 4−7).

But later he decided to institute this concubine, together with his son
by her, as heirs in succession to his wife (who apparently had no
children):

In the magistracy of Diokles son of Philistion, in the month of Eilaios, with the following intention and desire, Kleomantis son of Dinon freed his own foundling [slave] Eisias from the obligation to remain (*paramone*) with him, and remits the sum written in the *paramone*-agreement; together with Nikostratos, the son she bore during the period of *paramone*, whose name she changed to Kleomantis, so that they are to be free from anyone at all and have no obligations towards anyone in any way whatsoever.

And if the common fate of mankind befalls Kleomantis, all that is left behind by him is to belong to Sosyla for her own use. And if anything happens to Sosyla, then everything is to belong to Eisias and Kleomantis, and no one else is to have any claim in any way whatsoever. Eisias may do anything at all anywhere on earth, just as any other person.

Witnesses: Priests of Apollo: Diodoros, son of Philonikos, Dionysios son of Astoxenos, Damon son of Polemarkhos;
            Magistrates: Laiadas son of Melision, Nikon son of Nikaios;
            Private citizens: Strategos son of Philon, Xenagoras son of Habromakhos, Lamenes son of Eukrates, Evangelos son of Megartas, Agon son of Poplios.

27. Harpocration, s.v. *apostasiou*

Some *paramone*-agreements specify that the act of liberation is void if the freedman fails to obey his patron. Athenian law provided that if a patron sued his freedman for disobedience and he was acquitted, all obligations towards the patron would cease. The successful ex-slave would inscribe and dedicate a silver bowl, and calculations based on surviving inscriptions recording these dedications (*IG* 2,2.1553—78) suggest that there were about fifty cases a year in the period 340—320 BC.

This is a civil action allowed to patrons against their freedmen, if they cease to recognise them or seek legal protection from someone else or fail to do the other things required by the laws. Those found guilty have to become slaves once more, and those acquitted become absolutely free. It often occurs in speeches, like Lysias' *Against Aristodemos* and Hypereides' *Against Demetria, for Apostasy*.

28. Paulus, *apud* Festus p. 159

Manumission appears to have been so much more frequent in the Roman world than in Greece that there is some justification for seeing it as a temporary phase through which an outsider, if he had proved reliable, would pass to Roman citizenship. The reservations expressed by Greeks and by Romans themselves (**69–71**) only underline how normal manumission was. A Roman might free his slave informally, in the presence of his family council (*coram amicos*; cf. Pliny, *Letters* 7, 16.4 & 10, 104; for examples of records documenting informal manumission, L&R II, 67). But if the slave was to obtain full citizenship, certain procedures had to be followed (see No. 5, 17 above). There was a legal formula for manumission 'by the touch of the magistrate's rod' (*vindicta*), in the presence of a Roman magistrate with full powers (*imperium*).

A slave is said to be manumitted, when his owner holds that slave's head or some other part of his body and says 'I want this man to be free' and takes his hand away from him [literally, 'lets him go out of his hand'].

29. *Code of Theodosius*, 4, 7.1

Although it did not occur to Christians, any more than to anyone else in the ancient world, that slavery as such could be abolished, they felt that it was a humane and virtuous thing to manumit a deserving slave; many did this at the Easter ceremonies after a slave had served them for six years (see Gregory of Nyssa, *Oratio* 3 = *PG* 46,657D). Constantine recognised the special role of the Church in facilitating manumission in a letter to the Bishop of Cordova.

The August Emperor Constantine to the bishop Hosius.

If anyone grants freedom deservedly to his slaves in the bosom of the Church as a result of his religious feelings, he shall be held to have granted it with the same legal force as that with which Roman citizenship has formerly been bestowed by the performance of the traditional procedures. But this privilege will only apply to persons who make grants of freedom in the presence of their bishops.

To 'clerics' we grant in addition that they shall be held to have given the enjoyment of absolute freedom to their slaves not only when they have given them their freedom in the sight of the church and the body of the faithful, but also when they have made a grant of freedom or have ordered it to be given by any form of words at the hour of their

death; so that the slaves in question shall receive their freedom on the day of the publication of the Will, without the need for any witnesses or intermediary.
Dated 18 April 321 AD.

INTERPRETATION: If anyone wishes to manumit in the holy church, it suffices for him to wish to manumit in the presence of the presbyters, and he will know that when they receive their freedom they become Roman citizens. And if clerics should wish to bestow freedom on their own slaves, they shall attain full and complete freedom as Roman citizens even if the manumission takes place out of the sight of the presbyters, or is simply verbal, without confirmation in writing.

30. Cicero, *Philippic 8*, 11.32

Greek thinkers stressed the importance of setting a definite limit to the length of time a slave might expect to remain in servitude (206). Augustus' legal reforms (5) as well as epigraphical evidence (G. Alföldi, 'Die Freilassung von Sklaven') suggest that at Rome domestic slaves were frequently manumitted at about the age of thirty. Twenty or thirty years' slavery was an exceptional and harsh punishment (119). A Roman who had fallen into slavery as the result of capture in war redeemed his ransom with five years' service as a slave (*CTh.* 5, 7.2). In his attacks on Marcus Antonius, Cicero compares the six years since the start of Caesar's dictatorship in 49 BC to a full term of slavery for the Roman people.

After six years, members of the Senate, we can now hope for our freedom. We have suffered slavery for a longer period than careful and hardworking captives taken in war normally have to. Should we refuse to be wakeful, to be anxious, to make every effort, in order to give the Roman people back its freedom?

31. Augustine, *Sermon* 21.6 (= *PL* 38,145)

The different motives a Roman master might have for freeing his slaves are listed by Dionysius of Halicarnassus (No. 69 below); they include the desire to have a spectacular funeral, or to defraud the state corn supply (see No. 70 below). Other occasions for manumission are noted by Dio Chrysostom (No. 235).

    It was universally felt that manumission ought to be the just reward for good service, rather than the arbitrary gift it may often actually have been. Hence the great stress on the loyalty (*fides*) of slaves (see

Nos. 153 and 239).

For Christians, too, manumission was seen as the natural and just reward for loyal service (but by no means as ending a freedman's obligations towards his patron: see No. 242 below).

You lead the slave whom you are going to set free by the hand into Church; silence falls; the official record is read out, or you make a statement as to your intentions. You say that you are setting the slave free because he has been faithful to you in every respect. That is what you approve of and show that you respect, what you are rewarding with freedom.

32. *Digest* 40, 1: 'Manumissions'; 5: Marcianus, from *Institutes*, book 2

In theory, a slave's savings (*peculium*) were absolutely the property of his master (No. 8 above); nevertheless, the Romans recognised that a slave could use such savings to buy his freedom, and under the emperors the law was prepared to enforce such a contract.

If anyone claims to have bought himself free with his own money, he can lodge an accusation against the owner on whose good faith he has relied, and complain about the fact that he has not been set free by him. At Rome he can do this before the Urban Prefect, and in the provinces he may approach the governors, as the result of a Decree of the Divine Brothers [Marcus Aurelius and Verus] ; but with this proviso, that a slave who brings such an accusation but cannot prove it will be removed to work in the mines, unless his master prefers him to be returned to him to inflict a punishment upon him which must not be greater than this.

33. *ILS* 1519

A frequent occasion for freeing a slave was when the owner wanted his relationship with a concubine to be recognised as a legitimate marriage; this was one of the exceptions to the rule that a slave had to be over thirty (No. 5 above). There is a great number of inscriptions showing that a wife had previously been her husband's slave (see No. 171 below); frequently both had served as slaves in the same household, and when one of them was manumitted he (or occasionally she) could buy the master's rights over his spouse and then set her free.

To Titus Flavius Euschemon, freedman of Augustus,
who had been secretary for correspondence and also procurator of the
Jewish poll-tax; Flavia Aphrodisia set this up for her ex-owner and
husband, who well deserved it.

34. *Digest* 37, 15: 'The Duties Owed to Parents and Patrons';9: Ulpian, from *On the Edict*, book 66

The freedman was in no sense independent of his previous owner. His
obligations were both social and economic: it is to be noted that
obligations of social respect (*obsequium*) assimilate the freedman's
relationship to his patron to that of a son to his father.

The figure of father and patron ought always to be respected and
sacred in the eyes of a freedman or a son.

35. *Digest* 37, 14: 'The Rights of Patrons'; 1: Ulpian, from *The Responsibilities of Proconsuls*, book 9

Provincial governors must listen to complaints by patrons against their
freedmen and not deal with them lightly, since a freedman who does
not show due gratitude should not be allowed to get away with it.

Now if anyone fails to carry out their obligations to their ex-master
or ex-mistress or their children, he should merely be reproved and be
let off with a warning that he will be severely punished if he gives cause
for complaint again. Buf if he has behaved insolently or abused them,
he should be punished, perhaps even with a period of exile; and if he
physically attacked them, he should be condemned to hard labour in
the mines; and also if he has been responsible for spreading any malicious
rumours about them or inciting someone to lay an accusation against
them, or has initiated a law suit against them.

36. *Digest* 37, 14.19: from Paulius, *Opinions*, book 1

An ungrateful freedman is one who does not give due respect
(*obsequium*) to his patron or who refuses to look after the management
of his master's property or to act as his children's guardian.

37. Suetonius, *Claudius*, 25

On occasion the state might intervene drastically to stress the dependent status of freedmen and protect the interests of patrons (for Claudius' attitude to slaves, see Nos. **203**–4 below).

(1) He sold off for the benefit of the state (*publicavit*) any freedmen who pretended to the status of Roman equestrians. He reduced to slavery any who failed to show due gratitude or about whom their former owners had cause for complaint, and he told their advocates that he wasn't going through the formalities of a trial against a man's own freedman.

38. *ILS* 8365

The position of freedmen as members of their master's household (*familia*) just like his children and his slaves, is illustrated by large numbers of inscriptions giving them the right to be buried in the family tomb (see No. **175** below). This one from Rome is particularly specific.

Let there be unrestricted access, entry and inspection to this tomb for all my freedmen and freedwomen. My heir must let them have the key so that they may sacrifice as often as is necessary.

39. *ILS* 8283

Conversely, freedmen and freedwomen who failed to fulfil their obligations would be explicitly excluded from this right (this example is also from Rome; for others, see L&R II, 66. iii and iv).

To the Spirits of the Dead

Longina Procla made this for herself and for her freedmen and freedwomen and their descendants; except for the women who deserted me while I was still alive – they are not to have access or entry to this tomb.

40. *Digest* 38, 1: 'The Work-obligations of Freedmen' (*de operis libertorum*); 7: Ulpian, from *On Sabinus*, book 28

Apart from social respect (*obsequium*), Roman freedmen had another group of obligations towards their patrons which was much more concrete, and shows why Roman slave-owners may have felt that manumitting a slave need not be economically disadvantageous. When a slave was freed, he had to make a formal undertaking on oath to provide his master with his labour for a specified number of days each year (*opera* = a day's labour).

In order for there to be a legal obligation arising from the taking of an oath, the man who swears the oath has to be a freedman, and he has to swear the oath in order to attain his freedom.

(1) The following question arises. If someone leaves his freedman a legacy in his Will on condition that he swears that he will fulfil a quota of ten days' work for the benefit of his son, is he bound by such an oath? Juventius Celsus says that he is so bound, and that the reason why the freedman took the oath promising work-obligations isn't so very important; and I myself accept Celsus' opinion.

(2) He has to take the oath after he has been set free, if he is to be bound by it; and he is bound by it whether he takes it immediately after being freed or some time later. (3) He has an obligation to swear to provide work, gifts or services; the work can be of any kind whatever, so long as it is imposed in an honourable, just and legal way.

(4) A rescript from the Divine Emperor Hadrian states that the right to exact work-obligations is void against a person who has attained freedom as a result of a *fideicommissum* [a request made in a will].

(5) A judge will allow claims for work-obligations against a child, once the child has grown up; and on occasion such a claim will even be allowed while he is still a child, for such a person too might be able to provide services, if he happens to be a copyist or someone who calls out names or can do accounting, or if he is an actor or some other kind of entertainer.

41. *Digest* **38, 1.9; 6: Ulpian, from** *On Sabinus*, **book 34; book 26**

Since these obligations could be enforced at law, jurists provide much evidence about the different categories of *operae*. Thus, if a skilled freedman had agreed to provide his master with several days' labour at his craft, this labour could be bequeathed or allocated by the patron to someone else:

(9) Work-obligations do not exist automatically.
1. Those categorised as *officiales* [i.e. relating to the freedman's duties towards his former master] cannot be owed to anyone other than the patron, since their character resides in the identity of the individual who owes such an obligation and that of the individual to whom it is

owed. But those to do with manufacturing (*fabriles*) and others are such that they can be carried out by any kind of person, and for anybody. After all, if such a work-obligation resides in exercising a handicraft, then if the patron so orders it can be performed for someone else's benefit.

(6) Work-obligations which consist of manufacturing and any others which can be considered as providing money pass on to a patron's heir; but those which are *officiales* cannot be passed on.

42. *Digest* 38, 1.17: Paulus, from *The Rights of Patrons*

While patrons could go to law and obtain the rights owed them by their freedmen, these rights were not unconditional.

A judge should not listen to a patron who demands work-obligations which are impossible because of age or physical infirmity or which will damage the way of life which the freedman follows or hopes to follow.

43. *Digest* 38, 1.19: Gaius, from *The Provincial Edict*, book 14

Work-obligations must be imposed upon the freedman in such a way that even on those days when he is fulfilling these work-obligations he still has enough time to earn a sufficient income to feed himself.

44. *Digest* 38, 1.34: Pomponius, from *Commentary on Quintus Mucius*, book 22

It should be noted that work-obligations sometimes decrease or increase or become different in kind. When a freedman is ill, for example, those obligations which he had begun to fulfil, lapse. And if a freedwoman who undertook to carry out work-obligations attains a social status such that it would be unbecoming for her to undertake work for her patron, then these will lapse automatically.

45. *Digest* 38, 1.35: Paulus, from *The Julian and Papian Laws*, book 2

A freedwoman over the age of fifty cannot be forced to provide labour services for her patron.

46. Pliny the Elder, *Natural History*, 14, 5

While freedmen should not be seen as an 'entrepreneurial class', many ex-slaves and their sons were anxious to advertise their successful integration into citizen society by amassing wealth to an extent that citizens by birth did not need to. It may be noted that it is agriculture, not industry, that bestows respectability (see AVN 4 and 5 on the relative status of peasant farmers and craftsmen). The fact that at Athens a freed slave had no right to acquire land indicates the difference between the role of slavery there and at Rome.

There are a few examples from our own lifetime of outstanding success in vine-growing; they shouldn't be passed over, because readers ought to know what the rewards are which are most to be respected in any particular field.

(48) Acilius Sthenelus, a common man and the son of a freedman, won great honour by cultivating no more than sixty acres of vines in the territory of Nomentum (Mentana) and selling it for 400,000 Sesterces. (49) Vetulenus Aegialus, also a freedman's son, became famous in the district of Liternum in Campania, and was even more highly regarded because the land he cultivated had been Africanus' place of retirement. But the greatest honour has been accorded to Remmius Palaemon, also well known for his textbook on grammar [see 133, 23]; this too was thanks to the assistance of Sthenelus. Within these last twenty years, Palaemon bought for 600,000 Sesterces a country estate in the same territory of Nomentum, near the stopping-place ten miles from Rome. (50) The price of all suburban property is notoriously low, particularly in this region; he had obtained farms which had been ruined by neglect and whose soil was poor even by the worst standards. It wasn't for any particularly high motives that he wanted to cultivate this land, but primarily out of vanity, which was something he was well known for. While Palaemon pretended to be a farmer, the vineyards were prepared for replanting under Sthenelus' management, and the result was almost unbelievable: within eight years the unharvested vintage was auctioned to a buyer for 400,000 Sesterces.

(51) Everyone ran to have a good look at the heaps of grapes in these vineyards; the inefficient locals explained it away by saying that Palaemon was exceptionally well educated. Finally Annaeus Seneca (the greatest scholar of the time, with political influence which in the end destroyed him, and a man who certainly didn't admire things of no consequence) was so taken by this farm that he was not ashamed to admit to being defeated by a man whom he otherwise loathed and who was likely to make the most of such an admission; and he bought the

vineyards for four times the original price, after just ten years of careful cultivation.

47. Petronius, *Satyricon*, 75f

Writing at a time when some freedmen had been politically highly influential (see No. **176**), Petronius satirises the way an ex-slave could inherit his patron's estate and challenge the wealth of the landowning aristocrats who were supposedly his natural superiors.

I too used to be just what you are, but I have risen as far as this by my own merits (*virtute mea*). What men need is initiative, none of the rest matters. I buy well, I sell well; let others give you different advice ... Well, as I was about to say, it was thrift that brought me this good fortune. When I arrived here from Asia, I was just as big as this candlestick. Actually I used to measure my height against it day by day, and I used to anoint my lips from the lamp to get a beard on my face faster. Well, I was my owner's particular pet for fourteen years; there's nothing dishonourable in doing what your master orders. And I used to do my mistress's will too – you know what I mean: I won't spell it out, since I'm not the one to boast.

(76) But in accordance with the will of the gods, I became the master of the household, and took command of my master's little brain. And then? He nominated me co-heir with the Emperor, and I inherited an estate big enough for a senator. But no one is satisfied with doing nothing; I decided on a business career. I won't bore you with a long story: I built five ships, filled them with wine at a time when wine was equivalent to gold, and sent them to Rome. You'll suppose I'd planned what happened next: every single ship was wrecked. Fact, not fiction! In one day Neptune devoured thirty million Sesterces. Did I give up? Certainly not! I felt this loss as though it was nothing. I built other, bigger ships, better and more fortunate ones, so that no one should say I was not a courageous man. As you know, a great ship is a sign of great courage. I filled them with wine again, and bacon fat, and beans, and perfumes from Capua, and slaves. At that moment, Fortunata supported me most loyally – she sold all her gold and clothes and gave me one hundred *aurei*, cash. That was the yeast for my savings (*peculium*); what the gods will, happens quickly. On one voyage I made a round profit of ten million Sesterces. At once I bought back every estate which had belonged to my patron. I built a house, I bought slaves and cattle. Whatever I touched grew like a honeycomb. When I began to have more wealth than the whole of my community back home, I withdrew my hand; I retired from business life and drew an income

from advancing capital to my freedmen.

48. Pliny the Elder, *Natural History*, 18, 8

If a former slave was motivated to be more successful in order to assert himself, he also ran the risk of incurring the resentment of the free-born. This envy (*invidia*, Gk. *phthonos*) on the part of the rest of the community frequently expressed itself in terms of sorcery accusations (see Apuleius, No. **96** below).

(41) Caius Furius Chresimus had been set free from slavery; when he started getting much larger harvests from a fairly small farm than his neighbours did from very large ones, he became highly unpopular and was accused of abstracting other people's crops by sorcery.

(42) He was afraid that he would be found guilty at his trial before the Curule Aedile Spurius Albinus; so when the tribes were about to cast their votes, he brought all his farm equipment into the Forum and brought along his slaves, who were all healthy and well looked-after and well dressed (so Piso tells us), and his well-fashioned iron tools, heavy hoes and plough-shares, and well-fed oxen; and then (43) said, 'Here, Romans, is my sorcery, though I can't show you or bring into the Forum all the work I've put in at night and my early mornings or how I've sweated.' As a result they acquitted him unanimously.

49. *ILS* 8341

While some Roman freedmen managed to identify themselves with the ideal of the peasant farmer (Nos. **46** and **48** above), those who could not achieve the security represented by landed property saw their tomb as the best substitute – one reason why freedmen invested in particularly ostentatious funerary monuments. An inscription from Rome explicitly makes this connection.

Caius Hostius Pamphilus, freedman of Caius, physician,
bought this tomb for himself and for Nelpia Hymnis, freedwoman of Marcus, and for their freedmen and freedwomen and their descendants.

This is our eternal home, this is our farm,
these are our orchards, this is our tomb.

13 feet across, 24 feet deep.

50. *CIL* 6.22355A

The Roman *domus* provided foreigners who entered it as rightless slaves with a framework which enabled them not just to survive but to find a place in society as freed citizens. That the household unit satisfied emotional as well as merely economic needs can be seen not so much from epitaphs which freedmen had an obligation to erect for their patrons, as from those they put up for one another (from the tomb of the Memmii, Rome; see also Nos. 171—5).

In honour of Aulus Memmius Clarus

Dedicated by Aulus Memmius Urbanus to his fellow-freedman and dearest companion. I cannot remember, my most respected fellow-freedman, that there was ever any quarrel between you and me. By this epitaph, I invoke the gods of heaven and of the underworld as witnesses that we first met on the slave-dealer's platform, that we were granted our freedom together in the same household, and that nothing ever parted us from one another except the day of your death.

CHAPTER 4

MORAL INFERIORS

51. Xenophon, *The Householder*, 12

Associated with the compulsion to classify all men as either free or slave, came a tendency to assimilate this polarity to others: Greek and barbarian, intelligent and stupid, superior and inferior – and from there the shift to 'good and bad' was unavoidable. In spite of all the evidence that Greeks and Romans realised that *some* slaves were 'trustworthy, prudent, brave – and even philosophers' (Macrobius, *Saturnalia*, 46: see No. **243** below), there was an almost universal prejudice that slaves could not but be worse than their masters: 'There is no healthy element in the soul of a slave' (Plato, *Laws* = **80**, 264e below). Similar to the prejudices to be found in ancient and other societies directed by the middle-aged against the young, or by men against women (for example, in Aristophanes' comedies *Thesmophoriazusae* and *Ecclesiazusae*).

(18) It is hard to learn to do something well if the teacher's demonstration is bad; and when a master sets an example of carelessness, it is difficult for the slave to learn to be careful. (19) To put it briefly, I don't think I can remember a case of good slaves belonging to a bad master. I do however know of bad slaves who belong to a good master – and they're punished for it. If you want to make people capable of being managers, then you have to supervise their work, and examine it, and you have to be willing to reward those responsible for what has been done well, and you must not be frightened to punish as he deserves someone who is careless.

52. Salvian, *The Governance of God*, 8, 3

This assumption was just as much taken for granted by a Christian writer at the end of antiquity.

(14) No one doubts that all slaves are either like their owners, or they are worse – though the more usual thing is to find that they are worse. Since even good masters generally own bad slaves, it is easy to work out from this what sort of people all these slaves must have been, when

the wickedness of their owners made the character of slaves (bad enough in themselves) even worse.

53. Achilles Tatius, *Leukippe and Kleitophon*, 7, 10

Slaves appear as frequently in Greek romances as they no doubt did in the households of the wealthy members of the educated elite who read these works for their entertainment. While we should not assume that any particular episode was 'typical' in the sense that similar events frequently occurred or that it can be taken as a characteristic illustration of slave life in the ancient world, sentiments are expressed about the nature of slaves as a class which seem to have been widely held by the readers as well as the author. Here the wicked head slave Sosthenes has just been trying to seduce the heroine Leukippe.

(5) It seems that the maxim is true, that fear has the effect of paralysing the memory; at any rate Sosthenes was scared for his life, and was in such a state of shock that he totally forgot what he was just about to do, so that he didn't even lock the doors of Leukippe's little cottage. Slaves as a class are utterly cowardly whenever there is any cause for fear.

54. Salvian, *The Governance of God*, 4, 3

In the later Roman Empire, Christian intellectuals saw themselves as metaphorically the slaves of God (see Nos. 241–2); and when they attacked the vices of their wealthy congregations, they often compared their behaviour unfavourably with that of their own slaves. But an extenuation of the particular delicts of slaves only shows that it was taken for granted that slaves were bad. It is worth noting that this comprehensive list of the things that everyone knew slaves did wrong assumes that they are primarily consumers (on theft, see No. 83 below), not producers.

(13) Perhaps one of these rich men will object: 'but we just don't do the sorts of things that our slaves do. Among our slaves there are thieves and runaways; among them there are ones who are totally dominated by their appetites and by greed.' Of course these vices are typical of slaves – but there are more vices, and worse vices, which are typical of masters. Some masters must of course be excepted, but they are very few, and the reason I won't mention them by name is not to avoid appearing to praise them, but to avoid seeming to impugn those I

don't mention.

(14) Now the first point is that when slaves steal something, this is perhaps done under the pressure of necessity, since even if they are being provided with the standard ration, this corresponds to a customary norm rather than to what is satisfactory; it accords with the rule, but doesn't satisfy requirements. The resulting need makes the slaves' faults less blameworthy, since someone who was forced to commit a theft against his will stands accused of a theft for which he may be forgiven. The Bible itself seems in some ways almost to excuse the wrong-doing of all those who are in need when it says, 'A man who has stolen is not much to be blamed when he steals to fill a hungry belly' (*Proverbs*, 6, 30). He steals in order to fill a hungry belly: and we cannot make a serious accusation against those who are pardoned by the words of Scripture.

(15) What we have said about slaves stealing, applies equally to their running away, since it is not just material necessity but actual torture which drives them to run away. They are afraid of those who are in charge of them, of those who maintain silence among them (*silentiarii*), of their master's agents; so that they seem to be the property of each one of these every bit as much as of their masters. They are beaten and mishandled by them all. What more needs to be said? There are many slaves who actually run away *to* their owners, because they are terrified of their fellow-slaves. So we ought to blame their flight not on those who run away, but rather on those who force them to run away. These wretched individuals are subject to violence − they actually want to serve, but they are forced to run away. They don't by any means want to leave the service of their owners, but the savage treatment they get at the hands of their fellow-slaves doesn't allow them to serve.

(16) They are also called liars. But it is the fear of undergoing a brutal punishment that forces them to tell lies − they lie because they want to avoid being tortured. Is there anything surprising about a terrified slave preferring to tell a lie to being flogged?

(17) They are accused of being dominated by their appetites and by greed. This isn't surprising; someone who has frequently had to put up with hunger is much more likely to want to eat his fill. And even if he doesn't go without bread, he certainly has to go without delicacies, and he must therefore be forgiven for being greedy for something which he always has to make do without.

(18) The principal point I want to make about these vices typical of slaves is that if slaves are runaways, then you who are rich and noble are runaways too. Isn't anyone who departs from the law laid down by his master a runaway? So why are you rich men finding fault with your slaves? You're behaving exactly as they are. They run away from their masters, you from yours. But you are more to blame than they are,

since they may well be running away from a bad master, but you from a good one. And then you accuse your slaves of uncontrolled gluttony. This sin is rarely true of a slave, because they lack the means to satisfy it – but it is frequent with you, since you have the means.

55. Pliny the Elder, *Natural History*, 35, 36

This moral inferiority must imply that slaves are unworthy of the higher aspirations of human beings, from which they must be formally excluded (see AVN 51 on Athenian regulations banning them from taking exercise in the *palaestra* and – a particular humiliation – forbidding homosexual relations between free men and slaves).

(77) Painting has always had the honour of being practised by men of free birth and later of high status; there has always been a ban on teaching it to slaves. That is why there are no famous works of art, nor statues, made by anyone who was a slave.

56. Pliny, *Letters*, 10, 29 and 30

In principle slaves were banned absolutely from all those activities which made a man a citizen: the most important of these was fighting. For a slave to be found serving as a soldier was normally considered an unnatural violation of the slave/free distinction.

29: Pliny to Trajan.

The young officer Sempronius Caelianus has sent to me two slaves whom he found among the new recruits; I put off passing judgement on them because I wanted to ask you about the punishment appropriate, seeing that you are responsible for establishing and upholding military discipline. My main reason for hesitating is that although the men had taken the military oath, they had not yet been assigned to particular units. So I would be grateful, Master, if you would write to tell me what to do – especially since this will set a precedent.

30: Trajan to Pliny.

It was in accordance with my orders that Sempronius Caelianus sent these persons to you; it will be necessary to decide whether they appear to have deserved the death penalty. The point at issue is whether they volunteered, were conscripted, or were given as substitutes [i.e. by conscripts who did not want to perform their military service]. If they were conscripted, it was the recruiting procedure that was at fault;

if they were given as substitutes, the guilt lies with the men who presented them; if they came forward of their own accord, although they were aware of their status, then they will have to be punished. It is not really relevant that they had not yet been assigned to particular units; the truth about their background should have been made public on the very first day when they were passed for service.

57. Pausanias, 1, 29.7 and 32.3

Slaves naturally helped their masters when these went on a campaign, by carrying heavy equipment, preparing food, and assisting the wounded. Only on rare occasions, when a community felt that its very existence was threatened, would slaves be required to take part in the fighting — after first having been given their freedom. In his guide to the monuments for Athenians and allies who fell in various battles and were buried outside the north-western city-walls of Athens, Pausanias (no supporter of democracy) shows surprise that the Athenians were humane enough to pay tribute to the support given by their slaves.

And there is also the grave of the Athenians who campaigned against the people of Aegina before the Persian invasion. Even a democracy can make a just enactment — for the Athenians allowed their slaves to be buried publicly and had their names inscribed on a monument. It testifies that in the fighting they showed how well disposed they were towards their owners.

Other occasions on which slaves were manumitted and granted the privilege of fighting are listed by Macrobius (**243**, 30–4; see also **89**; **230**, Ch. 4.8; **235**, Ch. 21). According to Pausanias, the first such occasion was during the Persian invasion of Attica in 490 BC, repulsed at the battle of Marathon.

There is a grave in the plain for the Athenians; on it there are slabs containing the names of the dead arranged by their tribes; the other tomb is for the Plataeans from Boeotia and for the slaves — since this was the first occasion on which slaves fought too.

58. Isidore of Seville, *Definitions*, 9, 3

When manpower shortages led the Roman government to enlist slaves, the fiction that only free citizens could fight was maintained by buying the slaves from their masters and manumitting them first. This exception, in 216 BC, was recorded by Livy (who said 8,000 slaves were involved: 22, 57.11) and Valerius Maximus (who mentioned 24,000: 7, 6.1; L&R I, 65).

(38) It is known that slaves have absolutely never fought as soldiers, except after ceasing to be slaves; the exception was in the time of Hannibal, when the Romans were in such dire straits after the battle of Cannae, that they didn't even have the time to free their slaves first.

59. Dio Cassius, 48, 19

For Romans, one of the most horrifying things about the civil wars of the first century BC was that there was a great temptation for the warlords to ignore the status distinction between free and slave by allowing slaves to fight in their armies. Thus, Octavian used 20,000 slaves as rowers in his fleet in the war against Sextus Pompeius (Suetonius, *Augustus*, 16), but he was careful to have them manumitted first. There is virtually no evidence for the use of galley slaves by the navies of antiquity, at least under normal circumstances (Thucydides 7, 13.2 and Scipio's captives in No. 114 are clearly exceptions; see L. Casson, *Ships and Seamanship in the Ancient World* (Princeton, 1971), Ch. 13, *App.* pp. 322–6). At the same time, Octavian's propaganda made the most of the fact that Pompeius also used slaves – the Vestal Virgins ostentatiously prayed for the recapture of runaways (see No. 216 below), and when Octavian finally defeated Pompeius at Naulochus in September 36 BC, the free men and the former slaves in his army were treated quite differently. In his official biography, Augustus could describe Pompey's navy as though they were pirates.

(4) As a result Pompeius took over his fleet and received the great numbers of slaves who were arriving from Italy, and his power increased enormously. So many slaves were running away that the Vestal Virgins inserted a prayer into their ceremonies in order to stop the desertions of slaves.

60. Dio Cassius, 49, 12

(4) Of those who had supported Sextus Pompeius, the equestrians and senators were punished with some exceptions, while of the ordinary soldiers, those who were free were enlisted among Octavian's army, while the slaves were handed over to their masters for punishment. If no master could be found, they were crucified.

61. *The Achievements of Augustus*, 4.25

I freed the sea from pirates. Of the slaves who ran away from their masters in the course of this war and took up arms against the Republic, I recaptured thirty thousand and returned them to their masters to be punished.

62. *Code of Theodosius*, 7, 13.8

Even during the frequent military crises of late antiquity, the authorities were hesitant about enforcing levies of slaves (see Symmachus, *Letters*, 6, 58: 398 AD). In principle, slave status continued to disqualify anyone from military service, like other degrading activities, and landowners who supplied the imperial army with such worthless material were seriously punished.

The August Emperors Gratian, Valentinian and Theodosius: Edict to the Provincials.

We decree that no slave is to be offered for enlistment into the excellent squadrons of our military levies, nor anyone taken from an inn or who has been working in any notorious tavern or from the category of cooks or of bakers or any other category which is excluded from military service by its disgraceful occupation, nor people taken from prisons (*ergastula*).
(1) If anyone is reported for this offence on the information of any person to the Illustrious Gentlemen, the Masters of the Infantry and the Cavalry, they shall not be able to escape the penalty of a heavy fine on any excuse whatsoever. Not only will a stern penalty be imposed upon the man who offere such a recruit for enlistment, but he will also be punished by having to supply three worthier recruits.
Dated Constantinople, 29 January 380.

63. *Code of Theodosius*, 7, 13.16

But in a time of crisis, the Roman authorities were prepared to promise slaves their freedom in return for military service.

The August Emperors Arcadius, Honorius and Theodosius, to the Provincials.

When the attacks of our enemies have to be resisted, we order that attention be paid not just to the legal status of our soldiers, but also to their strength. Of course we believe that free-born persons are motivated

by patriotism; nevertheless, we exhort slaves too, by the authority of this edict, to offer themselves for the exertions of war as soon as possible, and if they take up arms as men fit for military service, they are to obtain the reward of freedom. They are also to receive a travel allowance of two *solidi* each. We particularly urge this service upon the slaves of those who are employed in the Imperial Armed Services, and also upon the slaves of our federated allies and of subject peoples, since it is clear that they are fighting the same war side by side with their owners.
Dated Ravenna, 17 April 406.

64. *CIL* 14.4178

Slaves were generally allowed to participate on equal terms in religious ceremonies (for example, in the Benevolent Society of Diana and Antinous at Lanuvium in Latium, *ILS* 7212 = L&R II, 70); but some cults treated slaves as unclean and excluded them, for specific reasons (see Athenaeus 262c, No. **80** below). This inscription from an altar also found at Lanuvium is so extreme that its authenticity has been doubted. If it does in fact refer to Mars as god of warfare, it would be an indication that this was thought an activity specifically reserved to free men.

MAVORTIO SACR. HOC SIGNUM A SERVO TANGI NEFAS EST.
Sacred to Mars [?] . It is a sin for this image to be touched by
a slave.

65. Appian, *Roman Civil Wars*, 2, 17

If slaves were 'bad', then any situation in which the slave/free polarity was not strictly adhered to gave cause for concern. Already in fifth-century Athens, an anti-democratic writer was uneasy about the fact that slaves were treated with as much respect as free men ('Old Oligarch' = pseudo-Xenophon, *Constitution of Athens*, 1.10; see AVN 74). There is no evidence from either the Greek or the Roman world that slaves could normally be identified by their clothing or hairstyle (shaving a slave's head was an exceptional punishment: see Nos. **156**, **191**, **218**; Achilles Tatius 8, 5.4). But if these distinctions were not upheld, the free population would be corrupted. Here Appian is talking about the degeneration of the urban plebs at Rome; after Caesar's assassination, Cassius tried to win their support with talk of political liberty, but this meant very little to them.

(120) The Roman plebs is very mixed up with immigrants. A freedman has the same civic rights as they have, and a man who is still a slave wears the same clothes as his masters; for the dress of the rest of the population, excepting the senators, is the same as that of the slaves.

66. Pliny the Elder, *Natural History*, 33, 8

Horror at the thought that the status distinction between free and slave might be ignored is frequently expressed by Roman writers of the first century AD. Ever since Augustus' reforms of the equestrian order:

(33) Even men who have been freed from slavery leap over these restrictions to attain the symbols of equestrian status ... and this became so widespread that one of the equestrians called Flavius Proculus accused 400 persons on this count to the Emperor Claudius when he was holding his census. Thus while this Estate has been clearly separated off from ordinary free men, it has become full of slaves.

67. *Digest* 1, 14.3: Ulpian, from *On Sabinus*, book 38

In the real world, persons whose legal status was that of a slave might even manage to get themselves elected to high public office.

Barbarius Philippus was a runaway slave, stood for the Praetorship at Rome and was elected Praetor Designate. Pomponius says that the fact that he was a slave did not prevent him from becoming Praetor; and in actual fact he did hold this office.

Now let's examine this question: if a slave has managed to elude recognition for some time, and has held the office of Praetor, what should our opinion about this be? Should all his judgements and decrees be null and void? Or should they be valid, for the sake of those who took cases before him according to the statutes or for some other reason prescribed by law? I personally think that none of his decisions should be overturned, for the more sensible interpretation is the following — that the Roman People has the right to entrust the powers of a Praetor to a slave, and even if it had known that he was a slave, it could have made him a free man. And *a fortiori* that ability must be recognised as residing in an Emperor.

68. Dio Cassius, 48, 34

It also required emphatic punishment to reassure public opinion that there was no danger that legal statuses were becoming confused; one of the most serious charges levelled against the Second Triumvirate (43 BC) was that it allowed non-Romans, serving soldiers, freedmen and even slaves, to become members of the Senate.

(5) Certainly a man called Maximus was about to enter upon the office of Quaestor when his owner recognised him and dragged him away. He was actually granted immunity because he had dared to stand for public office, but another runaway who was found to be one of the Praetors was thrown from the Tarpeian Rock on the Capitol, after having first been manumitted so that he could suffer this appropriate punishment [39 BC].

69. Dionysius of Halicarnassus, *Ancient History of Rome*, 4, 24

The period of the Roman civil wars may well have been a time of exceptional social mobility, and many free citizens felt that steps should be taken to reinforce the distinction between free and slave — as Augustus in fact did by the *Lex Aelia Sentia* (Nos. 5 and 6 above).

Those who believed that there was a clear and unbridgeable difference between slaves and citizens found the Roman practice of using slavery as a mechanism to integrate outsiders into their society highly objectionable. Greek opponents of Rome pointed to this Roman peculiarity as something highly unnatural; and Dionysius of Halicarnassus, as a Greek historian of Rome who tried to explain and defend Rome to his fellow-Greeks, felt he had to explain and extenuate the Romans' readiness to give citizenship to men who had been slaves.

The custom of enrolling in the four 'urban' tribes manumitted slaves who didn't want to go back to their home countries was traced back to the institution of the first census by King Servius Tullius (traditional dates 578—534). In Dionysius' account, Servius defends his action by claiming that it would make owners more careful not to liberate slaves if they did not deserve it, while the hope of becoming full citizens would be a greater incentive to serve more loyally. Two other arguments are listed: the number of potential soldiers would be increased, and so would the electoral support of the wealthy (whose freedmen clients would have votes). This leads Dionysius to digress:

(1) Since I have reached this part of my account, I think it essential to describe the attitudes which the Romans had at that time towards their

slaves, in case anyone should criticise either the king who first decided to give citizenship to people who had been enslaved, or those who accepted such a law, for abandoning sensible and fine traditions. (2) The Romans obtained possession of slaves through extremely legitimate procedures: either they bought from the state those who were 'sold under the spear' as part of the booty; or a general would allow those who took prisoners of war to keep them, together with the rest of the plunder; or else they obtained possession of slaves by buying them from others who were their owners as the result of one of these methods. (3) By allowing those who had lost their own country and their freedom in war, and had been useful to those who had enslaved them or had bought them from their captors, to have both these things restored to them by their owners, neither Tullius who established the rule nor those who accepted and continued it, considered that what they were doing could be criticised as shameful or harmful to the community. (4) Most of them were given their freedom as a reward for good conduct, and this was the best way of becoming independent of your owner. A small number bought their freedom with money they had earned by working dutifully and honestly.

But this is not the situation today: things are in a state of such confusion and the fine traditions of the Roman State are ignored and disgraced to such an extent, that people now buy their freedom (and immediately become Romans) with money which they have acquired through brigandage and robbery and prostitution and similar disreputable activities. (5) Slaves who have advised and supported their owners in poisonings and murders and crimes against the gods or the community receive their freedom from them as a reward; and others, so that they can draw the monthly dole of corn provided by the State or any other grant for poor citizens which leading politicians may be handing out, and then bring it to the persons who have given them their freedom; and others again as a result of their owners' frivolity or silly desire for popularity. (6) I personally know people who conceded freedom to all their slaves after their own deaths so that as corpses they would be acclaimed as good men, and so that there would be lots of people wearing the felt liberty-caps on their heads to follow their biers in the funeral procession; and according to what was said by those who knew, some of those in the processions were criminals who had just been freed from prison and had done things worthy of ten thousand deaths. But most people are horrified when they consider these almost indelible blots on the city's reputation; and they criticise this custom, since a powerful city which claims to dominate the entire world ought not to make such persons citizens. (7) There are many other traditions which one could condemn because they were instituted by the ancients but are totally perverted by men today.

I myself do not think that this law should be abolished, in case something even worse for the community should happen as a result. But I assert that it has to be amended as far as possible, and that great infamy and filth which cannot be cleansed should not be allowed to be introduced into the citizen-body. (8) I would prefer the Censors to look into this question, or alternatively the Consuls (since it calls for an office with great authority); they should investigate those who have become free each year – what sort of people they are and why and by what procedure they have been manumitted, just as they investigate the character of the equestrians and Senators. Then they should enrol among the tribes those they find worthy of citizenship, and allow them to stay in Rome; and they should expel from the city the mob of those who are corrupt and unclean – they should give this operation the plausible cover of founding a colony. I thought that since my subject required it, it was essential and right for me to say these things in reply to those who criticise the traditions of the Romans.

70. Suetonius, *Augustus*, 42

Other accounts confirm that the practice of manumitting slaves so that they would become entitled to receive the State corn-dole and would no longer have to be maintained by their masters was one of the reasons for Augustus' restrictive legislation. This continued to be a problem even in late antiquity (*CTh*. 14, 17.6: 370 AD).

(2) Once, when he decreed a distribution of largesse and discovered that a large number of persons had been manumitted and entered on the lists of citizens, he declared with great authority and firmness that those to whom nothing had been promised would not get anything; and he gave the rest a smaller sum than he had promised, so that the total allocated would not be exceeded. During one particularly serious famine, he adopted the unpleasant solution of expelling from Rome all slaves who were up for sale, all gladiatorial slave gangs, all non-Romans except for doctors and teachers, and even some of the household slaves.

71. Dio Cassius, 55, 13

The reason for Augustus' legislation was thus the feeling that only those who deserved it should be granted citizenship, and in particular that indiscriminate testamentary manumission should be controlled. Livy ascribes this point of view to a much earlier period (45, 15.5: 168 BC), but is probably reflecting the preoccupations of his own age. There is no evidence that Augustus was acting in the interests of Roman slave owners concerned about a possible decline in the size of the slave labour force.

In 4 AD, he held a partial census of those owning property worth more than 200,000 Sesterces, and introduced other reforms including the *Lex Aelia Sentia* (see No. 6 above).

(7) A lot of people were indiscriminately manumitting lots of slaves. Augustus set minimum age limits both for the person who intended to manumit somebody and for the man who was going to be freed. He also codified the rules according to which both the rest of the population and the masters themselves should behave towards freedmen.

72. Pliny the Elder, *Natural History*, 28, 14

The prejudice that slaves were inferior to their masters implied that it was a disgrace for a Roman of high status to depend upon his slaves for anything (a theme which frequently occurs in satirists like Juvenal).

(56) Self-restraint as regards eating is the most useful thing for health. Lucius Lucullus appointed a slave to control him in this respect, so that an old man who had celebrated a triumph incurred the ultimate indignity of having his hand restrained from touching any food even when he was dining in the Capitol; how disgraceful it is that he should have been more ready to obey his slave than himself!

73. Pliny the Elder, *Natural History*, 29, 8

If it was axiomatic (for a free Roman) that 'Roman and Greek' and 'free and slave' were as 'good and bad', then obeying a Greek slave was clearly unnatural — even if he was your doctor. Pliny had a personal interest in attacking Greek slave doctors, since he considered himself the only Roman who bothered to investigate the products of Nature, otherwise left over to these slaves:

(19) We deserve what we get [i.e. being murdered by physicians], since none of us wants to learn what he has to do for his health. We use other people's feet when we go out, we use other people's eyes to recognise things, we use another person's memory to greet people, we use someone else's help to stay alive; but what is worthwhile amongst Nature's products, what is useful to life, these are utterly neglected. The only things we keep for ourselves are our pleasures.

74. Lysias 5: *In Defence of Kallias, on a Charge of Temple-robbery*

In both Greece and Rome, the slave's inferiority was expressed by the fact that when he appeared as a witness in a court of law, he had to give evidence under torture (see Nos. **177–9**). Such evidence could be impugned by an advocate who exploited the free jury's prejudice that slaves were morally worthless.

(3) It is not right that you should think that the words of slaves are to be believed, while those of these men are not. You must remember that no one has ever lodged an accusation against Kallias before — neither any private citizen nor any magistrate — and that during the time when he has been living in this city, he has done many good things for you, and has reached this late stage in his life free from blame; while these slaves have done many wicked things throughout their lives, and have been responsible for disasters of all sorts, and now they are making these statements in order to gain their freedom — as though they deserved a reward for what they are doing . . .

(5) I think that this trial should not be thought to concern just the accused, but everyone in our community — for these are not the only people who own slaves; everyone else has slaves too, and when these slaves consider what has befallen the accused, they will not think about how to earn their freedom through some good deed for their masters, but rather how to earn it through some false accusation against them.

75. Pliny, *Panegyric on Trajan*, 42

A Roman orator who wished to denigrate an unpopular emperor like Domitian could accuse him of nothing more terrible than having relied upon the evidence of slaves to secure the condemnation of their masters (see No. **179**).

(1) It was not so much the Voconian and Julian laws that enriched the Imperial Account and the State Treasury, as the charge of high treason — the one single way to accuse those who were invulnerable to any other accusation. You, Trajan, have completely removed any fear of this; you have been satisfied with that real superiority which none lacked so much as those who insisted upon their own majestic status. (2) We can trust our friends again, we are respected by our children, we are obeyed by our slaves; they respect their masters, and obey them, and they keep them. (3) For no longer are our slaves the emperor's particular friends, but we are, and the Father of the State no longer thinks that he is dearer to other men's slaves than to his own citizens. You have freed

us from the fear of an accuser within our own households, and you have removed the threat of what I would call a slave war by means of the straightforward principle of public safety. By doing this, you have benefitted the slaves no less than their masters: for you have made us secure, and them better men. (4) You do not want this policy of yours to be praised, and perhaps it should not be praised. Nevertheless, it is most welcome to those of us who remember an emperor who incited slaves to lay capital charges against their owners, who instructed them as to the accusations which he was going to punish as though they had already been made — a real and inescapable evil which every slave-owner had to suffer so frequently if his slaves were as wicked as the emperor was.

76. Livy, 26, 27

The relationship between masters and slaves should not be interpreted as one of semi-permanent conflict (see Ch. 10). Nevertheless anyone who owned a slave who had cause to hate him might find that information about his intentions was being betrayed to his enemies — particularly in a period of political strife like the Hannibalic War. There had been strong support for Hannibal in Capua, and in 210 BC certain Campanians were suspected of terrorist attacks in Rome itself.

Complaints about the way the war was going were interrupted by a fire which began in several places near the Forum on the night before the Quinquatrus festival. The so-called seven shops (later called the 'five') and the silversmiths' shops (now called the New Shops) caught fire at the same time, then several private houses (there were no large public halls in those days), the State Prison, the Fishmongers' Forum, and the King's House; the Temple of Vesta was saved with difficulty, particularly through the assistance of thirteen slaves whom the state subsequently bought and set free. The fire raged continually for a day and a night, and because the flames had broken out in several widely separate places at the same time, there was no doubt that it had been started intentionally. So with Senatorial authority, the Consul announced at an assembly that anyone who stated who was responsible for starting the fire would be rewarded with money if he were a free man, and with his freedom if he were a slave. As a result of this reward, a slave belonging to the Calavii of Campania (his name was Manus) informed against his masters and against five young Campanian nobles whose parents had been beheaded by Quintus Fulvius. He said that they were responsible for this fire and were going to start others all over the place if they weren't arrested. So they and their slaves (*familiae*) were apprehended. At first the informer and his story were scornfully denied — he had run away from his owners on the previous day after being beaten as a punishment, and his resentment and disloyalty led him to exploit the coincidence of the outbreak of these fires in order to invent this accusation. But when they were interrogated in his presence, and a public interrogation of their accomplices in this crime began in the Forum, they all confessed, and the guilty masters and slaves were punished; the informer was given his freedom and a reward of twenty thousand bronze Asses.

77. Livy, summary of book 77

While the state authorities were clearly pleased when a slave betrayed a foreign master, their attitudes were highly ambivalent towards a slave who betrayed one of their own class — even if he was on the other side in a civil war. In 88 BC, Marius' supporter, the tribune Publius Sulpicius Rufus, had tried to deprive Sulla of command of an important war against Mithridates, and Sulla responded by occupying Rome.

Publius Sulpicius was hiding on a country estate and then dragged out and executed as the result of information laid by his slave. The slave was manumitted so that he could be given the reward which had been promised to informers, and then thrown down the Tarpeian rock as a punishment for the crime of having betrayed his master.

78. Publilius Syrus

In the writings of the educated elite, slaves as such are invariably 'bad', even if particular slaves might be 'good'. There is virtually no evidence about how slaves themselves came to terms with the analogy between 'free/slave' and 'good/bad'. Perhaps the animal fables of Aesop (who was believed to have been a slave) expressed some ideas about how the privileged and the disadvantaged should treat one another. In the collection of sayings compiled by the ex-slave Pubilius Syrus in the first century BC (see No. **108** below), there are a small number which explicitly refer to slavery. Some of them show a point of view quite unlike the ordinary prejudices of Greeks and Romans.

(414) There are less risks in being tame: but it makes you a slave.

(489) It is beautiful to die instead of being degraded as a slave.

(519) Whoever helps his country is the slave of his people.

(538) Modesty is also a kind of slavery.

(596)   If you serve wisely you will have some share in the master's role.

(616)   If you don't like being a slave, you will be miserable; but you won't stop being a slave.

79. Petronius, *Satyricon*, 57

One of the guests at Trimalchio's dinner makes fun of his host's establishment. Another freedman expresses annoyance at this and testifies that those who were not landowners with inherited wealth might be proud of their achievements too.

What has he got to laugh about? His father didn't have to pay for him with gold when he was a baby. So you're a Roman gentleman; and I'm a king's son. You ask why in that case I served as a slave? Because I sold myself into slavery myself; I preferred to become a Roman citizen than be a tax-paying subject. And now I hope that my life is such that no one can laugh at me. I am a man among men, I walk about holding my head up with pride; I don't owe anyone a bronze As; I've never been taken to court; no one's ever come up to me in the Forum and said, 'give me back what you owe me'. I've bought a bit of property and some silverware; I keep a household comprising twenty persons and a dog; I bought free the woman I've lived with, so that no one else should get his hands on her; I paid one thousand *denarii* for my own freedom; I was made a member of the College of the Six Priests of Augustus without having to pay a contribution; I hope to die in such a way that I won't be ashamed of it when I'm dead. . .

CHAPTER 5

STATUS SYMBOL OR ECONOMIC INVESTMENT?

80. Athenaeus, *The Banqueting Sophists*, 6, 262–73

One of the few passages of any length dealing with slavery to be found in the ancient writers occurs in this collection of literary references arranged in the form of a discussion between various guests at a dinner party. The scene is supposedly set in Alexandria around the year 200 AD; most of those present are Greeks, but characters based on the two famous jurists Ulpian and Masurius Sabinus provide some interesting comments from a Roman point of view. Athenaeus is more concerned to show how widely read he is in Greek literature than to provide a systematic treatment of the subjects he touches on. Consequently his narrative is particularly useful for the excerpts it contains from earlier sources.

But it is hardly a sufficient basis for attempts to reconstruct the development of Greek slavery over the centuries, although a number of points do emerge. While there are references to chattel-slaves as objects of value in the earliest literary sources (Homer, *Odyssey* 17.322; 24.278f.), it was felt that slaves had only recently become widespread (263b; see Herodotus 6.137 = AVN 15), and that this process took longer in some parts of the Greek world than in others (264c). Although the hypothesis that slavery developed to provide labour for new 'industries' *c.* 600 BC is fallacious, there may be a connection between the large numbers of slaves on Chios and the importance of wine in the island's economy (265b: on the suitability of slaves for viticulture, see Columella, 1, 9.4 = **149**).

The figure for slaves in Aegina is impossible and that for Athens ambiguous: if genuine, it probably simply refers to all members of the household who were not listed as adult male citizens or Metics.

Despite the myth that the virtuous Romans of old owned only a few slaves (273b), some Roman slave-holdings were vast (Tacitus mentions a household of 400 kept in Rome alone, apart from the owner's rural slaves: *Annals* 14, 43.4), and Athenaeus clearly thought that the purpose of owning such large numbers of slaves was primarily to demonstrate one's wealth and status (272e; 273c). This was not true only of Romans – Hellenistic kings like Antiochus IV sought to impress their subjects by organising processions involving hundreds if not thousands of slaves (Polybius, 30, 25.17); it was a mark of extreme indignity for an exiled monarch like Ptolemy VI to arrive at Rome accompanied by just four slaves (Diodorus Siculus, 31, 18: 164 BC).

The fact that slave-holdings were huge does not allow valid deductions to be made about the greater or lesser availability of slaves as the result of warfare, about the proportion of slaves in the population as a whole, or about the proportion of citizens who owned slaves — they are rather a sign of the increasing concentration of wealth in a small number of particular households. Thus it is not surprising that there continue to be references to slave-holdings numbering thousands from late antiquity (the estate of Melania the Younger in the early fifth century is the best example) even if the total number of slaves may have been less than in the first century AD.

Two separate remarks made by the physician Galen suggest that in his city of Pergamon in the second century AD, there may have been 120,000 adults, of whom 40,000 were slaves (5, p. 49 Kühn); for what it is worth, this implies a substantially higher proportion of slaves than in rural regions of Roman Egypt for which tax-lists survive.

Cults Excluding Slaves

Demokritos finished what he had to say and asked for a drink from the so-called 'decanter of Saurias'.

Who is this Saurias? asked Ulpian. As he was about to list a whole series of similar questions, a crowd of house-boys appeared around us bringing in things for the meal. Demokritos started speaking again and talked about these people.

I myself, my friends, have always been amazed at how much self-restraint slaves in general have, considering that they are in contact with so many tempting things. They don't keep their hands off them just because they are afraid, but also because that is how they have been trained — and I don't mean the sort of training given by Pherekrates' 'Slave-teacher', but one which they acquire by habit.

And it isn't because this sort of thing is forbidden — as it is when they sacrifice to Hera on the island of Cos: for Makareus says in book three of his *Coan Antiquities* that when the Coans sacrifice to Hera they don't allow any slave to come into the temple or to taste any of the things that are prepared for the festival. And in *The slave who couldn't be sold*, Antiphanes says:

Looking at half-eaten cream cakes and fowl lying here in front of us; and the women tell us that it is not right for a slave to eat any of these things even when they are left over.

and Epikrates, in his version of *The slave who couldn't be sold*, makes one of the house-slaves complain and say:

> What is more hateful than to be called to a drinking party with
> 'Boy, boy' — and that by some adolescent who hasn't grown a
> beard yet; or to have to bring in the chamber-pot and have to look
> at half-eaten cream cakes and fowl lying there in front of us; and the
> women tell us that it isn't right for a slave to eat any of these things
> even when they are left over. What makes me really angry is that
> they call those of us who do eat any of these things greedy gluttons.

(e)   It is clear when we compare these lines that it was Epikrates who
borrowed the verses from Antiphanes.

Dieukhidas says in his *Megarian Antiquities*:

> Once upon a time on the islands which lie between the territory of
> Cnidos and Syme — called the Islands of the Curses — an argument
> took place amongst the companions of Triopas after the latter's
> death. Some of them went off to Dotion, some stayed with Phorbas
> and went to Ialysos, while some joined Periergos and put in at
> Kameiros.
>
> This is said to have been the occasion when Periergos cursed
> Phorbas, which is why the islands are called the Islands of the Curses.

(f)

> Phorbas was shipwrecked and swam across to a spot at Ialysos called
> Skhedia, together with Parthenia, who was the sister of Phorbas and
> Periergos. It so happened that Thamneus was out hunting at Skhedia,
> and when he came across them he invited them to stay at his home
> as his guests. He sent a house-boy to tell his wife to prepare some-
> thing suitable since he was bringing some guests home.

(263)

> But when he got home he found that nothing had been prepared,
> so he put the grain in the mill himself and did all the other appro-
> priate things, and in this way he entertained his guests. Phorbas was
> so pleased with his hospitality that when he died he ordered his
> friends to have his funeral carried out by free men; and this has
> remained customary for sacrifices in honour of Phorbas. The
> assistants are free men, and it is sinful for a slave to come near.

Origins of Slavery; Semi-servile Statuses

(b)   Now since this question of house-boys was one of the points Ulpian
asked about, let us also consider a quotation about them, from a
text which I happen to have read a long time ago.

In *The Savages*, Pherekrates says:

> For in those days there was no Manes and no Sekis to be anyone's
> slave, but women had to do all the hard work around the house

themselves. And in addition they had to grind corn early in the morning so that the village would echo to the noise of the mills.

And in *Ankhises*, Anaxandrides says:

> Slaves have no city of their own anywhere, my friend, and Fortune inflicts all sorts of changes upon them. There are many who are not free right now, but tomorrow they will be registered as citizens of the Deme of Sounion, and in two days' time they'll be playing their part in public life. There is a divinity that directs each man's course.

In book eleven of his *Histories*, the Stoic Poseidonios says:

> Many persons who are unable to manage their own affairs because of the weakness of their intellect, hand themselves over to the service of men who are more intelligent, so that they may be looked after by them and provided with whatever they need, and may themselves give back to their masters all the service they are capable of giving through their own work. It was in this way that the Mariandynians placed themselves under the domination of the people of Heraklea, promising to serve them for ever, so long as they provided them with what they needed. They added the condition that none of them should be sold beyond the borders of Heraklea, but that they should stay within their own country.

It is probably for this reason that the epic poet Euphorion calls the Mariandynians 'bringers of gifts':

> Let them be called bringers of gifts, trembling before their lords.

And the Aristophanic writer Kallistratos says that they called the Mariandynians 'bringers of gifts' in order to avoid the resentment caused by the term 'dependant' — just as the Spartans do with their Helots, the Thessalians with the *Penestai*, and the Cretans with their *Klarotai*. The Cretans call the house-slaves they have in their cities 'Gold-bought', but they call those in the countryside, who are native and have been enslaved in the course of war, *Aphamiotai*. The term *Klarotai* comes from the fact that they have been shared out. In book three of his *Histories*, Ephoros says:

> The Cretans call their slaves *Klarotai* because of the lot which is cast for them. There are certain traditional festivals for them at Kydonia, and while they are held, free men do not go into the city; the slaves are in control over everything and are entitled to whip

the free men.

In the second book of his *Cretan Antiquities*, Sosikrates says that the
(264) Cretans call their public slaves *Mnoia*, the ones they own privately
Aphamiotai, and their subjects *Perioikoi*. Dosiades too gives a similar
account in the fourth book of his *Cretan Antiquities*.

The Thessalians use the term *Penestai* for those who are not slaves
by descent but were taken in war; the comic playwright Theopompos
develops this meaning when he talks of:

the wrinkled counsellor of a labouring (*penestēs*) master.

In the second book of his *Thessalian Affairs* (if this history is in fact
genuine), Philokrates says that the *Penestai* are also called *Thettaloiketai*
(house-boys of Thessaly). In the third book of the *History of Euboea*,
Arkhemakhos says that:

(b)   those of the Boeotians who came to live in the territory of Arne and
did not later move on to Boeotia itself, but came to like the country,
gave themselves up to the Thessalians to be their slaves. The conditions
of the agreement were that they would neither carry them off out of
the country nor kill them, while they were to work the land on their
behalf and pay the rent contributions that were assessed. Consequently these people who stayed and handed themselves over in
accordance with this agreement were originally called 'those who
stayed behind' (*Menestai*), but now they are called *Penestai*. And
many of them are wealthier than their masters.

(c)   Euripides too, in the *Phrixos*, calls them 'servers' (*latriai*) in these
words:

Servant-toiler, belonging to my ancient household.

In the ninth book of his *Histories*, Timaios of Tauromenion says that
in ancient times it was not the ancestral custom for the Greeks to be
served by slaves they had bought for money. He writes as follows:

Everybody criticises Aristotle for having been wrong about the
habits of the people of Locris. For it was not an accepted custom
among either the Locrians or the Phocians for people to buy themselves maidservants or house-boys except in accordance with a
contract made for a stated period of time. Indeed they say that
the first person to be attended by two maidservants was the wife of
Philomelos, who seized control of Delphi [355/4 BC]. Similarly

Mnason, the associate of Aristotle, became most unpopular with the people of Phocis after he had bought one thousand slaves, on the grounds that he had taken away necessary employment from the same number of citizens. For it had been customary for younger people to work as servants for older members of their own families.

Plato

In the sixth book of the *Laws* [776b–8a], Plato says:

> The question of slaves is a difficult one in every respect ... Of all Greek institutions it is perhaps the Spartan system of Helots which gives rise to the greatest doubts and disagreements, with some people considering it a good thing and others not. The slave system of the Herakleots, who have enslaved the Mariandynians, is less controversial, as is the Thessalian class of *Penestai*. When we have studied these and all other types, what should we decide to do about the acquisition of house-boys? ... For there is no element in the soul of a slave that is healthy. A sensible man should not entrust anything to their care. As the wisest poets [Homer, *Odyssey*, 17, 322] puts it:
> 'When the day of slavery catches up with a man,
> Wide-seeing Zeus takes away half of his mind.'

> ... This form of property is not easy. This has in actual fact been demonstrated many times – by the frequent revolts of the Messenians, by all the difficulties that have occurred for those states whose citizens keep many slaves who speak the same language, and by all the acts of robbery and sufferings inflicted by the so-called roving bandits of Italy.
> Anyone who considers all these points will be quite uncertain what ought to be done about things of this sort. There are two safeguards that one may take: first, those who are going to be slaves must not come from the same country of origin, and in so far as it can be arranged they must not speak the same language; and secondly, they must be properly looked after – and not just for their sakes; anyone who wishes to pay proper regard to his own interests should never behave arrogantly towards his slaves. ... One ought to punish slaves according to strict justice instead of making them conceited by giving them the odd word of advice as one would a fellow-freeman; every word spoken to a house-slave ought to be a direct command; never at any time should an owner joke with his house-slaves, whether they are women or men. A lot of people foolishly like to act like this towards their slaves, and by making them conceited they make life much more difficult both for the slaves who have to

obey, and for themselves in managing them.

The Chians the First to buy Chattel Slaves

The Chians were the first Greeks that I know of who used slaves they had bought for money, as Theopompos narrates in book seventeen of his *Histories*:

(c)
> After the Thessalians and the Spartans, the Chians were the first Greeks to use slaves, but they didn't obtain them in the same way as these did. For as we shall see, the Spartans and Thessalians constituted their slave population out of the Greeks who had previously inhabited the territories which they now control – the Spartans taking over Achaean territory, the Thessalians that of the Perrhaiboi and the Magnesians; and they call the people they enslaved *Helots* and *Penestai* respectively. But the Chians have acquired people who are not Greek-speakers to be their house-slaves, and pay a price for them.

That is what Theopompos tells us. In my opinion God punished the people of Chios for this – for in later times they were engaged in a long war because of their slaves. At least Nymphodoros of Syracuse tells the following story about them in his *Voyage along the Coast of Asia Minor*:

(d)

(e)

(f)
> The Chians' slaves ran away from them and made off into the mountains, where they gathered in large numbers and did a lot of damage to their country estates. The island is rough and covered with trees. There is a story which they tell that a little before our own time there was a certain slave who ran off to make his home in the mountains. Since he was a brave man who had a lot of luck when it came to fighting, he came to lead the runaways in the same way as a king leads an army. After the Chians had organised many expeditions against him which failed to achieve anything, Drimakos (for that was the runaway's name) saw that they were being killed for no good reason, and he made them the following proposal: 'Chian owners: what you have been suffering because of your house-slaves is never going to stop. How can it, since it is in accordance with an oracle that has been given by a god? Now if you make a truce with me and allow us to live in peace, I shall ensure that there will be many benefits for you.' So the people of Chios made a treaty with him and agreed on a truce for a certain period of time, and he prepared some measures and weights and a special seal. He showed these to the Chians and said that, 'I am going to

take anything that I take away from any of you in accordance with these weights and measures, and when I have taken whatever I need, I shall leave your warehouses sealed up with this seal. And I shall interrogate any of your house-slaves that run away about what their reasons are; and if anyone seems to me to have run away because he has been treated intolerably in any way I will keep him with me: but if their story does not convince me, I will send them back to their owners.' When the other house-slaves saw that the Chians were prepared to accept this arrangement, they ran away much less frequently, since they were afraid of being interrogated by Drimakos. At the same time the runaways who were with him were much more afraid of Drimakos than of their own masters, and treated him with great respect, obeying him as though he were their commanding officer; for he punished those who were guilty of breaches of discipline, and allowed no one to plunder the fields or to commit even a single act of injustice without having obtained his consent. At festival time, he would set out and take from the fields wine and any animals suitable for sacrificial purposes which their owners themselves would [† not] hand over. And if he found out that anyone was plotting to lay an ambush for him, he would take his revenge on them.

The city of Chios had announced that it would give a lot of money to anyone who captured Drimakos or brought them his head; and so, in the end, when he had grown old, he called his boyfriend to a particular place and told him that, 'I have loved you more than anyone else and you are my favourite and like a son to me, and so on and so forth. Now I have lived for long enough, while you are a young man in the best years of your life. So what ought to be done? You ought to become an upright and respected citizen. And since the city of Chios is going to give a lot of money to the man who kills me, and has promised him his freedom, it is you who must cut off my head and bring it to the Chians, take the money from the city and live happily ever after.' Although the young man objected, he convinced him to do this; so he cut off his head and received from the Chians the money that had been promised, buried the body of the runaway and then went home to his own country. Later the Chians suffered a lot of vandalism and theft because of their house-slaves, just as they had before; and since they remembered how fair Drimakos had been to them when he was alive, they erected a shrine to him out in the countryside, and dedicated it to the Kindly Hero. And even today runaway slaves bring the first fruits of everything they steal to him. And it is also said that he appears to many Chians while they are asleep and warns them when their house-slaves are plotting against them; and those to whom he appears go to the

(e)   place where the hero's shrine stands and sacrifice to him.

Now that is the account given by Nymphodoros. But I have found that in many manuscripts the text does not mention Drimakos by name. I don't suppose that any of you are unaware of the story which the wonderful Herodotos tells of Panionios the Chian, and what he so rightly suffered when he made free born boys into eunuchs and sold them [see No. **102** below]. Both the Peripatetic writer Nikolaos and the Stoic Poseidonios state in their histories that the citizen population of Chios was enslaved by Mithridates the Cappadocian and handed over to their

(f)   own slaves in chains to be resettled in the land of the Colchis. In this way God truly showed how angry he was with them because they were the first people to use human chattels that had been bought, while the † citizens [*or*: most people] carried out any necessary services by doing the work themselves. Perhaps these events were behind the proverb which Eupolis uses in his play *The Friends*: 'a Chian has bought himself a master'.

Athens and Samos

The Athenians were concerned for the fate of slaves as well as of other persons, and enacted a law to the effect that there could be criminal actions for insulting behaviour against slaves too. In his speech *Against Mantitheos, on a charge of assault*, the orator Hypereides says:

(267)   They [the lawmakers] decided that an accusation could be submitted against a man who has behaved insolently not just when the behaviour effects free persons, but even when it was directed at a person of slave status.

In his first speech *Against Lykophron*, Lykourgos too seems to be saying the same thing, and so does Demosthenes in his speech *Against Meidias* [see No. **183**]. In his *Seasons of the Siphnians*, Malakos tells the story of how some slaves of the Samians, a thousand in number, founded the city of Ephesus. These men had previously withdrawn to the mountain which is on the island of Samos and done the Samians a

(b)   lot of harm. But as the result of an oracle, the Samians made a truce with these slaves in the sixth year of their revolt, on certain conditions: they were allowed to leave unharmed and sailed away from the island, landing at Ephesus. The Ephesians are their descendants.

Words for Slaves

Writing in book two of *On Concord*, Khrysippos says that the difference between a slave (*doulos*) and a house-boy (*oiketēs*) is this, that freedmen continue to be slaves [i.e. are slaves 'by nature'], while *oiketai* are those who have not been set free from ownership. 'For the *oiketes'* — he says — 'is a slave who is subject to ownership.'

Kleitarkhos says in his *Dictionary* that the following words exist for slaves: *azos, therapōn, akolouthos, diakonos, hypēretēs, hepamōn, latreus.* Amerias says that those house-slaves who work in the fields are called *herkitai.* And Hermonax says in his *Cretan Dictionary* that *mnōtai* are indigenous house-slaves, while Seleukos says that *azoi* are male or female attendants, *apophrasē* and *bolizē* refer to female slave personnel, a *sindron* is a slave born of someone of slave status, an *amphipolos* is a female attendant of the Lady of the House, while the *propolos* is the woman who walks before her. In book two of his *Constitution of Sparta,* Proxenos says that among the Spartans, female attendants are called *khalkides.* In his *Laertes,* Ion of Chios uses the word dependant (*oiketēs*) for 'slave' when he says:

Go quickly, *oiketēs,* and shut the house
so that no human being may come in.

When Akhaios refers to the satyr in his *Omphale,* he says: 'How good he was to his slaves, how good to his house.' What he is strictly saying is that he behaved well towards his slaves and towards his dependants. It doesn't have to be said that an *oiketēs* can be anyone who is staying in your house, even if he is a free person.

Utopias in Comedy

When the writers of Old Comedy talk about life in the old days, they say that at that time no use was made of slaves, in passages like the following:

Kratinos in *Riches*:

Once upon a time Kronos was their king, in the days when they played knuckle-bones with loaves of bread, and in the athletic schools payment was made with great lumps of ripe barley as good as the coinage of Aegina.

Or Krates in *The Beasts*:

— Then there shall be no one who may own a slave or a slave girl, but each man, each old man, shall have to serve himself?
— By no means: for I am going to make everything walk about on its own.
— How is that going to help?
— Each object will come to him when he calls for it. Put yourself down next to me, table. That one — get yourself ready. Get kneading, my sweet little kneading-trough. Fill up, jug. Where's the cup got to?

Go and get yourself washed. Cake, come along over here. The pot ought to empty out the cabbages. Get moving, fish: − 'but I'm not yet toasted on the other side!' − Then why don't you turn yourself over − and cover yourself with oil and salt!

Athenaeus gives us several further excerpts from the comic dramatists Telekleides, Pherekrates, Nikophon and Metagenes referring to the automatic arrival of food and drink. These passages illustrate the extent to which slaves could be seen as living machines (see No. 2 above), providing the rich with goods which the peasant citizens who watched these comedies had to work to produce. Anxieties about food were naturally universal in the primitive agrarian societies of the ancient world.

There follows an episode which is standard in the literary genre of the symposium, the *topos* of the interruption from an unpleasant guest. The Cynic Kynoulkos complains that all these quotations about food make him feel famished, and he wants the discussion to cease so that the guests can get on with the meal. He is firmly put in his place by Ulpian, who points out that intellectual discussion is immensely superior to material sustenance; and although the Cynic makes as though to leave, the opportune arrival of food persuades him to stay, quoting a line which the comic poet Metagenes had adapted from Homer (*Iliad*, 12, 243):

The best omen of all is to stay and fight for one's dinner.

Spartan and Other Serfs

(271b) When he had shut up, Masurius Sabinus said: Some points connected with this account of slavery haven't yet been resolved. So [quoting the poet Philoxenes of Kythera], 'I too am going to compose a love song' for my wise friend Demokritos. In his *History of the Carians and the Leleges*, Philippos of Theangela mentions the Lacedemonian Helots and the Thessalian *Penestai*, and says that in the past, and indeed today, the Carians use the Leleges as their house-boys. Phylarkhos, in book
(c) six of his *Histories*, says that the Byzantines, too, had the same master-and-serf relationship towards the Bithynians as the Spartans had towards the Helots. As regards the group of persons among the Spartans called *Epeunaktoi* ('married in') − these too are slaves − Theopompos gives the following clear account in book thirty-two of his *Histories*:

Many Spartans had died in the war with the Messenians. The survivors didn't want their shortage of manpower to become known to the enemy, so they made some of the Helots marry each of the widows of the dead men. Later they made them citizens and called them 'those who married in' because they had been selected as husbands in the place of the men who had been killed.

The same historian notes in book thirty-three that there are some slaves called the *Katōnakophoroi* ('sheepskin-coat wearers') among the people of Sicyon, whose position is similar to that of the *Epeunaktoi*. Menaikhmos in his *History of Sicyon* gives a similar account. And Theopompos in book two of his *History of King Philip* says that the people of Arcadia possess retainers of a similar status to Helots, to the number of 300,000. The people called *Mothakes* who live among the Spartans are free men, but they do not have the status of Spartans. In the twenty-fifth book of his *Histories*, Phylarkhos says this about them:

> The *Mothakes* are brought up together with Spartans; for each boy of the citizen class chooses one or two or sometimes even more to be brought up with him, depending upon the means at the family's disposal. So the *Mothakes* are free, although they are not Spartans, and they share the Spartan education system. They say that Lysander himself, the man who conquered the Athenians at sea, was one of these, and that he became a citizen because of his noble character.

In book two of his *Messenian History*, Myron of Priene says:

> The Spartans freed their slaves on many occasions. They called some of them 'released', some 'persons without masters', some 'defenders', others — whom they assigned to their naval expeditions — 'master-seamen' and others 'new citizens'. They all had a different status from Helots.

In book seven of his *Greek History*, Theopompos says of the Helots that they are also called *Heleatai*. He writes as follows:

> The conditions of the Helot race are in every respect inhumane and horrible. These people were enslaved by the Spartans a long time ago; some of them originate from Messenia, while the *Heleatai* formerly inhabited the territory called Helos in Lakonia.

Numbers of Slaves in Greece and Rome; Slave Revolts

Timaios of Tauromenion actually contradicts himself (and Polybios of Megalopolis in book twelve of his *Histories* criticises him for this) when he says that it wasn't customary for the Greeks to acquire slaves — for this 'Contradictor of Timaios' (as Kallimakhos' follower Istros

calls him in the essay he wrote criticising him) himself said that Mnason the Phocian owned more than a thousand slaves. And in the third book, the 'Contradictor of Timaios' says that the Corinthians were so rich that they owned 460,000 slaves (*douloi*). I suppose that that's why the Pythia called them 'those who measure out rations'. In
(c) book three of his *Chronicles*, Ktesikles says that at Athens during the †hundred and tenth† [? 117th = 312/308 BC] Olympiad, Demetrios of Phaleron took a census of everyone who was resident in Attica, and he found that there were 21,000 Athenians, 10,000 Metics and 400,000 dependants (*oiketai*). According to the noble Xenophon in his essay *On the Revenues*, Nikias the son of Nikeratos had a holding of one thousand slaves whom he hired out to work in the silver mines for Sosias the Thracian; his rate was that he should get an obol a day for
(d) each of them. Aristotle, in his work on the *Constitution of Aegina*, says that amongst them too there were at that time 470,000 slaves (*douloi*). Agatharkhides the Cnidian says in book thirty-eight of his *European Affairs* that some of the Dardaneis possessed a thousand slaves, others even more. In peacetime all of them worked on the land, but in war they were called up in units officered by their own master.

Larensius said in reply to these points:

In contrast every single Roman — you know this very well, my dear
(e) Masurius — buys himself the greatest number of slaves he can. Very many of them own ten or twenty thousand or even more — but not because of the income, as with Nikias (who was so incredibly wealthy by Greek standards); most Romans have the greatest possible number so that they can accompany them on their excursions. In contrast, most of these tens of thousands of Athenian slaves were chained and worked in the mines. The philosopher Poseidonios, whom you have frequently mentioned, says that they even revolted and killed the men
(f) who were guarding the mines, took control of the acropolis at Sounion and ravaged Attica for a long time. This was the moment when the second slave revolt was taking place in Sicily. There were many of these, and over a million house-slaves lost their lives. The rhetor Caecilius who came from Kale Akte wrote a history of the slave wars. Then there was the gladiator Spartacus; at the time of the wars against Mithridates, he ran away from the Italian city of Capua and made a vast number of slaves revolt (he was a slave himself, a Thracian by race); for a considerable period of time he overran the whole of Italy, and
(273) day after day a lot of slaves poured in to join him. He would have caused my fellow-countrymen some quite unprecedented exertions if he hadn't been killed in the battle against Licinius Crassus — and the same goes for Eunous in Sicily.

The Romans of ancient time showed more moderation and were superior in every respect. Polybios and Poseidonios relate how when

Scipio Africanus was sent out by the Senate to organise all the kingdoms of the world so that they would obey their proper rulers, he took just five slaves along with him, and when one of them died during the journey he sent off to his relatives to buy him another in his place and send him to him. Cotta tells us in the essay on the Roman constitution which is written in our own Latin language, that when Julius Caesar, whose legate he was, was the first of all human beings to sail over to the British Isles in a fleet of a thousand ships, he took only three slaves with him in all. What a contrast to Smindyrides of Sybaris, my Greek friends − when he set out for his wedding to Agariste the daughter of Kleisthenes, he took a thousand slaves with him as an expression of his ostentation and immoderate wealth − they included fishermen and bird-catchers and cooks. This man wanted to demonstrate what a luxurious life he was living, as Khamaileon of Pontus records in his book *On Pleasure* (this is the same book as is also ascribed to Theophrastos).

81. Apuleius, *Defence*, 17

In the mid-second century AD, the African Latin writer and philosopher Apuleius was accused of having used sorcery to persuade a wealthy widow called Pudentilla to marry him. The prosecution had used several of the stock arguments available in ancient rhetoric − that Apuleius had shown that he lacked all moderation and self-restraint by manumitting three slaves on the same day; and alternatively, that the fact that he was accompanied by only one slave showed him up as a disreputable figure of low social status whom the court should not trust. Apuleius had no difficulty in pointing out the contradiction. But it is interesting that he had to explain the absence of a retinue by reminding the court that philosophers like himself didn't care for status. He wasn't sure the jury would be persuaded by this; so he advanced a much stronger argument: the traditional stories about Roman generals who were poor or unostentatious show that you can be highly virtuous even if you have no slave retinue. The frequency of this myth about the behaviour of great figures from the Roman past (see No. **80**, 273b above) only underlines the importance to wealthy Romans of possessing and displaying slaves as symbols of high social status.

I myself have no idea whether you keep slaves of your own to work your farm or have an agreement for the exchange of labour with your neighbours, and I don't care. But you have information that at Oea I manumitted three slaves on one and the same day, and your barrister used this and other points that you had made to him to blacken my character — even though he had said a little earlier that I had gone to Oea accompanied by only one slave. I do wish you could explain to me how I was able to manumit three out of one slaves, unless that was magic too. Are you so blind — or just so habituated a liar? 'Apuleius went to Oea with one slave'; then after muttering something in between, 'On one day, Apuleius manumitted three slaves at Oea.' Even if you had said that I had come with three slaves, it wouldn't be credible that I had manumitted them all; but even if I had done that, why on earth should having three slaves be better evidence of poverty than manumitting three freedmen evidence of opulence? Do you really not know how to go about accusing a philosopher, Aemilianus? You refer to ownership of a small number of slaves as a cause for shame, while I ought to be claiming it as something to be proud of, since I know that not just philosophers (of whom I claim to be one) but even Commanders of the Roman people were proud to own few slaves. Your barristers omitted to mention any of the following facts: that after he had been consul, Marcus Antonius only had eight slaves at home, that Carbo, when he seized power, had one less than that, that Manius Curius, famous for having won all those prizes for valour, who led three triumphal processions through the same city gate, Manius Curius had just two camp followers! Here was a man who had won one triumph over the Sabines, one over the Samnites, and one over Pyrrhus; and he had fewer slaves than triumphs. And there was Marcus Cato, who didn't wait for others to preach about him, but himself recorded in his speeches that when he went out to Spain as Consul he brought only three slaves with him from Rome; and when he got to the government mansion, they seemed too few for his needs, so he ordered two extra slaves to be bought from the counter in the forum, and took the five of them to Spain. In my opinion Pudens would either have ignored this line of attack completely if he had read about these things, or else he would have preferred to criticise an escort of three slaves as too many for a philosopher rather than as a sign of poverty.

82. Petronius, *Satyricon*, 53

Although it is dangerous to look to novelists for concrete evidence about particular questions such as statistics of the number of slaves the 'average' Greek or Roman might have owned, they can tell us about the attitudes they expected their readers to share. The descriptions of Trimalchio's vast household may or may not be indications of the resentment felt by Romans at the power and wealth of some imperial freedmen in the first century AD; they certainly show that the higher the status a man aspired to, the greater the number of his slaves had to be, and the greater the specialisation of each man's job.

An accountant (*actuarius*) diverted the desire to dance which had over-come Trimalchio by reciting something that sounded like the official Roman gazette:
    'July 26th. On Trimalchio's estate at Cumae: born: boys 30, girls 40. Taken from the threshing-floor to barn: 500,000 *modii* of wheat. Oxen broken in: 500.
    Same day: slave Mithridates crucified for cursing the life (*genius*) of our master Gaius [Trimalchio].
    Same day: deposited in strong-box because no suitable investment possible: 10,000,000 Sesterces.
    Same day: fire in the gardens at Pompeii, broke out at the house of the manager, Nasta.'
    'What was that,' interrupted Trimalchio, 'When did I buy any gardens at Pompeii?'
    'Last year,' said the secretary, 'that is why they had not appeared in the accounts yet.'
    Trimalchio became flushed with anger and said: 'I forbid any estates that have been bought for me to be entered in my accounts if I have not been told about it within six months.'

83. Pliny the Elder, *Natural History*, 33, 6

Moralistic diatribes attacking ostentatious display often single out the ownership of large numbers of slaves with specialised functions — frequently contrasted with an idealised picture of 'early Rome' where things were different. Pliny the Elder interrupts his discussion of the different uses of seal rings to declare:

(26) Nowadays even food and wine has to be sealed up in order to be protected from theft. This is due to the legions of slaves, the crowd of outsiders in our homes, and the fact that we need someone just to remind us of the names of our slaves [the *nomenclator*]. In the days of old there were just single slaves belonging to Marcus and Lucius (*Marcipores Luciporesve*), part of their masters' kin-groups who took all their meals in common with them; there was no need to lock up any-thing in the house to keep it from the household slaves.

84. Seneca, *Dialogue 9: The Tranquillity of the Mind*, 8.5—9

Philosophers claimed to distinguish themselves from the common run of (rich) men by doing without large slave retinues (see No. 81 above).

The idea that individual self-sufficiency was something for everyone to aim at was clearly at variance with the fact that wealthy Romans felt they needed to display slaves. It is interesting that Seneca can argue that slaves cost money, time and trouble to keep — not that they are an 'investment' and bring their owner an income.

(5) Now look at the heavens; you will see that the gods are naked, they give everything and keep nothing for themselves. Do you think that someone who has laid aside those things which mere chance has bestowed is poverty-stricken, or is he rather like the immortal gods? (6) Do you think that Pompey's freedman Demetrius, who wasn't ashamed to be richer than Pompey, was also happier? Every day he used to go through the list of slaves he owned as though he were an army commander, though he should have considered himself well off if he just had two under-slaves (*vicarii*) and more spacious sleeping quarters. (7) Diogenes had just one slave who ran away from him, and when he was told where he was, he didn't think it worthwhile to bring him back. 'It would be dishonourable,' he said, 'if Manes could survive without Diogenes, but Diogenes couldn't survive without Manes.' I think that what he meant was this: 'You go and mind your own business, Fortune, you have no claim on Diogenes any longer: my slave has run away, and I've got my freedom back.' (8) Slaves require a clothing and food allowance; you have to look after the appetites of all those greedy creatures, you have to buy clothes, you have to keep a watch on those hands ever ready to steal things; you have to make use of the services of people who are always breaking down in tears and who hate us. How much happier is a man whose only obligation is to someone whom he can easily deny — himself! (9) But since we don't have that much self-reliance, we should at least reduce our inherited wealth so that we are less exposed to the damage Fortune can inflict on us.

85. Lysias 24: *On Behalf of a Cripple*

As a result of its imperial expansion, Athens was one of the wealthiest Greek states and could afford to grant a subsistance allowance of two obols per day to physically disabled citizens. The *Constitution of Athens* states that those owning property worth less than three minae could apply to the *Boulē* (executive council) for this grant. This speech written by Lysias on behalf of a disabled citizen implies that even poor Athenians would have looked upon ownership of a slave assistant as an investment to provide an income.

(5) I think that you are all aware of the truth about this supposed great

income which my trade provides me with, and the other circumstances in which I find myself; I shall nevertheless say a few words on the subject. (6) My father didn't leave me anything, and I only stopped supporting my mother when she died two years ago. I don't yet have any children who could provide for me. My craft can only bring me very limited assistance, and I can only exercise it with difficulty; and I am quite unable to buy (*ktēsasthai*) anyone to take it over from me. I have no other source of income apart from this grant; if you take that away from me, I will be in danger of suffering very great hardship.

86. Demosthenes 27: *Against Aphobus*

Some of the slave craftsmen owned by Athenians brought them a rent in money which augmented the income they drew from their agricultural estates. We know from inscriptions that slave, Metic and citizen workers would all receive identical wages (e.g. the Erechtheum building accounts, *IG* 1.2,374 col. 2,5ff). But the slaves (and freed slaves, No. **94** below) then had to transfer part of their wages, or their profits as craftsmen, to their owners. Aeschines mentions two obols a day for a craftsman (**91**); at this rate, one mina 'rent' would represent 300 working days.

(9) The size of my property is clear from the witnesses' statements. The rate of tax assessed for a property worth fifteen talents is three talents; and that was the amount they agreed should be paid in tax. You will see even more clearly how great this estate was if you listen to the details: for my father, men of the jury, left behind two workshops, each with highly skilled craftsmen. One had thirty-two or thirty-three cutlers, each one worth five or six minae, and even the least skilled of them were worth not less than three minae; they provided him with an annual income of thirty minae before tax. Then there were twenty furniture-makers who had been given to him as security for an outstanding debt of forty minae; they brought him twelve minae before tax. There was also cash to the value of one talent which had been loaned out at the rate of one drachma [per mina per month]; the annual interest on this came to more than seven minae. (10) These were the items that brought in an income, as my opponents themselves will agree; the capital amounts in all to four talents and 5,000 drachmae, and the annual interest on all this comes to fifty minae.

87. Xenophon, *Revenues*, 1

The use of slaves in the Athenian silver mines is the most large-scale example of slave-holding as a means of obtaining an income. Xenophon's pamphlet contains various proposals for increasing the income of the Athenian state: one is that the state should do what private citizens like Nikias had already been doing (Athenaeus refers to this passage in No. **80**, 272c above), and invest in slave miners.

(13) To explain more clearly my ideas about state grants, I will now show how the silver mines can be organised in the way which is most useful for the community. I don't however think that anyone is going to be surprised by what I am going to say, as if I had discovered the solution to anything particularly complex. For some of the things I shall talk about we can all see with our own eyes as they exist today, and we have heard similar things from our fathers about the way things were in the past. (14) But what is surprising is that although the community realises that there are many private individuals who make a lot of money out of mining, it does not follow their example. Those of us who are interested in the subject will have heard a long time ago how Nikias the son of Nikeratos owned a thousand men who worked in the silver mines and hired them out to Sosias the Thracian on condition that he paid him a clear obol a day per man and always maintained the number of workers at the same level.

(15) Hipponikos also had six hundred slaves whom he leased out in the same way, which brought him an income of one mina a day before tax. Philemonides owned three hundred, which brought him half a mina, and I suppose other people's incomes were in proportion to their means. (16) But why do I have to talk about days gone by? Even today there are many men in the silver mines who are leased out in this way. (17) If my proposals were to be put into practice, the only thing new would be that, just as private individuals who buy slaves are provided with a continuous income, so the community too should acquire public slaves, until there would be three for each Athenian citizen. (18) Anyone who wishes should examine my plan point by point and judge whether what I say is feasible.

As regards the cost of buying these men: it is clear that the public treasury can find the money more easily than private individuals. And it would be easy for the Council to make an announcement that 'anyone who wishes should bring his slaves' and buy those who are brought along. (19) And once they have been bought, why should anyone be less willing to hire slaves from the treasury than from a private person, if he can get them on the same conditions? After all, they rent temple property and houses from the state, and buy the right to collect taxes.

(20) In order to keep the slaves that the treasury has bought in good condition, the treasury could require guarantees from those who hire them, as it does from those who farm taxes. (Someone who has bought

the right to farm a tax actually has greater opportunities for fraud than someone who hires slaves — (21) for how can you detect public money when it is being smuggled out of the country, since privately owned money looks exactly the same? But how could anyone steal slaves who have been branded to show that they were state property, if there were a penalty decreed for anyone who traded in them or exported them?)

So up to this point it appears to be possible for the community to acquire and keep men. (22) If one goes on to consider how a sufficient number of people could also be found to hire such a large workforce, one should be encouraged by the thought that many of the people who are already operating in the mines will hire state slaves in addition, since they have substantial means, and many of the men who are now working there are getting old, and there are many other Athenians and foreigners too who do not have the will or the physical strength to work with their own hands, but would be delighted to provide an income for themselves by acting as managers. (23) If we had twelve hundred slaves at first, it is likely that there would be not less than six thousand as a result of this source of income after five or six years. If each man brings in an obol a day nett, then the income from this number of slaves would be sixty talents a year. (24) If twenty of these were invested in the acquisition of further slaves, the community could use the other forty for anything else it required. When the number of ten thousand has been reached, the income would be one hundred talents. (25) But anyone who can still remember what the income from slaves was before the Decelean affair [see No. **211** below] will testify that the community would receive a good deal more than this.

88. Varro, *Agriculture*, 1, 16

The independence of the household unit (not to be confused with the kin-group) is one of the ideals of many peasant societies. Naturally, this self-sufficiency is relative: one may provide one's own food and clothing for one's dependants, but there are some goods one has to go to the market to buy, and there are some services that can only be provided by people who have been trained to exercise special skills. But when such professionals — smiths, doctors or cooks (Pliny, *NH* 18,109), for example — are outside the household, one can never be certain that they will be available exactly when they are needed. Thus a major motive for owning slaves was so that these specialists would be in the household whenever they were needed: a rich man did not own a doctor or high-class hairdresser just for the fees from their outside clients, but so that they would be available to serve him at any time, as an independent doctor would not. Varro points out that owning your own specialised craftsmen is even better than having a market nearby or friendly neighbours.

(3) Similarly, if there are towns or villages nearby, or even just well-stocked fields and estates belonging to wealthy owners, so that you will be able to buy cheaply from them anything you need for your own farm and can sell them your own surplus products — for instance stakes or poles or reeds — then your farm will be more profitable than if things have to be brought in from far away, and frequently it will even bring more profits than if you are able to provide these goods yourself by having them produced on your own farm. (4) For this reason small-holders prefer to have people who live in the neighbourhood under a yearly contract so that they can call on their services (under this heading come doctors, fullers and carpenters), rather than keep their own on their estate; for the death of a single craftsman can wipe out the estate's profitability. But rich landlords generally entrust all these functions of a great estate to members of their own household. If towns or villages are too far from their farm, they make sure that they have some smiths on the estate as well as the other essential craftsmen, so that the slaves on the farm won't have to leave off working and idle about on work days as though they were on holiday, instead of making the farm more profitable by getting on with their tasks.

89. Hypereides, fragment 29

If one of the reasons for owning slaves was that they were economically profitable, the question arises whether the civilisation of classical Athens and Rome would have been possible without the economic basis of slave labour. The ancient evidence for calculations of the total number of slaves, or the proportion of slaves to free men, is weak (see No. **80**, 272b–d above).

The tenth-century Byzantine lexicon called the *Suda* contains this excerpt from a speech in which the anti-Macedonian politician Hypereides seems to have suggested after the battle of Chaeronea (338 BC) that resistance against King Philip could be continued if citizenship were extended to slaves and others. He put forward a proposal:

that first of all those [slaves] working in agriculture and in the silver mines and elsewhere in the country, who were more than 150,000, and then those who were in debt to the state treasury and those who had lost their civic rights and those who had been disenfranchised and the resident aliens . . .

90. Lysias 12: *Against Eratosthenes*

There are a few passages in fourth-century orators which give precise and probably reliable figures for the numbers of slaves which particular individuals owned. But there is no way of telling just how typical these figures are: Lysias and his father and brother were Metics who were debarred from investing their wealth in land; and the demand for weapons in the last years of the Peloponnesian war suggests that their shield factory was exceptionally large.

(19) They took seven hundred shields that belonged to us, and all our gold and silver, so much copper and jewellery and furniture and clothing for women as they had never dreamed they would get hold of, and one hundred and twenty slaves: of all these things they kept the best for themselves and handed over the rest to the state treasury.

91. Aeschines 1: *Against Timarchus*

Specifications of property in slaves tend to mention only craftsmen who paid their owner a fixed rent; there is little mention of domestic servants or agricultural slaves, whose contribution to productivity would have been difficult to calculate in money terms, although they were clearly used to work the land of the rich at least (No. 139).

(97) His father left him an estate which anyone else would have found sufficient to provide a liturgy; but he wasn't even able to keep it for himself. There was a house at the back of the Acropolis, a country estate at Sphettos and another at Alopeke, apart from nine or ten slave craftsmen who were skilled at producing shields, each of whom brought him an income of two obols a day, while the manager (*hēgemoñ*) of the workshop brought in three. And in addition there was a woman who was skilled at weaving flax, who marketed her first-class products in the Agora, and an embroiderer, and also some men who owed him money, and then all his furniture.

92. Pliny the Elder, *Natural History*, 33, 47

There are indications that Athenaeus was right (272de, No. 80 above) to think that the wealthiest Romans owned slaves on an entirely different scale from the Greeks. Although initially simply a quantitative difference, the size of Roman slave-holdings tended to make the ideal that slaves were part of the household increasingly ineffective; Roman writers tended to distinguish privileged 'urban' slaves providing household services from 'rustic' slaves working in agriculture (126).

There is no absolutely reliable basis for estimating the total number of slaves in Roman Italy (e.g. from figures given by Pliny, *NH* 33,56, for proceeds from the 5 per cent manumission tax: cf. Brunt, *Manpower*, App.7, p. 549). Inscriptions relating to members of a religious association at Minturnae show that in about 100 BC, of 127 households owning slaves, only two are recorded as having more than three (one seven, the other between 14 and 16); papyrus evidence from Egypt suggests a similar distribution (94).

One of the problems about the literary evidence is that what was thought worth noting down was almost always what was exceptional. Isidorus had inherited the estate of one of the Metelli, a leading political family of the late Roman Republic.

(134) In later years we saw many freed slaves who were richer than Crassus — not long ago during Claudius' reign there were three at once, Callistus, Pallas and Narcissus. Let's suppose that these three are still running the government and not say a word about them. On 27 January 8 BC, Caius Caecilius Isidorus, freedman of Caius, stated in his Will that although he had lost a great deal in the civil wars, he left 4,116 slaves, 3,600 pairs of oxen, 257,000 other animals, sixty million Sesterces in coined money; and he ordered eleven hundred thousand to be spent on his funeral.

93. Apuleius, *Defence*, 93

The estate owned by Apuleius' wife Pudentilla, part of which she gave away to her sons by a previous marriage, is another indication of the huge wealth owned by the Roman elite, even in the provinces. It has been suggested that agricultural slavery was particularly prevalent in North Africa, as an inheritance from Carthaginian times, but there is no conclusive evidence that the use of chattel slaves by the Carthaginians was particularly widespread.

I suggested to my wife — whose property, as my opponents would claim, I was in the process of destroying — I suggested to her, and finally convinced her, to give back to her sons without delay the money which belonged to them and which they were asking to be returned, as I explained above, in the form of land at a rate well below the real value which they themselves had assessed; and also that she should give them the most fertile fields belonging to the family estate and a large and well-appointed house and a large quantity of wheat, of barley, of wine and olives and of all the other produce, and also slaves numbering hardly less than four hundred and a substantial number of valuable cattle, so that she could make them satisfied with the portion of the estate she had handed over to them and leave them with the hope that they would inherit the rest.

94. The Will of Akousilaos: Oxyrhynchus Papyrus 3, 494

One of the sources of evidence for estimates of the 'average' number of slaves a wealthy family might own (see No. 92 above) are Wills, most of them on papyri from Egypt. There are instances mentioning three slaves (see L&R II, 71: 191 AD), six slaves (P. Strasbourg 2, 122: 161–9 AD, and P.Oxy. 6, 907: 276 AD), eleven slaves (in a certificate of emancipation, P.Tebt. 2, 407: 199 AD), eighteen slaves (apparently on an agricultural estate: P.Mich. 5, 326: 48 AD); and one very exceptional case of a family owning somewhere between 59 and 70 slaves (P.Oxy. 44, 3197: 111 AD).

This Will, dated 156 AD, is interesting not just as an example of testamentary manumission, but also because it gives a widow the right to services and money revenues or 'rent' (*apophora*) from these freedmen and women.

If I end my life without having amended these dispositions, then I set free in the name of Zeus, the Earth-goddess and the Sun, my slave bodies (*doula somata*) Psenamounis (also called Ammonios) and Hermas and Apollonous (also called Demetria) and her daughter Diogenis and my other slave woman Diogenis, because of the goodwill and love they have shown towards me. I leave to my wife and cousin Aristous (also called Apollonarion), daughter of Herakleides, son of Dionysios (also called Akousilaus), and of Herais, daughter of Alexandros, because she has been well disposed towards me and has shown herself entirely faithful, any furniture and equipment and gold and clothing and jewellery and wheat and vegetables and household produce and stock that I may leave, and all debts owed to me, whether set down in writing or not. I appoint my son Deios, born to me by my above-mentioned wife Aristous (also called Apollonarion), if he survives me; and if not, his children; to be heir to the property I leave and to the other slave bodies and to any children that will be born to the above-mentioned female slaves; but my wife Aristous (also called Apollonarion) is, for the duration of her own life, to have the use of and all income (after tax) as well as the services and revenues (*apophora*) of the slave bodies who are to be set free upon my death.

95. Diogenes Laertius, *Lives of the Philosophers*

The details of the testamentary dispositions made by famous philosophers which Diogenes Laertius includes in his biographies are almost
certainly fictitious, but they do give an impression of the number of
slaves which the educated Greek-speaking readers of the Second Sophistic
would have expected a gentleman (albeit a philosopher) to own.

Book 5: Aristotle

(13) My daughter is to have three women to attend her, whom she is to
choose herself, in addition to the little girl she already has and the boy
Pyrraios. (14) I want Ambrakis to be freed when my daughter is married
and given five hundred drachmae plus the slave girl she has now; Thales
is to be given one thousand drachmae and a slave girl, in addition to the
little girl I bought whom she has now. (15) Apart from the money given
him already to buy another slave, Simon is either to have a slave bought
for him, or be given the equivalent in cash. When my daughter gets
married, Tykhon is to be freed, and so is Philon and Olympios and his
child. None of the slaves who served me is to be sold, they must all be
used; and when they have reached the appropriate age, they are to be
given their freedom according to their deserts.

Book 5: The Philosopher Lykon

(72) This is my Will concerning those who serve me (*therapeuontōn*):
Demetrios was freed a long time ago; I remit the money he owes for
his freedom and give him five minae, a cloak and a tunic, to reward
him for all the work he has done for me during my life. I also remit
Kriton from Chalcedon the money he owes me for his freedom and
give him four minae. I also manumit Mikros; let Lykon [his nephew]
look after him and see to his education for six years from this date.
(73) I also manumit Khares; let Lykon look after him. I leave him two
minae and the manuscripts of my public lectures; the unpublished
writings are for Kallinos, who is to edit them carefully. I give to Syros,
who is already free, four minae and Menodora; if he owes me anything,
I remit it. I give to Hilare five minae, a carpet, two pillows, a blanket
and whichever bed she chooses. I also manumit Mikros' mother, Noemon,
Dion, Theon, Euphranor and Hermias; Agathon is to remain for two
more years and then be given his freedom, and the litter-bearers
Ophelion and Poseidonios are to remain for four more years. (74) I
give Demetrios, Kriton and Syros a bed each and whatever blankets
Lykon thinks fit out of those that I leave behind.

In Epicurus' Will (10, 21), four slaves are manumitted; Straton (5, 63)
manumits four and leaves one slave to a friend; Plato (3, 42) frees one

and leaves four to his heirs.

96. Apuleius, *Defence*, 47

The paucity of reliable evidence for any statistical estimate of the number of slaves that existed at any period in antiquity is shown by the fact that some scholars have used this passage as the basis for serious calculations. But the context makes it clear that the only reason why Apuleius says that precisely fifteen slaves constitute a household (*domus*) or a prison (*ergastulum*) is that his accuser had claimed that he had carried out a magic rite in the presence of that number of slaves.

As far as I know these magic rites are something covered by the law, and right from the earliest times they have been forbidden because of the incredible business of enticing corn from one field to another. As a result, they are secret as well as disgusting and frightening, and involve staying up at night and hiding under cover of darkness and avoiding witnesses and saying the spells silently, in the presence of very few free men. Yet here you are suggesting that fifteen slaves were in attendance! Was this some kind of wedding reception or some other celebration or similar feast? Are these fifteen slaves taking part in the magic rites as if they had been appointed the fifteen State Commissioners for Religion? For what reason would I have invited such a number — far too many for the secret to be kept? Fifteen free men make a community, the same number of slaves a household, and if they are chained they constitute a prison. I suppose such a large number might have been needed to hold down the sacrificial victims for the duration of the ceremony: but the only victims you've mentioned have been chickens . . .

97. Xenophon, *Memorabilia*, 2, 5

Attempts to assess the relative productive 'efficiency' of slave and free labour are pointless, not merely because of the absence of statistical evidence, but also because what was bought was the slave's person, not his labour. Thus even in the same city at the same time, the range of 'values' was enormous. However, we can use the ratio between the price of a slave and the annual income he brought his owner (No. 86) to give us some idea of the minimum number of years a slave will have had to serve before being allowed his freedom.

(2) Antisthenes — said Socrates — do friends have different values, like slaves? For one slave may be worth two minae, another less than half

a mina; one five minae, another even ten. Nikias, the son of Nikeratos, is said to have paid one talent for an overseer for his silver mines. So I wonder whether friends, just like slaves, may not have different values.

98. Pliny the Elder, *Natural History*, 7, 12

Like the literary evidence about the size of slave-holdings, that for prices is slanted towards the exceptional and remarkable. What does emerge is that high prices, like large numbers, were eagerly accepted as a display of the owner's wealth and status.

(56) When Marcus Antonius was already a triumvir, the dealer Toranius managed to sell him as twins two particularly attractive slaves, one born in Asia and the other north of the Alps — they were that similar. But the fraud was brought to light because of the slaves' accents, and Antonius angrily complained about the high price he had paid (200,000 Sesterces), amongst other things. But the clever trader replied that that was actually why he had asked for such a high price — there was nothing wonderful about twin brothers looking alike, but to find such a similar appearance in two persons who belonged to quite different races was really something that was beyond price; and he managed to make Antonius think this so surprising (a feeling highly convenient to the trader) that although he was busily arranging the proscriptions and had just been in a terrifying rage, this man ended up thinking that no other items that belonged to him were better symbols of his high status.

99. Pliny the Elder, *Natural History*, 7, 39

(128) The highest price I have been able to discover that has been paid for a man born in slavery up to the present day was when the political leader Marcus Scaurus offered 700,000 Sesterces for the grammarian Daphnis, who was being sold by Attius of Pisaurum (Pesaro). In our own time this figure has been greatly exceeded by actors buying their freedom with their earnings — even in the days of our ancestors, the actor Roscius is supposed to have earned 500,000 Sesterces per annum. I don't suppose anyone thinks the man whom Nero manumitted for 13,000,000 Sesterces is relevant in this context; he was responsible for financing the recent Armenian war fought because of Tiridates, and the money was payment for the war, not just for the man — just as the 50,000,000 Sesterces for which Clutorius Priscus bought Sejanus' eunuch Paezon was payment for lust and not for beauty. He paid this outrageous price at a time when the city was in mourning, and no one

had the time to complain about it.

100. Diocletian's Edict on Maximum Prices: *ZPE* 34 (1979), 177

Official documents provide too small a sample to allow us to deduce 'average' prices (see Nos. **23–6** above, **105** below and AVN 75). Diocletian's edict imposing maximum prices during a time of rapid inflation is of limited value since it tells us nothing about prices a few years earlier or later. But it does give an idea of relative prices between slaves and other goods, or between different classes of slaves: the ratios between men, women and children are very similar to those we find in *paramone*-agreements (see Hopkins, *Conquerors and Slaves*, Ch. 3). We may also compare the wages laid down for one day's work (as at Athens, no distinction is made between slave and free): 25 *denarii* for labourers, and for skilled workers between 50 *denarii* and 150 (for a picture-painter): see L&R II, 140.

[Prices of slaves:]
[?Male slave or eunuch or young slave?]

Between the ages of 16 and 40:	30,000 *denarii*
Female of age above-specified:	25,000 *denarii*
Man between 40 and 60:	25,000 *denarii*
Female of age above-specified:	20,000 *denarii*
Boy between 8 and 16; also girl of age above specified:	20,000 *denarii*
Man (*homo*) over 60 or under 8:	15,000 *denarii*
Female of age above-specified:	10,000 *denarii*

With regard to a slave trained in a skill, agreement is to be reached between buyer and seller with regard to the sex and age and the type of skills, in such a way that the price may not exceed double that fixed for a slave.

CHAPTER 6

SOURCES OF SLAVES

101. Aristophanes, *Wealth*, 510–26 (with Scholia)

The jurist Marcianus listed those methods of obtaining slaves which Roman law recognised as legitimate (No. 4): fraudulent self-sale, capture in war and descent from a female slave. Romans, unlike some Greeks, did not accept that a foundling became the slave of the person who raised him. Dio Chrysostom discussed the moral objections to these and other grounds for holding people as slaves (No. 235 below).

Ownership of a slave could be acquired through inheritance, donation or sale — always assuming that the vendor was the slave's legitimate owner (see Varro, No. 150, Ch. 4 below). The literary evidence suggests that the traders who introduced slaves into a community were frequently suspected of having stolen or kidnapped their wares.

Poverty: But if Wealth weren't blind, if he distributed himself in equal shares to everyone, there wouldn't be a single person who would bother to exercise any craft or skill. And if these disappeared, who would work as a smith or build ships or sew clothes or make wheels or shields or bricks or run a laundry or a tannery or break up the soil by ploughing in order to reap Demeter's harvest — if you could live without bothering about any of these things?

Khremylos: You're talking rubbish. All the labours you've just listed could be done for us by our slaves.

Poverty: And where would you get your slaves from?

Khremylos: We'd buy them for money of course.

Poverty: But who would have an incentive to trade in slaves if he was already well off?

Khremylos: Some merchant would come from Thessaly in the hope of making a profit — that's where most of the men who kidnap slaves come from.

Poverty: But the logical conclusion of your argument is that not a single slave-trader would be left. Would anyone who was rich risk his life in such a profession? Of course not — you will be forced to plough and dig and do all the other hard work yourself, and your life will be twice as unpleasant as it is now.

One of the Scholiasts has commented:

'Slave-trader' doesn't just refer to someone who drags free men off into slavery, but also to someone who removes slaves from their masters and brings them under his own control in order to take them somewhere else and sell them. The Thessalians are here being attacked for indulging not just in these practices, but in piracy too.

102. Herodotus, 8, 104f.

It is ironical that ancient writers – almost all of whom presumably owned slaves – were so hostile to those who traded in them. Dealers in eunuchs were particularly despised: Herodotus tells how, after the battle of Salamis, Xerxes sent some of the children of his harem away to Ephesus.

He sent Hermotimos, whose place of origin was Pedasus, to look after these children; this man was the most important of his eunuchs, (105) and took a greater revenge for the wrong done to him than anyone else we know about. A Chian called Panionios had bought him after he had been taken captive by the enemy and offered for sale; this man made his living in the most horrible [literally, 'unholy'] way – when he had bought any boys who were particularly attractive in appearance, he castrated them and took them to Sardis or Ephesus to sell them for a lot of money (amongst non-Greeks, eunuchs are worth much more than ordinary male slaves because of their total loyalty). Since he made his living in this way, Panionios had castrated a lot of people including this one. But Hermotimos was not unfortunate in every respect, for from Sardis he was taken to the Persian king together with some other presents, and in due course Xerxes came to respect him more highly than any of his other eunuchs.

103. Strabo, 11, 2.3

Just as in early modern West Africa, many slaves were bought from 'barbarian' tribes (like Tacitus' debt-bondsmen: see No. 20) at recognised 'Ports-of-Trade'. Amongst the exporting countries were Britain (Strabo, 4, 5.2) and the Black Sea (see Strabo, 7, 3.12, No. 12 above). Side was the 'Port-of-Trade' for those kidnapped in central Anatolia (Strabo, 14, 3.2); Ephesus (No. 13 above) may have been an exchange like Delos, where Romans bought their wares from the eastern slave-merchants.

Where the river Don flows into the Sea of Azov, there is a city called Tanais, after the name of the river; it was founded by the Greeks who controlled the Bosporos, but was recently destroyed by King Polemon for refusing to recognise him. It was the central place of exchange between the nomadic tribes of Asia and Europe and the people who sailed across the Sea of Azov from the Bosporos; the former brought slaves and hides and whatever else nomads have to offer, and in exchange the latter traded them fabrics and wine and all the other things pertaining to civilised living.

104. The Edict of the Curule Aediles

From an early date Greek communities seem to have regulated the conditions under which slaves were bought and sold: sales had to be publicly proclaimed, and take place in the town square (partially no doubt so that the authorities could collect the sales-tax). At Athens, the vendor had to state whether the slave suffered from certain specified illnesses, or had been guilty of murder and might thus pollute his new master's household (see Plato, *Laws*, 11, 916).

At Rome, similar regulations were enforced by the magistrates responsible for the public markets, although here a tax on selling slaves was only introduced in 7 BC; it is significant that the corresponding tax had here been levied on manumissions — the *vicesima libertatis*. Among the points which had to be declared was whether a female slave was incapable of bearing children (*Digest* 21, 1.14.3), whether the slave had ever committed a capital offence, tried to commit suicide, or been set to fight the beasts in the arena (*Digest* 21, 1.1). Revealing the ethnic origin of a slave was also required. On noxality, see No. 8 above.

That section of the Edict of the Curule Aediles which regulates the sale of slaves, reads as follows:

> Care must be taken that a notice is written out for each particular slave, in such a way that it is possible to find out exactly what diseases or defects each one has, whether he is liable to run away or loiter about at will, or is not free from liability for a claim for damages (*noxa*). (Aulus Gellius, *Attic Nights*, 4, 2.1)

Those who sell slaves must state the *natio* of each at the sale; for the *natio* of a slave frequently encourages or deters a prospective buyer; hence it is advantageous to know his *natio*, since it is reasonable to suppose that some slaves are good because they originate from a tribe that has a good reputation, and others bad because they come from a tribe that is rather disreputable. (*Digest* 21, 1.31 (21): Ulpian, from *The Edict of the Curule Aediles*, book 1)

Similar information also had to be given in tax forms declaring property:

When entering slaves, you must ensure that their *natio*, age, duties and skills are entered separately for each. (*Digest* 50, 15.4 (5): Ulpian, from *The Census*, book 1)

105. Buying a Slave: Dacian Sales Contracts

In 1855, a number of wax tablets was found at Verespatak in Transylvania, the Roman province of Dacia. They date to the middle of the second century AD, and include a number of documents confirming the sale of slaves (Bruns, 132; for other examples, see L&R II, 52). In accordance with the Roman law of contract (see Crook, *Law and Life*, Ch. 6), the vendor is associated with a guarantor or 'second vendor' to stand surety for him should the buyer be dissatisfied (in some of these documents, the surety is specified as twice the sale price; see Varro, No. **150**, 4f. below).

Claudius Julianus, soldier of the century of Claudius Marius in the Thirteenth Legion 'Gemina', has bought and taken ownership of the woman called Theudote, or any other name she may have, a Cretan by race, for 420 *denarii, apocatam pro uncis duobus* [the interpretation of this phrase is uncertain], from Claudius Philetus, with Alexander Antipatris asked to act as guarantor.

This woman was handed over in good health to the above-mentioned buyer. And in case anyone should remove from his possession this woman or anything pertaining to her, with the result that the above-mentioned buyer or anyone else who may be concerned is unable to have use and profit and proper possession of her, the above-mentioned soldier Claudius Julianus requested that in that case he should be given in good faith as much valid money as the value abstracted or taken from that woman or the value of whatever was done that was illegal; and Claudius Philetus promised that it would be given in good faith. Alexander Antipatris stated that he would guarantee it.

And Claudius Philetus said that he had received and had the price of 420 *denarii* for the above-mentioned woman from the above-mentioned soldier Claudius Julianus.

Done in the Camp of the Thirteenth Legion 'Gemina', 4th October in the consulship of Bradua and Varus [160 AD].

Signatures: of Valerius Valens, Thirteenth Legion 'Gemina'.
                of Cineaus Varus.
                of Aelius Dionysus, veteran of the legion.

of Paulinus.

of Julius Victorinus.

[in Greek]   I, Alexander Antipatris the guarantor, have signed.

[in Latin]   of Claudius Philetus, the actual vendor.

106. Strabo, 14, 5.2

Delos had been made a free port by Rome in 166 BC, largely in order to damage the prosperity of Rhodes; it became the main centre for Italian merchants in the Eastern Mediterranean, and thus one of the markets where pirates sold their captives. The effect of Rome's weakening of the Seleucid monarchy was a whole series of civil disorders in Syria and Cilicia, which led to a massive increase in the slave trade.

Responsibility for making the Cilicians turn to piracy lies with Tryphon and with the ineffectiveness of the succession of kings who at that time ruled Syria together with Cilicia. As a result of Tryphon's rebellion, others also revolted, and the rivalry between one Seleucid brother and another put the whole area in the power of anyone who attacked it. The export trade in slaves was a major cause of all this criminal activity, as it had become extremely profitable. They were easy to capture, and the important and extremely wealthy centre of the trade was not very far away — the island of Delos, where tens of thousands of slaves could be received and despatched again on the same day, so that there was a saying, 'Trader, dock here, unload, your cargo's already been sold.' The reason was that after the destruction of Carthage and Corinth, the Romans had become extremely rich and made use of large numbers of slaves; and as pirates could see how easy it was to make money in this way, they sprang up all over the place, and raided and traded in slaves themselves. The kings of Cyprus and Egypt co-operated with them because of their hostility to the Seleucids, and the Rhodians weren't friendly towards the Seleucids either, so that they had no help from any-one; and all the time the pirates pretended to be slave-dealers and carried on their activities unhindered. The Romans themselves didn't care very much at that time about the area to the south-east of the Taurus Mountains; they did send Scipio Aemilianus to inspect the cities and peoples of the area, and then some others later on. They came to the conclusion that it was all due to the incompetence of the government, but didn't dare to put an end to the rule of Seleukos Nikator's successors, since they had themselves confirmed that rule.

107. Pausanias, 4, 35.6

Although piracy was a major source of new slaves during the period of
the great expansion of slavery in the Roman world in the second century
BC, it was not recognised at all in law. The victim of a pirate raid could
claim back his freedom if he could prove it to the satisfaction of a
Roman magistrate; but his chances of success might be minimal in
practice (see Nos. **14** above and **230**, 3 below). Here is a description of
such a pirate raid; the Illyrians had overrun Epirus during a period of
anarchy after the death of Queen Deidameia in *c.* 232 BC.

When the Illyrians had experienced the exercise of power, and felt that
they wanted more and more of it, they built a fleet and plundered any
other ships they came across, and they put in at Mothone and anchored
there, pretending that their intentions were peaceful. They sent a
messenger to the city to ask for wine to be brought down to the ships
for them. A few men came down, and the Illyrians bought the wine at
the price asked for by the Mothonians and themselves sold them some
of the merchandise they were carrying. When more people arrived from
the city on the next day, they allowed them also to make some profitable
business deals. In the end, women as well as men came down to the
ships to sell wine and obtain things from the visitors in exchange. At
this point the Illyrians violently seized many of the men and even
greater number of women; they put them on board their ships and sailed
back to the Adriatic, leaving the city of Mothone depopulated.

108. Pliny the Elder, *Natural History*, 35, 58

The extent of the enforced immigration into Italy caused by piracy
and slave-hunting is illustrated by a passage from Pliny; he cannot resist
making the point that it is unnatural for ex-slaves to win power and
influence, but he also cannot help revealing that many of these despised
slaves had recently formed the intellectual elite of the Hellenistic world.
'Publilius' is Publilius Syrus (see No. **78** above); Manilius' grandson wrote
a surviving astronomical treatise dedicated to Tiberius; for Staberius Eros,
see No. **133**, 13 below.

(199) There is another kind of chalk which is called 'silversmith's',
since it makes silver shiny, but it is very low grade and our ancestors
decided to use it to mark the finishing line in the Circus, and to mark
the feet of slaves brought from overseas to be sold. Among slaves of this
kind there was Publilius from Antioch who was the first author of
mimes, and his cousin Manilius the first astrologer, also from Antioch;

and Staberius Eros the first grammarian — our great-grandfathers could see them all arrive on the same ship. (200) Why should anyone have to mention these men, since they are famous for their literary productions? Among the men they saw on the slave-dealer's platform was Sulla's Chrysogonus, Quintus Catulus' Amphion, Lucius Lucullus' Hector, Pompey's Demetrius and Demetrius' Auge — although some believe that she too was Pompey's property — Marcus Antonius' Hipparchus, Sextus Pompeius' Menas and Menecrates, and others besides, whom I cannot all list; they became rich at the cost of Roman blood and the lawlessness of the proscriptions.

(201) This chalk marks the crowds of slaves up for sale, and the fickleness of a Fortune which has brought us disgrace. We ourselves have seen how such people became so powerful that the Senate decreed them the insignia of ex-praetors on the orders of the emperor Claudius' wife Agrippina; they arrived with chalk on their feet, and virtually returned to the same places with a retinue of lictors bearing fasces wreathed with laurel.

109. Seneca, *Dialogue 5: On Anger*, 3, 29

Slave-owners were well aware of the psychological effect that their change of status had on free men who became slaves. Many advised against buying outsiders as slaves, since home-born slaves (*oikogeneis, vernae*) were much more likely to remain loyal to a master they had known all their lives (see Nos. **124**, **206**, below). On the other hand, Stoics like Seneca felt that one ought to show special sympathy towards someone who had only recently been enslaved.

(1) How vile to hate someone you should praise — and how much more vile to hate someone for something because of which he deserves to be pitied; namely because as a captive who has suddenly fallen into slavery, he holds on to some remnants of his former free status and fails to hurry to perform sordid and difficult services; because he is a bit slow as a result of his previous inactivity and can't keep up with his owner's horse or carriage on foot; because he is exhausted by having to be alert all the time and falls asleep; because he has been transferred from being a slave in Rome with all its holidays to the toil of the farm, and can't put up with this strenuous work or doesn't approach it with enthusiasm.

110. Pausanias, 5, 21.10

Even under the more ordered conditions of Roman rule, free citizens continued to go in fear of being kidnapped and sold as slaves (a tomb at Ravenna mentions a free-born Parthian sold to Rome as a slave: *CIL* 11, 137 = *ILS* 1980 = L&R II, 72). The effect was that the slave lost all links with the community of his birth; if he were freed (and was not lucky enough to obtain Roman citizenship) he would be assumed to belong to the community where he had first been sold — for instance, the Cilician trading ports of southern Anatolia. In the course of his account of the monuments at Olympia, Pausanias lists the men who had won both the 'pancration' and the wrestling match; we know from other sources that Nikostratos' victory was at the 204th Olympics, in 37 AD.

The seventh man to win both prizes was Nikostratos, from the Coastal Cilicians, although he had nothing to do with Cilicia except in theory. Robbers kidnapped this Nikostratos from Prymnessos in Phrygia while he was still a baby; he belonged to an important family. Someone or other bought him when he was brought to Aigiai, and some time later this man had a dream: it seemed that a lion's pup was lying underneath a bed on which Nikostratos was asleep. When he grew up, Nikostratos won many other victories as well as the pancration and wrestling at the Olympics.

111. Suetonius, *Augustus*, 32

Even in Italy free men might be abducted to serve, illegally, as slaves, and the government repeatedly had to send out commissions to ensure that men who had been free had their rights restored to them. In two passages, Suetonius mentions an inspection by the later emperor Tiberius. A shortage of volunteers for Augustus' wars on the Rhine and Danube meant that he was particularly concerned that free men should not be diverted from military service.

(1) Many evil precedents that were harmful to public order had either carried on from the habitual lawlessness of the civil war period, or had actually arisen since peace had been restored. Brigands went about openly carrying swords, which they claimed were for self-defence, and in the countryside travellers were kidnapped without discrimination between slave and free, and held in the prisons (*ergastula*) belonging to the landowners; and numerous gangs had been formed, calling themselves 'new guilds' for no co-operative purpose other than crime. So Augustus controlled brigandage by erecting police posts at suitable

points, inspected slave prisons and dissolved all guilds other than the lawful traditional ones.

112. Suetonius, *Tiberius*, 8

Meanwhile Tiberius had been entrusted with two official posts: organising the grain supply, which was insufficient, and sorting out the slave prisons (*ergastula*) throughout the whole of Italy. Their masters were suspected of holding and imprisoning not just travellers but also those who had gone to the extent of hiding in these places out of fear of being called up for military service.

113. Diodorus Siculus, 23, 18

While kidnapping free persons or other people's slaves was strictly speaking illegal, prisoners captured in a just war which had been formally proclaimed by due ceremony were legitimately enslaved, if they hadn't been massacred. The Romans had no doubts that any war they engaged in was just, and the captives their property: if they could not arrange to be ransomed, they had to face slavery – as after the capture of Palermo by the Romans in 259 BC.

(4) The Romans attacked continuously and broke down the city wall with their battering-rams; they got control of the outer city and slaughtered a lot of people. The rest fled to the old city, from where they sent ambassadors to the Consuls to ask them to spare their lives. (5) It was agreed that those who gave two minae per person could go free, and the Romans then took control of the city. The money that was found there covered the agreed ransom for fourteen thousand persons, and these were set free. The rest, thirteen thousand of them, and all the other material, were sold as booty.

114. Polybius, 10, 17.6–15

There were few restrictions on what Roman commanders might choose to do with the slaves they captured; they might be distributed to the troops as booty, or sold for the benefit of the state, or the proceeds might be used to erect a public building at Rome (or remain in the pockets of the commander and his officers). On some occasions, captives could become state property, as at the conquest of the Carthaginian capital of Spain, New Carthage, by Scipio in 210 BC. Here too the promise of manumission was a great incentive for loyal work (see No. **206** below).

The military tribunes were organising the distribution of the booty; and after all the captives had been collected together – there were a little under ten thousand of them – the Roman commander first ordered all the men of citizen status with their wives and children to be marshalled separately, and all the craftsmen. When this had been done, he called up the citizens, told them to be favourably disposed towards Rome and to remember how well they had been treated, and let them go back to their own homes. They wept with joy at this unexpected redemption, and prostrated themselves before the commander as they left.

Then he told the craftsmen that, for the moment, they were public slaves of Rome; but he proclaimed that if they co-operated and worked hard at their particular crafts, and if the war against Carthage proceeded as he hoped, they would be given their freedom. He ordered them to register their names with the Quaestor, and appointed a Roman overseer for each group of thirty; there were about two thousand of them altogether.

From those who were left, he selected those whose strength, appearance and age made them most suitable and mixed them in with his ships' crews, so that he increased the total number of sailors by half, and in addition manned the ships he had captured; the crews of each of these ships were a little under double the number they had been before. Eighteen ships had been captured, and he had originally had thirty-five ships. He promised these men too that they would get their freedom if they co-operated and worked hard, once the war with Carthage had been won. By adopting this approach towards the captives, he made the citizens well disposed and loyal both towards himself and towards Rome generally, and he gave the craftsmen a great incentive to work because they hoped for their freedom.

115. Polybius, 15, 4.1

The Romans felt no obligation to allow an enemy to surrender on terms rather than enslave them (202 BC).

Publius Scipio made arrangements to protect the fleet and left Baebius in charge of it; he himself went from one Carthaginian city to the next, and no longer agreed to terms for those who freely surrendered to him; he used violence to enslave them and show how angry he was with the enemy because of the treachery of the Carthaginians.

116. *2 Maccabees*, 8, 8–11

With the progressive disintegration of the Seleucid empire in the second century BC, the occasions on which whole communities were liable to enslavement in war multiplied. The Bible gives a very one-sided account of the attempts by Seleucid generals to suppress the struggle for independence of one subject group, the Jews, who were quick to take advantage of Rome's defeat of Antiochus III.

Philippos realised that this man (Judas Maccabaeus) had become very successful in a short period of time, and was achieving more and more success as a result of his good fortune; so he wrote to the governor of Coele-Syria and Phoenicia, Ptolemaios, to help him carry out the royal policy. Ptolemaios quickly put at his disposal Nikanor son of Patroklos, who had the title of King's Friend, First Class, with no less than twenty thousand men of diverse ethnic origin, in order to destroy the entire Jewish people. He sent along with him as his commander a man called Gorgias, who was extremely experienced in military affairs. Nikanor expected to finance the tribute of two thousand talents [imposed by Rome] which the king had to pay, out of the Jewish prisoners he hoped to capture, and immediately sent messengers to the cities along the seacoast with invitations to auctions of Jewish slaves, promising that he would sell them ninety slaves for one talent; he had no idea of the judgement that was about to fall upon him from the Almighty.

117. Polybius, 28, 14 (= 27, 16)

The dividing line between a recognised war and acts of piracy was not always clear; the general insecurity which resulted from Rome's systematic destruction of any powerful Hellenistic state that might be a rival opened the door to atrocities of every kind. Thus during the third Roman-Macedonian war:

[Polybius says] that at this time [i.e. 170/169 BC] the people of Kydonia did something horrible and universally agreed to be in breach of treaty obligations. Many things of this sort have occurred in Crete, but what happened then seemed even worse than their normal behaviour. They didn't just have a treaty of friendship, but even reciprocal citizen rights with the people of Apollonia, and generally shared all the rights that men are thought to possess; there was an agreement supported by sworn oaths to this effect, which was kept in the Temple of Idaean Zeus; but they broke the treaty, captured the Apollonians' city, slaughtered the men, carried off everything there was as booty, divided up the women and children and the city and its territory, and kept them for themselves.

118. Strabo, 7, 7.3: excerpting Polybius, 30, 15(16)

In the course of the third Macedonian war, the Romans made one of the largest hauls of slaves on record (see Livy, 45, 33.8–34.7 = L&R I, 77; also Plutarch, *Paullus*, 29).

Polybius says that after his destruction of Perseus and the Macedonians, Aemilius Paullus captured seventy cities in Epirus (most of these belonged to the Molossians), and that one hundred and fifty thousand human beings were enslaved.

119. Suetonius, *Augustus*, 21

The brutality and insecurity of the second century BC were exceptional; but even under Augustus the Romans did not doubt that they had the right to enslave those captured in a just war. Suetonius cites Augustus' treatment of prisoners of war as evidence of his clemency. Similar conditions were imposed when other conquered tribes were sold 'under the spear': for instance twenty years' servitude for the Alpine Salassi in 25 BC (Dio, 53, 25.4).

(2) And the most serious punishment he ever inflicted on those who frequently or treacherously rebelled was to sell the captives on the condition that they should not serve as slaves in any neighbouring territory, and should not be set free before thirty years had passed.

120. Aelian, *Different Stories*, 2, 7

It has been suggested that states which were unable to obtain slaves through warfare had to turn to other sources to supply their needs for slave labour. There are frequent references in Greek literature and Egyptian papyri to the exposition of unwanted children as a source of slaves. While Boeotia was one of the few Greek states which discouraged infanticide, a foundling (*threptos*) had no right to appeal against having to serve as a chattel slave.

There is a particularly just and humane law at Thebes that no Theban may expose his child or condemn it to death by abandoning it in a deserted place. If the child's father really is in dire poverty, then whether the child is male or female he must bring it in its swaddling bands to the magistrates as soon as the mother's labour has ended, and they must take the baby and give it to whoever will pay them the least amount of money for it. An agreement must be made with this person stipulating that he should look after the baby and is to have it as his male or female slave when it has grown up, and to use its labour in return for having looked after it.

121. Suetonius, *Grammarian* 5

A free-born Roman citizen could not legally forfeit his status without his own consent; but in the ancient world many free-born children were abandoned (*expositi*) by parents who could not or would not bring them up, and raised as foundlings (*threptoi, alumni*) by someone whose slaves they effectively became (scc Pliny, *Letters*, 10, 65 and 66 = L&R II, 107).

In theory a Roman citizen could claim back his freedom even after many years' service as a slave (No. **14**); but being free was not necessarily thought to be preferable to belonging to another man's household.

(21) Gaius Melissus was born at Spoleto; he was free-born, but abandoned because of an argument between his parents. Because of the interest and efforts of the man who brought him up, he received a higher education, and was presented as a gift to Maecenas to use as a grammarian. Because he realised that Maecenas liked him and accepted him as he would a friend, he retained the status of a slave even though his mother claimed his freedom on his behalf, and he preferred his present status to that due to his true birth. For this he was soon freed, and became friendly with Augustus; and it was he who appointed him to look after the arrangement of the library in the Portico of Octavia.

122. *Code of Theodosius*, 5, 10.1: 'Persons Who Buy New-born Children, Or Take Them To Bring Them Up'.

The principle that someone born as a citizen always had the right to demand to be restored to that status was never questioned – although Constantine effectively vitiated that right by decreeing that the foundling had to pay his master full compensation. This apparent departure from Roman tradition has variously been explained as due to eastern Mediterranean influence, or to pressures from slave-owners concerned not to lose their labour force. It is best paralleled by legislation requiring a Roman citizen who had been captured in warfare but later ransomed to serve as a slave for five years in order to pay off the ransom (*CTh.* 5, 7.2: 408 AD).

The August Emperor Constantine, to the Italians.

In accordance with the decisions of earlier Emperors, any person who lawfully obtains a new-born child in any manner and intends to bring it up, shall have the right to hold it in a state of slavery; so that if after a series of years anyone asserts that it is free, or claims it as his own slave, that person must provide another similar slave or pay an equivalent price.

(1) For when someone has made a contract and paid a just price, his possession of that slave shall have such validity that he shall have unrestricted rights even to sell him to pay off a debt of his own. Anyone who attempts to disobey this law is subject to punishment.
Dated Serdica (Sofia), 18 August 329 [or 319?].

123. *Code of Theodosius*, 3, 3.1: 'Fathers Who Have Sold Their Children'.

Later emperors reasserted the traditional interpretation of the law: the work the foundling had done for the man who had brought him up was sufficient recompense.

The August Emperors Valentinian, Theodosius and Arcadius, to the Praetorian Prefect Tatianus.

All those whom the pitiable misfortune of their parents has reduced to slavery because they needed some money in order to live, are to be restored to the free status they had before. And no one ought to ask for the price to be repaid to them, if he has had the benefit of using a free person as his slave for a considerable period of time.
Dated Milan, 11 March 391.

INTERPRETATION: If a father is forced by poverty to sell a child of free birth, he cannot remain in perpetual slavery; he is to be restored to his proper free-born status, even without paying back the cost of his purchase, if he has made a recompense by means of his services.

124. *Digest* 5, 3: 'On Recovering an Inheritance'; 27: Ulpian, from *On the Edict*, book 15

Qualms about the morality of acquiring slaves from slave-traders are unlikely to have been the reason for the general belief in ancient writers that the best slaves were those born within the household from slave mothers; the contrast with practice in some other slave societies (e.g. Brazil) shows that the Greeks and Romans saw slaves as members of their household, and not simply as labour to be exploited.

The proportion of home-born slaves clearly fluctuated; for instance, Delphi *paramone*-inscriptions suggest an increase over the course of the second century BC, as the 'market' for newly-captured slaves shifted to Italy. It is unlikely that the ancient slave populations can have reproduced themselves without the continuing addition of new slaves from outside (see Brunt, *Manpower*, pp. 148–52). However, the eagerness of owners for their slave women to have children does not mean that they were pressed for labour once warfare no longer provided so many new slaves from the time of Augustus on; it is rather a sign of the high status of *vernae* relative to bought slaves. A slave woman who was unable to bear children was obviously less valuable – *Digest* 21, 1.14 (3) specifies that a vendor's failure to reveal that a female slave was over fifty or sterile leads to a defective sale. But this does not mean that female slaves were bought to 'breed' labour:

Although the offspring of female slaves, and the offspring of such offspring, are not to be considered to be 'fruits' (since women slaves cannot properly be bought for this purpose, to breed offspring), they nevertheless go to increase the inheritance; and there is no doubt that the person who possesses them, or has fraudulently arranged to avoid having possession of them after an action for recovery has been initiated, has to hand them over.

125. Isidore of Seville, *Definitions*, 5, 27: 'The Punishments Decreed by the Laws'

One other source of servile labour was not included in Marcianus' list (No. 4 above) because it was not slavery in the strict sense: condemnation to hard labour as a result of a court sentence (*servitus poenae*). But the convict was no one's property, not even the state's, any more than any other prisoner was; he had merely permanently lost his civic rights. The period of servitude might be for life or for a fixed term (for instance two years for an unjustified appeal against a court sentence: *CTh*. 1, 5.3); and unlike slavery, this condition was personal and could not pass to one's descendants. For cases of *servi poenae*, see Nos. 7, 32 and 138.

(31) 'Mines' are where exiles are taken to excavate veins of metal or to cut blocks of marble on the surface.

(32) *Servitus* (slavery) is so called from 'keeping safe'; for in ancient times those who were kept safe in a war were called *servi* (slaves). This alone is the most extreme of all possible penalties, and for a free person it is much more serious than any other punishment — for when one's freedom is lost, everything else is lost with it.

CHAPTER 7

DOMESTIC SLAVES AND RURAL SLAVES

126. *Digest* **32, 99: Paulus, from the single-volume work** *The Meaning of the Term 'Equipment'*

The uniform condition ascribed to slaves by Greek and Roman legal codes masks the fact that they performed a wide variety of different economic roles, all of which might equally be performed by dependants of free or citizen status. The actual living and working conditions of slaves might differ greatly. Slaves who worked on an estate which their master rarely visited were far less likely to develop any personal feelings towards the head of their household than those who saw him daily — particularly in the Roman period, when some masters owned thousands of slaves, with many of whom they can have had virtually no personal contact. Sending a slave away from the urban household to work on a country estate was considered a punishment and a degradation (**109, 236**).

Roman jurists developed a clear distinction between the 'urban family' and the 'rural family'; although largely a distinction of status, it corresponds to a great extent to the division between slaves who provided services and those engaged in agricultural production, and by late antiquity rural slaves were considered as producers permanently tied to the land they worked (like other *coloni*), while the 'urban family' could still be treated by the owner like other moveable property (*CTh*. 6, 35.1; 12, 1.6; 10, 8.4).

When 'urban slaves' have been specified in a legacy, some authorities distinguish property in urban slaves not by place, but by the type of work done, so that even if they are on a rural estate, they are considered to be urban slaves so long as they do not do agricultural work. It should also be said that any slaves whom the head of the household used to list among his urban slaves, should be held to be urban slaves; this can most effectively be checked from the family journal or from the ration lists.

(1) Doubts may arise about whether slaves used for hunting or fowling should be included amongst the urban or the rural slaves. They should be listed as belonging there where the head of the household kept them and fed them.

(2) Mule-drivers perform an urban service, unless the testator had them allocated specifically to rural work.

(3) Some authorities think that a slave who is the child of a slave woman who belongs to the urban group but was sent to an estate in the country to be brought up belongs to neither group; we should consider whether he doesn't belong to the urban group — that seems to be much more sensible.

(4) When a legacy specifies 'slaves who are litter-bearers', then a slave who is both a litter-bearer and a cook passes to the legatee.

(5) If 'home-born slaves' (*vernae*) are left to one man, and 'messengers' (*cursores*) to another, then any who are both home-born and messengers will be classified as messengers: for a particular type always takes precedence in law before a general class. If there are any slaves who fall into two types or two classes, then they will generally be shared between the legatees.

127. *ILS* 1514

The kinds of services provided by slaves in Greek and Roman households were similar to those required from dependants in other societies. Diogenes Laertius' account of the Wills of his philosophers gives us some idea of the number of personal slaves there might be in a wealthy man's retinue, including litter-bearers and a secretary (No. **95** above). Romances like *Leukippe and Kleitophon* show that slaves would be used to provide background music at mealtimes (1, 5.4), as messengers (1, 12.1), doorkeepers (2, 26.1), concubines (2, 26.1), to wake you up in the morning (1, 6.5) and generally as attendants; they would be beaten mercilessly if their master was angry with them (4, 15.6). An inscription from Rome shows that a finance officer of Tiberius who was himself a slave was accompanied on a trip to the capital by sixteen of his own under-slaves (*vicarii*); their functions are all specified, except for that of the single woman amongst them.

To Musicus Scurranus [slave] of Tiberius Caesar Augustus, superintendent of the Gallic Treasury for the province of Lyon: [dedicated] to him, as he well deserved, by those of his under-slaves who were with him at Rome when he died:

Venustus, buying agent	Agathopus, physician	Facilis, attendant
Decimianius, treasurer	Epaphra, in charge of silver	Anthus, in charge of silver
Dicaeus, attendant	Primio, in charge of wardrobe	Hedylus, chamberlain

Mutatus,	Communis,	Firmus,
attendant	chamberlain	cook
Creticus,	Pothus,	Secunda.
attendant	attendant	
	Tiasus,	
	cook	

128. Xenophon, *The Householder*, 7

Xenophon describes how the wealthy landowner Iskhomakhos instructs his young wife in her duties, which include training her slave attendants. Their skills are not very different from those required of their mistress.

(41) You have some enjoyable tasks of your own, like when you take a girl who knows nothing about spinning wool, and make her skilled in it, and she becomes worth twice as much to you; or when you take a girl who knows nothing about management or the duties of a servant, and you make her skilled and trustworthy and a good attendant, so that she becomes worth any sum at all; or when you have the opportunity to reward those in your household who are self-controlled and useful, and to punish anyone who seems to be bad . . .

129. The Nurse: *ILS* 8532

It was of course the more unpleasant, troublesome and time-consuming domestic tasks that were given to slaves. Despite the social pressures on mothers to nurse and look after their own children, those who could afford it preferred to leave them to nurses, bought or hired (see Tacitus, *Dialogus* 28f.); Quintilian (*Inst. Or.*, 1, 4f. = L&R II, 73) discusses how important the right choice of nurse is even before he mentions the role of parents. By no means all nurses were slaves or freedwomen, rather than poor citizen women, but some inscriptions explicitly mention nurses who had been slaves (see No. 136 below).

To the Spirits of the Dead.
To Servia Cornelia Sabina, freedwoman of Servius.
Servius Cornelius Dolabella Metillianus
made this for his nurse and 'mummy' (*nutrici et mammul.*), who well deserved it.

130. Quintilian, *Educating an Orator*, 1, 1

The slaves who were closest to their masters were the ones who had looked after them when they had been children: for women, their nurse, and for men normally the *paedagogus*, the slave who had accompanied them to school every morning and had generally been responsible for protecting and assisting them. Even the law recognised how deep the friendships between these slaves and their masters might be (see No. 5, Ch. 19 above).

But although the educational role of these slaves was crucial, they were often appointed merely because they were useless for any other kind of work: when Pericles saw a slave fall from a tree and break his leg, he is said to have remarked that he had just become a *paedagogus* (Stobaeus, *Florida*, 4.209).

(8) What was said about nurses should also be said about the playmates with whom the child you want to become a great orator is going to be brought up. There is an additional point to make about tutors; they should either be thoroughly well educated (which I would prefer) or else they should be aware of their lack of education. Nothing is worse than those who have got a little beyond the alphabet and falsely persuade themselves that they are very knowledgeable. For they think it insults their dignity to give way to those whose job it is to teach, and they imperiously and sometimes brutally impose their own stupidity on their charges as though they had some claim to authority (which is what makes all people of this kind inordinately proud). And their foolishness is equally harmful to their charges' character, certainly if it was Alexander's tutor Leonides who infected him with some of his vices (so Diogenes the Babylonian says); as a result of the education he had received as a child, these vices clung to him when he had grown up and was already the greatest of kings.

131. Pliny the Elder, *Natural History*, 12, 32

As with doctors (No. 73 above), so with *paedagogi* it was felt to be somehow unnatural for a free man to be under the control of a slave, even if he was just a child. This resentment felt by the Greek and Roman elite at having once had slaves as their special companions expressed itself in frequent jokes about *paedagogi* (for example, in Roman comedy; see Martial, 11.39, and No. **240** below). When Pliny illustrates the exceptional expense of frankincense, he tells how the world's greatest conqueror had once been told off by a slave.

(62) When as a boy Alexander the Great was heaping piles of incense onto an altar, his *paedagogus* Leonides told him that he would be able to invoke the gods in such a lavish way once he had conquered the peoples who produced incense; and when he had won control over Arabia, he sent a ship laden with incense to him, telling him to worship the gods unstintingly.

132. Seneca, *Letters*, 27

Other functions performed by slaves were to remind their master of the names of the people he met (the *nomenclator*), and even to provide entertainment by memorising poetry: this case presses to absurdity the idea that a slave is a mere tool extending his master's faculties.

(5) There is another type of knowledge which does allow us to use the assistance of others. I remember that there was a very rich man called Calvisius Sabinus. He inherited a freedman's estate, and his mind too: never was it so scandalous that a man should have wealth. His memory was so bad that he would sometimes forget the name Ulysses, or Achilles or Priam — persons we all know as well as we know our tutors. No slave assigned the job of reminding us of people's names (*nomenclator*), no matter how old, ever made so many mistakes in imposing names on humble clients rather than repeating them properly, as Sabinus did when he mentioned Trojans and Greeks. Yet he wanted to appear to be an educated man. (6) The following solution occurred to him: at enormous expense he bought some slaves, one to memorise the whole of Homer off by heart, another Hesiod, and one each assigned to the nine lyric poets. That he paid an enormous price for them isn't surprising — he couldn't find any for sale, and had to contract for them to be trained. After he had acquired this slave gang, he started pestering his dinner guests. He kept some of them stationed at the end of his couch and would continually ask them for some lines of poetry to quote — though he'd often forget in the middle of a word. (7) Satellius Quadratus was someone who went in for cheating stupid rich men, and therefore also for flattering them and, consistently enough, for making fools of them: he suggested he should get a gang of grammarians to stand in for the slaves who have to clear up the left-overs. When Sabinus said that these slaves had cost him 100,000 Sesterces each, he said, 'The same number of book-cases would have been cheaper.' But Sabinus' attitude was that, whatever anyone in his household knew, he knew. (8) Satellius also tried to persuade him to go in for wrestling: Sabinus was a pale and weak invalid whose reply was, 'How could I — it takes all my energy to stay alive.' 'You mustn't say that,' came the riposte, 'don't you see

how many slaves you own who are in excellent health?'

133. Suetonius, *Grammarians*

While some slaves were treated as mere mechanical devices assisting their owner's intellectual activity (as readers, *lectores*, or shorthand clerks, *notarii*: see Pliny, *Letters*, 3, 5.12 and 15), others could themselves play an important role in the development of Latin philology and literary criticism.

(7) Marcus Antonius Gnipho was born in Gaul of free birth, but was abandoned, then manumitted and educated by the man who brought him up; some say that this was at Alexandria, where he lived with Dionysius Scytobrachio, but I'm not prepared to believe this because the chronology doesn't fit at all. He is said to have been extremely talented, with an unparalleled memory, as learned in Greek as in Latin, with a pleasant and easy-going character; and he never made any agreement about getting paid — so that he obtained more, as a result of the generosity of his pupils. He first taught at the house of the divine Julius, who was still a boy at the time, and later at his own home.
(11) According to some sources, Publius Valerius Cato was the freedman of someone from Gaul called Bursenus; he himself asserts in the pamphlet entitled 'Indignation' that he was born free and left an orphan, and that that was how he was so easily stripped of his inheritance during the lawless period of Sulla's dictatorship.
(12) Cornelius Epicadus was the freedman of Lucius Cornelius Sulla the Dictator; he became an official herald (*calator*) of the College of Augurs, and also very close to Sulla's son Faustus, which is why he always maintained that he was a freedman of both. He also finished the last book of Sulla's autobiography, which Sulla had left incomplete.
(13) Staberius Eros was a† Thracian bought at a public sale, and later set free because of his interest in literature. Amongst others, he taught Brutus and Cassius. Some people say that he was endowed with such nobility of character that during Sulla's dictatorship, he accepted the children of the proscribed at his classes without charging them any fee.
(15) Lenaeus was the freedman of Pompey the Great and went with him on almost all his expeditions . . . The story is told that when he was still a slave (*puer*) he escaped from his chains and fled back to his own country, where he taught literature; he sent his master the price he had cost him, but was manumitted for nothing because of his excellent character and scholarship.
(23) Quintus Remmius Palaemon of Vicenza is said to have been the

house-born slave of some woman. He was originally a weaver, but then learned letters when he accompanied his master's son to school.
(27) Lucius Voltacilius Pilutus is said to have been a slave, and even to have been chained up in the old-fashioned way as a door-keeper, until he was set free because of his intelligence and interest in literature, and assisted his patron in making legal accusations in court.

134. Xenophon, *The Householder*, 9

The most important domestic slave was the manager, since he or she would allow the master the leisure required for participation in civic affairs (see No. 2, Ch. 23). Iskhomakhos says that he had personally trained his managers (*epitropoi*) to be careful and loyal agents, and the head of the women slaves is also treated with respect.

(11) When we chose our manageress, we considered which woman seemed to us to show the most temperance with regard to food and wine and sleep and intercourse with men, and in addition which one seemed to be endowed with the best memory and to be the most circumspect (so that she would avoid being punished by us for carelessness) and most keen to please us so that we would reward her in return. (12) We taught her to be well disposed towards us by communicating our joy to her when we were pleased, and asking for her sympathy if there was something which disappointed us. We trained her to want the household to prosper, by making her know all about it and making sure she shared in its success. (13) And we encouraged her to develop a sense of justice by giving more honour to the just slaves than to the unjust ones, and pointing out to her that their lives had more riches and more freedom than those of the unjust. And that was the position which we entrusted to her.

135. Seneca, *Letters*, 12

Nineteenth-century abolitionists were keen to argue that apart from being immoral, slave labour was less economic than that provided by a free labour market. One of the points they made was that a capitalist employer did not have to concern himself with that section of the workforce which was sick or too old to work, whereas slave-owners did have to look after such people. The number of functions which might usefully be performed by old and feeble slaves was limited; they could become *paedagogi* (Nos. 130–1 above), *nomenclatores* (No. 132) or door-keepers. Seneca's story about how he failed to recognise his old playmate is an illustration of the callous ancient attitude to old age generally; and also an instance of the immediate tour of inspection of an estate a master had not seen for a long time, recommended by the agricultural textbooks (No. **149**, Ch. 6 below).

(1) Wherever I turn, I see indications that I'm getting old. I was visiting a suburban estate of mine and complaining about the expense of the dilapidated building. My manager told me that this wasn't the fault of neglect on his part – he was doing everything, but the fact was that the building was old. Actually this house was built under my own super-vision – what is to happen to me, if stones of the same age as myself are in such a crumbling state? (2) I was upset at what he had said and used the next suitable occasion for an outburst of anger. 'These plane-trees are obviously not being looked after,' I said; 'there aren't any leaves on them; the branches are all knotted and parched, and the bark is flaking off those squalid trunks. That wouldn't happen if someone was digging round them and giving them water.' He swore by my own soul (*genius*) that he was doing whatever he could, that there was no respect in which his efforts were falling short – but they were old. Between ourselves, I planted them myself; I saw their first growth of leaves. (3) I went up to the entrance. 'Who,' I said, 'is that decrepit fellow? How suitable that he should have been moved to the door – he's clearly waiting to move on. Where on earth did you get hold of him? What possessed you to steal a corpse from someone else?' But the fellow said to me, 'Don't you recognise me? I'm Felicio – you used to give me puppets at the Saturnalia. I'm the son of your manager Philositus, I was your playmate when I was little.' 'The man's absolutely mad.' I said. 'Now he's turned into a little boy and a playmate of mine. Could be true though – he's toothless as a child.'

136. Pliny, *Letters*, 6, 3

An old family retainer who was particularly close to his or her master might be pensioned off with a small estate – but one assumes that this will have been rare.

Greetings from Gaius Plinius to Verus.

I thank you for taking over the running of the little farm which I had presented to my old nurse. It was worth 100,000 Sesterces when I originally gave it to her; but afterwards the income declined and the value of the estate fell accordingly; with you managing it, it will recover its former value. You must remember that it is not trees and soil with which I have entrusted you (although I've done that too), but rather with a gift that I had made, and that it is as important to me who gave it as to her who received it, that it should be as profitable as possible.

137. *Digest* 14, 5.8: Paulus, from *Decrees*, book 1

Slaves could be used to do those jobs which were unpleasant or risky or took up a lot of time, and therefore ranked as low status in the eyes of ancient agrarian societies: shipping, manufacture, trade and banking. Much entrepreneurial activity was the particular sphere of freedmen (see No. **47** above); there is a certain amount of evidence about the role of slaves and freedmen in Roman brick and pottery production (see Burford, *Craftsmen*). A notable freedman banker was Pasion († 370 BC), who was so successful that he was, exceptionally, granted Athenian citizenship (his career is well documented by Isocrates' *Trapeziticus* and many of Demosthenes' speeches). But so long as the agent was still a slave, his master was legally responsible for all his undertakings, and this might land him in serious difficulties. Here the jurist Paulus tells how one of the Severan emperors rejected his opinion on a verdict which had been appealed against.

Titianus Primus had appointed a slave to make loans and accept pledges as security for these loans. But in addition, this slave made a habit of taking over debts owed to grain-merchants by purchasers and paying them off. The slave ran away, and the person who was responsible for recovering the price of the grain brought an action against the master on the grounds that the slave was his agent. But Primus denied that an action could be brought against him on this account, since the slave had not been appointed to undertake deals of this kind. When it also emerged that the same slave had undertaken various other deals and rented a granary and paid off debts owed by a number of people, the Prefect of the Corn Supply gave a ruling against the owner. I stated my own opinion, which was that this seemed to be analogous to giving surety for bail: he had paid off other people's debts, but had not himself incurred any debts on their behalf. It is not normal for an action to be allowed against a master on these grounds, and the master did not appear to have given any such orders. The Emperor, however, upheld the Prefect's ruling, since the master had given the impression that he had appointed the slave to act on his behalf in everything.

138. Hippolytus, *Refutation of all Heresies*, 9, 12.1ff.

A curious case of fraud by a slave banker is told by an early Christian
theologian. Hippolytus is attacking a rival theological tradition which
he accuses of having tainted Christianity with Greek philosophical
ideas going back to Heraclitus. In classical rhetoric, criticism of a person's
ideas was thought to be immeasurably strengthened by an attack on the
teacher — an invective. One of the recognised elements of a classical
invective was to accuse the opposition of coming from a low social
background: here Hippolytus tells us how his opponent and rival for
the Papacy, Callistus, was not just of servile origin, but also incompetent
in business and disloyal to his master.

He happened to be the house-slave of someone called Carpophorus,
a Christian believer belonging to the Emperor's household. Carpophorus
entrusted a considerable sum of money to him, since he seemed to be a
reliable person, and told him to invest it profitably in banking. He took
the money and set up a bank in what is called the 'Public Fish-Market',
and in time several quite significant deposits were lodged with him on
behalf of widows and other Christians, since the legal responsibility lay
with Carpophorus. But Callistus managed to waste it all and got himself
into a hopeless situation. When this had happened, someone informed
Carpophorus, who said that he would require Callistus to present his
accounts for inspection. When Callistus heard about this he could see
the danger that he would be in from his master and ran away to escape
by sea. He found a ship at Portus ready to set sail and went on board
prepared to go anywhere the ship might be sailing to. But even this
didn't enable him to get away unnoticed, since someone had told
Carpophorus what had happened, and he went down to the harbour as
a result of this information and tried to get on board the ship. But the
ship was at anchor in the middle of the harbour, and the captain was
in no hurry to set sail, and Callistus saw his master when he was still
a long way off. Since he was on board ship, he saw that he couldn't
avoid being recaptured; he didn't think his life was worth living for
and he thought that he was finished and threw himself into the sea.
But the people on the shore all started to shout and the sailors jumped
into their boats and pulled him out against his will. In this way he was
given back to his owner and carted off to Rome, and his master put
him to work in the tread-mill. Some time went by, and then — as so
often happens — some fellow-Christians came to Carpophorus and
asked him to release the runaway from his punishment, saying that
he had admitted to them that there were some people with whom he
had deposited the missing money. Carpophorus was a humane man and
said that he didn't care about recovering money he had lost himself;

on the other hand he was concerned about the sums that had been deposited by others, since a lot of people had complained that they had entrusted their deposits to Callistus because the legal responsibility lay with Carpophorus. Yet he accepted their arguments and ordered Callistus to be freed from the tread-mill. But he didn't have anything with which to pay back his creditors, and because he wasn't able to run off again because he was being kept under guard, he worked out a plan to get himself killed: one Saturday, pretending that he was going to meet his creditors, he went to the synagogue where the Jews assembled, and got up and created a disturbance. The Jews were upset by his behaviour and started insulting and beating him and dragged him off to the Urban Prefect, Fuscianus. Here they made a statement to the following effect: 'The Romans have agreed that we can recite in public the laws of our ancestors, and then this fellow comes along and stops us by causing a disturbance and proclaiming that he's a Christian.' Fuscianus, from the judge's bench, was very angry with Callistus on the basis of the evidence presented by the Jews; and someone went and told Carpophorus what had occurred. Carpophorus hurried off to the Prefect's court and shouted, 'Lord Fuscianus, I beg you, don't believe this man, he isn't a Christian at all but wants to get himself killed because he's made away with a lot of money belonging to me, as I shall show you.' The Jews assumed that this was a trick on the part of Carpophorus to have him released on this pretext, so they appealed to the Prefect in an even more hostile manner. He gave in to them, had Callistus whipped and sentenced to be sent to the mines in Sardinia.

In the end Callistus managed to get his name on to a list of Christian prisoners who were pardoned by Commodus at the instigation of his concubine Marcia, who was herself a Christian; he returned to Italy and was elected Pope – quite unjustifiably, according to Hippolytus.

139. Xenophon, *The Householder*, 5

From the point of view of production, slavery may be seen primarily as a mechanism for achieving a quantitative increase in the productivity of the household unit, rather than as a separate 'mode of production'. In Hesiod (*Works and Days* 406) and Homer, slaves provide domestic services and are not used in agriculture; such work is carried out by dependant tenants or day-labourers (*Odyssey* 11,489; 18,356–64). But in the classical period, slaves are found providing additional labour for work on the land in Chios (see No. **80**,265b) and Corcyra (Thucydides 3, 73). The fact that only twelve of the seventy-nine slaves whose occupations are specified on Athenian apostasy records worked on the land (see No. 27) may mean that slaves were more frequently used in domestic service and industry than in agriculture, or more probably that agricultural slaves were far less likely to win their freedom. For the rich at least, the use of agricultural slaves is taken for granted. Thus Xenophon praises agriculture because a man who is experienced in controlling agricultural slaves will also be a good army officer.

(14) Farming also trains men to assist each other as a team. When you campaign against an enemy, you use men; and working the land requires men too. (15) So if you are going to be a good farmer, you must make your workers co-operative and willing to obey you; and when you lead men against an enemy you must try to achieve this too, by giving rewards to those who behave as brave men should, and punishing those who lack discipline. (16) It is just as necessary for a farmer to give his workers frequent encouragement as for a general to encourage his troops. Slaves have no less need of something good to hope for than do free men — if anything, more, so that they may stay with you willingly.

140. Aristotle, *Politics*, 7, 9

Aristotle believed that all those who did agricultural work should have a lower status than leisured gentleman citizens. In actual fact classical Athens was a society of peasant farmers who worked the land themselves, side by side with their sons and any slaves they may have had; Aristotle was thinking of the ideal of Sparta, where the Helot population liberated the citizens for political and military activity.

(9) If I am to state my own preference, the people who cultivate the land should be slaves; they should not all come from the same tribe or nation, and they should not be too courageous. This will make them useful workers and safe from the danger of revolt. As a second best, they should be non-Greek-speaking serfs (*barbarous perioikous*) with natural characters as similar as possible to those I have indicated. Those of them who are used on private estates must be private property, and those used on community land public property. I will discuss on a separate occasion how slaves ought to be treated, and why it is better if freedom is held out as a prize to all slaves.

141. Appian, *Roman Civil Wars*, 1, 1

At Rome, slaves did not liberate the peasant farmer to take part in democratic politics, but to fight to conquer an empire. For the wealthy, there were great advantages in using slave rather than free labour. The best ancient analysis is given by Appian in the introduction to his account of the civil strife which led to the fall of the Roman republic.

(7) When the Romans had won control over one part of Italy after another through warfare, they took part of the land and built settlements there, or if there were towns there already, they selected settlers from amongst their own people. They intended these colonies to fulfil the functions of garrisons; on each occasion when they won control of land through war, they immediately allocated any that was being worked to their colonists, or else sold it or leased it out, while as regards the land which was then lying fallow as a result of the fighting (and that was the greater proportion), they proclaimed that since they didn't have the time to divide it up into lots, anyone who wished to work it could do so in the meantime for an annual rent of one-tenth of the crops harvested each year, and one-fifth of the fruit. Similar assessments were decreed for those who had herds of cattle or smaller livestock. This was done with a view to increasing the population of Italy, which seemed to them to be particularly able to endure hard work, so that they would have allies to call upon in that country. But they achieved the exact opposite. What happened was that the rich got hold of most of that land which was not distributed as allotments, and as time passed they assumed that no one would take it away from them; and they persuaded the poor owners of small farms bordering on their own to sell them, or even seized some farms by violence, so that they came to cultivate huge estates instead of individual farms; and they used bought slaves as cultivators and herdsmen, so that they wouldn't have to depend upon free men who could be called away from their work to serve in the army. And owning slaves was very profitable because they produced lots of children so that the number of slaves relentlessly increased because they weren't liable to military service. Those property-owners who were powerful became extremely wealthy, and the number of slaves increased throughout the country, while the Italians became fewer and poorer, oppressed by poverty, by taxes and by military service. And even if there was a period when they weren't away on campaign, they sat around without employment, because the land was owned by the rich and they used slaves to work it instead of free workers.

(8) For these reasons the Roman people became concerned that they might no longer have enough Italian allies, and that these vast numbers of slaves might constitute a danger to their government of Italy. But they didn't see how things could be put right since it wasn't easy, nor entirely fair, to deprive so many men of such a large amount of property

which they had possessed for such a long time, including trees they had planted themselves and buildings and equipment. With great difficulty the Plebeian Tribunes introduced a law that no one should have more than 500 *iugera* of this land, and shouldn't graze more than 100 cattle or 500 lesser animals on it. To give effect to these provisions they ordered landowners to employ a certain proportion of free men, who would watch over what was going on and submit reports.

They included all these things in a law and reinforced it with an oath and decreed a penalty, and they thought that the land that was left would soon be distributed to the poor in small allotments. But no one took any notice either of the law or of the oaths.

142. Suetonius, *Julius*, 42

The danger that the presence of slaves caused to civil society was recognised, not because of the possibility of slave revolts, but because of the threat it posed to the survival of the peasants on whom the Roman elite depended for service in the army.

In order to restore the declining population of Rome, he decreed that no citizen over twenty and under † forty who had not been inducted into the army should be away from Italy for more than three years at a time; nor should anyone who was a Senator's son go abroad, except in attendance upon an officer or magistrate, and those who engaged in ranching should have not less than one-third free-born persons among their herdsmen.

143. Livy, 6, 12

Complaints about the lack of free manpower, especially for military purposes, occur in Lucan (7, 387–439 and 1, 158–82), Seneca Rhetor (*Excerpt.Controv.* 5, 5) and Livy (7, 25.9); here Livy has been wondering how it was possible for the Volsci and the Aequi to find the soldiers to fight Rome year after year in the fifth and fourth centuries BC. He had been unable to find any explanation in his sources, but:

It is plausible . . . (5) that there was then a vast number of free persons living in the same places in which there is hardly the tiniest seed-bed for soldiers left today, and which only the Romans' slaves stop from becoming a desert.

144. Pliny the Elder, *Natural History*, 18, 4

The contrast between contemporary slave gangs and the old Roman peasant heroes who worked smallholdings themselves was frequent in rhetoric (see Nos. **80**–**1** above); but the use of chained slaves was not merely a rhetorical *topos* (**146,149** Ch. 9.4). In contrast to the times of Cincinnatus:

(21) Nowadays farmwork is done by feet which have been chained, by hands which have been punished, by faces which have been branded; but the earth which we call our mother and claim to work for is not so stupid that we should think that she is not displeased and angry that this work is done by the labour of such slaves. Should we be surprised that we do not get the same profits from slave prisons as used to be got from the labour of Roman commanders?

145. Pliny the Elder, *Natural History*, 18, 7

One assumption which it is not safe to make is that the use of large numbers of disciplined slave workers led to increased efficiency by allowing the kinds of economies of scale which may have been possible on the cotton, sugar or coffee plantations of the New World. One reason for this was that it was felt that slave workers needed a great deal of supervision (see, for example, No. **149** below); the other was that ancient technology had not developed the kinds of tools and techniques which prove more profitable where the scale is larger. Hence there arose the paradox that the 'best' estate in terms of size was not the 'best' in terms of profits — and once again we find that size is a function of display, not of profitability.

(36) The worst thing for a farm is to be worked by slaves housed in a prison — like anything else that is done by men who have no hope. It may seem rash to quote an old maxim, and perhaps you won't believe it if you don't think about it carefully: 'Nothing is more pointless than having the best farm to cultivate.' (37) Lucius Tarius Rufus, who rose to the consulship from an extremely humble background as a result of his military ability, was in most respects as thrifty as the heroes of old; but in order to enhance his glory, he wasted a fortune of 100 million Sesterces which had been presented to him by the Divine Augustus on buying and cultivating land in Picenum — so that his heir had to repudiate the estate.

So does farming mean disaster and starvation? Not at all: but moderation is the best standard in all things. (38) Having a good farm is essential, but having the largest one of all (*optime colere*) is disastrous, except when the farmer can cultivate it with the labour of his own children or with persons he has to feed in any case.

146. Pliny, *Letters*, 3, 19

Romans knew that a larger estate would mean some improved efficiency, but these economies were unconnected with the actual method of exploiting the land, and were outweighed by other considerations. This letter also reminds us of the universal threat of debt hanging over every peasant farmer. The reference to slaves in section 7 does not mean that Pliny considered replacing the tenant smallholders of this estate (at Como in northern Italy) with slaves: the slaves are among the farm tools the tenants had to sell to pay off their debts (for slaves as part of the equipment (*instrumentum*) entrusted to tenants, see *ILS* 6675, Ch. 43).

Greetings from Caius Plinius to Calvisius Rufus.

(1) I would like to include you amongst my advisors in a matter concerning my household, as I always do. An estate is being offered for sale which borders upon and is even partially surrounded by my own. There are many things which I find attractive about it, and some important ones which deter me. (2) I am attracted primarily by the advantages of joining up the two estates; then there's the fact that both estates could be inspected on a single visit (which is not only pleasant, but has material advantages too); they can be managed by the same agent, and virtually by the same foremen; there will only be one house to maintain and furnish – the other one will only have to be kept in a decent condition. (3) My comparison takes into account the cost of furniture, slaves to look after the house and the garden, tool-makers, and the personnel and materials needed for hunting. It makes a great deal of difference whether you can keep them all in one place or have to have them spread out among several.

(4) On the other hand, I fear that it would not be wise to concentrate so much property which could be affected by the same climatic and other disasters; it seems safer to insure oneself against the uncertainties of Fortune by having one's property in different places. And indeed changes of scenery and climate are quite enjoyable, as is travelling from one farm to another.

(5) But the most crucial thing to consider is that these fields are fertile, rich and well irrigated; they consist of pasture, vineyards and woodland which provides trees and thus a steady if moderate income. (6) However, the advantages of the soil have been diminished as a result of bad cultivation. The previous owner frequently foreclosed on

debts, and although this enabled him to cut down the tenants' rent arrears in the short term, he destroyed their long-term resources so that the arrears soon increased again. (7) So these fields will have to be stocked with slaves, who cost more if they are honest; I don't use chained slaves anywhere, and no one there does either . . .

147. Columella, 1, 7

Discussions of whether to have your land cultivated by free tenants or slaves refer to the system of management, not the nature of the workforce: tenants might use slaves too, and some tenants would be just as much absentees as the landlords themselves.

The ancient consensus — which was not necessarily correct — was that, as long as the farm manager was competent, slaves would produce greater surpluses everywhere except on marginal land, and on land so far away that the owner could not supervise it regularly.

(1) The landowner must be as careful in selecting his workforce as in other things. These may be either tenants (*coloni*) or slaves, who may be loose or chained. He should treat his tenants in a pleasant and easy fashion, and should be more insistent that they work properly than that they pay their rent, since they will find this less offensive and it will be generally more advantageous — for when land is properly cultivated, it will generally bring in profits and never losses, unless there is a major disaster due to climatic conditions or brigands; and the tenant will therefore not dare to ask for payments to be remitted. (2) But the owner should not insist on his strict legal rights in respect of every single one of the obligations he has imposed upon his tenant, like the date when rent is due to be paid, or demanding additional little exactions like firewood; remembering about these things gives rural workers more trouble than expense. So we should not insist on our legal rights, since absolute justice is absolute torture, as our ancestors said. But we shouldn't abandon our rights completely either; as the money-lender Alfius is said to have remarked — and how right he was — 'even the best debts become bad if they are not called in'.

(3) I myself remember how as an old man Publius Volusius, an extremely wealthy ex-consul, used to say that the most fortunate farm was one whose tenants were local people who had been born there and effectively inherited the place and stayed there because they were familiar with it right from their childhood. So I believe absolutely that frequent changes of tenants are bad for a farm; but renting to a tenant who lives at Rome and prefers to have the land cultivated by his slaves than by himself is worse. (4) Saserna used to say that you would get law suits rather than

rents from this sort of person; and that is why we should be careful that if we cannot farm the estate ourselves or through our own slaves, our tenants are rural people and do not change frequently. But this should only happen in areas which have been abandoned because of a bad climate or infertile soil. (5) If the climate is only moderately healthy, and the soil moderately fertile, then you will always get a higher return from an estate you look after yourself than from tenants — and you will even get a higher return if it is looked after by a manager, unless this slave is particularly incompetent or corrupt. And if he does suffer from either of these vices, there can be no doubt that he generally does so, or at least is encouraged to do so, as the result of a mistake on his master's part, since his master could have made sure that he was not put in charge in the first place and that he was removed if he had already been appointed.

(6) But when farms are a long way away, so that the head of the household finds it difficult to visit them, then any kind of cultivation by free tenants is preferable to that of slave managers; particularly for arable farming, since a tenant can do minimal damage to such a farm, as he can to vineyards and orchards, while slaves can do a lot of harm. They may hire out oxen and not pasture other cattle properly and not plough properly and claim that they have sown far more seed than they in fact have and not look after what they have sown to make it grow properly, and lose a lot of the harvested grain during threshing as a result of theft or incompetence. (7) They may steal it themselves or fail to take proper precautions against other thieves or just not compile trustworthy accounts. The result is that neither the manager nor the slaves do their work properly and the reputation of the estate declines. That is why I think that a farm of this kind should be let to tenants if, as I said, the owner cannot be there himself.

148. Varro, *Agriculture*, 1, 17

Varro's remarks about the agricultural labour-force contain references to the use of children by those who couldn't afford slaves, to serfdom, and to incentives both for overseers and others.

(1) I shall now discuss the instruments by means of which the land is tilled. Some theorists divide these into two parts, the men, and the men's tools, without which they cannot work the land; others prefer a threefold classification, the class of instruments endowed with speech, that which is inarticulate and that which is speechless. That endowed with speech includes slaves, the inarticulate includes cattle, and the speechless wagons. (2) All fields are worked by human beings, whether

slaves or free men or both; they are worked by free men either when these people work their own land, as many poor people do together with their offspring, or when they are hired labourers, when major agricultural operations like the vine harvest or hay-cutting are carried out by means of the hired labour of free men: or else by those persons whom the Romans used to call 'debt-bondsmen' (*obaerati*) and of whom there are large numbers even today in Asia Minor and Egypt and Illyricum. (3) My opinion about these people as a class is the following: it is better to work unhealthy land with hired labourers than with slaves, and even in healthier districts, for the more important agricultural operations like bringing in the produce of the vintage or the harvest. As regards the kinds of qualifications these people should have, Cassius [C. Dionysius of Utica, an agricultural writer of the early first century BC] writes:

> You should obtain labourers who are able to put up with hard work, not less than twenty-two years old and quick to learn the work of the farm. You can assess this on the basis of how they carried out their previous duties, or by asking those of them who are newly engaged what they had been accustomed to do for their previous employer.

Slaves ought neither to be fearful nor brash. (4) Those put in charge of them should know how to read and write and have some culture; they should be honest and older than the hired labourers I mentioned above — for they will be more prepared to obey them than they would younger men. In addition it is particularly important that whoever is in charge should have practical experience of farming. For he shouldn't just give orders but also work himself, so that his subordinates imitate his example and realise that he has been put in charge of them for a good reason, because he knows more about it than they do. (5) And they must not be allowed to enforce their orders by beatings rather than words, so long as this is likely to achieve the same result. Nor should several slaves of the same ethnic origin be obtained; household difficulties tend most frequently to arise from this cause. Overseers are to be encouraged with rewards to work more efficiently, and care must be taken that they have some property (*peculium*) of their own and women slaves to live with them, by whom they can have children; this makes them more reliable and more attached to the farm. It is because of these family ties that the slaves of Epirus are highly regarded and highly expensive. (6) The goodwill of overseers should be won by treating them with a certain degree of respect, and as for those labourers whose work is better than that of the others, they ought to be consulted about what work is to be done, because in that case they will not think that they are looked down upon so much but rather that their employer has some consideration for them. (7) They can be made more keen on their work by being more generously treated as regards food rations or clothing or exemption from work or permission to graze some animal of their own on the farm or other things of this kind, so that if anyone has been ordered to do a particularly unpleasant job or has been punished for something, he can be reconciled by these privileges and his goodwill and loyalty towards his master restored.

149. Columella, 1, 8

In the mid-first century AD, Columella gave the following advice about the selection of managers and labourers, and their tasks. He also refers to the ideal that a farm should be as self-sufficient as possible (8.8), to the danger that a manager will exploit his position of authority to behave brutally or sadistically (8.10 and 16ff., on the *ergastula*), and to the incentive of marriage (8.5). He advises masters against letting their managers undertake business deals on their behalf; disagrees with Plato about sharing a joke with one's slaves, at least those one rarely saw (8.15: see No. **80**, 265b above). While 8.19 is no evidence for the systematic breeding of slaves in Roman times, it does prove that manumission was not universal, or even normal, for agricultural slaves.

The Manager

(1) The next thing to consider is which slave to put in charge of which particular office and what jobs each should be assigned to. My first advice is not to appoint as manager one of those slaves who are physically attractive or someone out of the ranks of those who have performed specialised services in the city household. (2) This kind of slave is dedicated to sleep and idleness, and because he has been used to leisure, gymnastics, race-courses, theatres, dicing, wineshops and brothels, he dreams of this nonsense all the time; and when this sort of thing is applied to farming, the owner doesn't just lose the value of his slave, but of his whole property. You should choose someone who has been hardened to agricultural work from childhood and tested by experience. If there isn't anyone like this, you should put someone in charge who is already used to hard work as a slave. (3) He should no longer be a young man, since this will detract from his authority to command since old men don't like to obey some youngster; nor should he have reached old age yet, or he will not have the stamina for work of the most strenuous kind. He should be middle-aged and fit and know about agriculture, or at least be so dedicated that he will be able to learn quickly. There is no point in having one man in authority and someone

else to point out what work has to be done, (4) as a man who is just learning from one of those under him what ought to be done and how to go about doing it won't really be able to insist that it gets done. Even someone who cannot read and write can supervise an estate properly, as long as he has a first-rate memory; Cornelius Celsus says that a manager of this kind brings his master money more often than he brings him his accounts; because he is illiterate he can't cook the figures so easily, and he won't dare to do so through a confederate who would know exactly what was going on. (5) Whomever you appoint as manager, you must allocate him a woman to live with him and keep him in check and also to help him in various things. The manager should also be told not to be on particularly good terms with any one of the slaves on the farm, let alone with anyone from outside. But occasionally he should confer a mark of distinction on any slave whom he sees working hard, and dedicated to the jobs assigned to him, by inviting him to eat with him on a feast day. He must not make any religious sacrifices except if the master has told him to. (6) He must not let fortune-tellers or sorceresses onto the farm; both of these types of silly superstition cause unsophisticated people to spend money and result in wrongdoing. He should not spend his time in the city or at markets except to buy or sell something which concerns him. (7) As Cato says, the manager should not go out a lot; he should not go beyond the boundaries of the estate except to find out about some agricultural technique, and even then he should only go to places from which he can get back [on the same day]. He must not allow any new tracks or paths to be made on the estate; and he should not receive anyone as a guest unless he is a friend or close relative of his master.

(8) Those are the things he must be told to avoid; and he must be urged to make sure that twice as many metal tools and instruments are kept stored away in good condition as are required by the number of slaves, so that nothing will ever have to be borrowed from one of the neighbours; for the expense in terms of the slave's labour being lost outweighs the cost of providing such extra equipment. (9) He should dress and clothe the slaves in a functional rather than an attractive way, so that they are protected against storms, frost and rain; long-sleeved coats, patchwork cloaks and hoods afford protection against all of these. If they have these, the weather will never be so bad that there isn't some work they can do out in the open. (10) He should not merely be skilled at agricultural work; he should also have such personal qualities — insofar as this is possible in a slave — that he will exercise his authority neither carelessly nor brutally, and should always be giving encouragement to some of the better slaves, and should not be too hard on those who are less good, so that they will fear him for being severe rather than hate him for being cruel. He will achieve this if he keeps watch

over those under his authority so that they don't do anything wrong, instead of finding that he has to punish delinquents as a result of his own incompetence. (11) There is no better way of controlling even the most worthless man than by insisting that he does his work, and that what is due should be completed; and by insisting that the manager is always at his post. In that way those who are responsible for particular jobs will be keen to carry out their tasks properly, and the other slaves will be so exhausted by their work that they will be more interested in rest and sleep than in fun and games.

(12) I approve of several excellent ancient precepts which are now no longer practised — that a manager should not ask one of his fellow-slaves to do anything for him unless it is on the master's business; that he should take all his meals in the presence of the slaves and should be served with the same food as they. In this way he will make sure that the bread has been baked properly and that everything has been prepared hygienically. He should allow no one to leave the farm unless he has sent him himself, and he should not send anyone away unless it is absolutely necessary. (13) He should not do any business for himself and should not use his master's money on deals involving animals or anything else, as this sort of dealing distracts the manager's attention and will make it impossible for him to settle his accounts satisfactorily with his master because he will have stock instead of money. In general, you have to make absolutely sure that he does not think that he knows what he doesn't know, and that he should always try to learn about things he is ignorant of. (14) It is good to do something knowledgeably, but it does much more harm to do it wrongly — for there is one single basic principle in agriculture, which is to do whatever needs doing just once; since everything has already been ruined if there was a mistake due to ignorance or incompetence which had to be put right, and things will not grow again later in such a way as to restore what was lost and produce profits to make up for the losses of the past.

The Labourers

(15) These are the rules which should be adhered to with regard to the other slaves; I do not regret having followed them myself. One should address those rural workers who have not behaved improperly in a friendly way more frequently than one would one's urban slaves. When I realised that such friendliness on the master's part relieved the burden of their continual labour, I often joked with them and allowed them to joke more freely. What I do quite often nowadays is discuss some new piece of work with them as though they were more knowledgeable than I am, and in this way I can find out what each one's attitude is and how intelligent he is. And I've noticed that they are much more willing to start a piece of work when they think that they've been consulted about it

and that it was actually they who first suggested it.

(16) There are some things that every careful man recognises: that he must inspect the slaves in the farm prison (*ergastulum*) to check that they're properly bound and that the actual building where they are kept is sufficiently strong and whether the manager has either tied any-one up without the owner's knowledge or set him free. For the manager has to be absolutely obedient both in not setting free without the owner's permission anyone whom he has ordered to be punished in this way, and in not setting free before the master has found out about it anyone whom he has decided to chain up on his own initiative. (17) The head of the household should inspect this type of slave correspondingly more carefully, and make sure that they are not being maltreated as regards clothing and other rations, in proportion as they are under the control of a greater number of superiors — managers, foremen and prison-keepers — and are more vulnerable to suffer injustice, and also become more dangerous if they have been badly treated as the result of anyone's sadism or greed. (18) That is why the master should ask both them and those who are not chained up (since these are more likely to be trusted) whether they are being treated in accordance with his instructions, and he must himself taste their food and drink to see that it is acceptable, and check their clothing, their fetters and their foot-wear. He must frequently give them an opportunity to complain about anyone who makes them suffer as a result of cruelty or dishonesty. I personally will sometimes punish those responsible for justifiable com-plaints in the same way as I will severely punish those who incite the slaves to disobedience or criticise their overseers slanderously; and conversely I will reward those who work hard and diligently. (19) I have also given the mothers of large families — who ought to be honoured when they have had a certain number of children — freedom from work and sometimes even manumitted them when they had raised several children. If there were three children, they were exempted from work, if more, they got their freedom in addition. [This passage has been interpreted as evidence of systematic breeding of slaves in Roman times.] If the head of the household behaves justly and carefully in this way, he will find that his patrimony increases greatly. (20) He should also remember to worship the farm gods whenever he arrives from the city on a visit; and if there is time, he should start his tour of inspection at once, or otherwise on the next day, and visit every part of his estate and try to work out how much discipline and supervision have declined as a result of his absence, and whether there are any vines, trees or crops that are missing; and he must count his cattle, his slaves, the farm tools and the furniture. If he has made a habit of doing all these things over a period of many years, then discipline will remain good when he reaches old age, and, however infirm he becomes with

the years, he will never be scorned by his slaves.

(Ch. 9.1) I should also say something about the kind of physical and mental faculties appropriate to each particular job. We should put men who are hard-working and utterly abstemious in charge of the flocks and herds. Each of these points is much more relevant to this particular job, since they will have to be continuously on the look-out and very skilled. (2) Intelligence is a necessary, but not a sufficient, quality for the ploughman, if a loud voice and large physique do not give him the necessary authority over his oxen. But he must be gentle as well as powerful; if the oxen are both to obey his commands and not be worn out by their work and by being beaten, and thus survive for longer, then he must terrify them rather than be brutal to them. I will deal with the tasks of shepherds and cowherds in greater detail elsewhere [books 7, 1–7 and 6, 1–26 respectively]. (3) All I want to say here is that strength and physique are irrelevant to these, but essential to ploughmen. Anyone who is particularly tall will become a ploughboy, both for the reason I mentioned just now, and because, of all agricultural activities, ploughing is least exhausting to a tall man, since he is able to stand up straight and rest his weight on the plough handle. A common labourer may be of any height whatsoever, as long as he is able to sustain hard work. (4) Vineyards do not need tall men, but rather broad and powerfully built ones, for they are better at digging and pruning and the other things required here. It is not so important as in other kinds of agricultural work that the men should be honest, since they will be working with others and under supervision; troublesome slaves are also often more intelligent, and this is what is needed in viticulture – the worker shouldn't just be strong, but also have good judgement. That is why vineyards are often worked by slaves in chains. (5) But there is nothing that a good man cannot do better than a bad man if he is as nimble – I have to add that, or someone might think that I preferred to work my land with dishonest rather than honest slaves.

It is also my view that the jobs done by different slaves should be kept separate, so that everyone doesn't do the same thing. (6) That is not to the farmer's advantage: no one thinks that any particular job is his own responsibility, and when he does work hard the advantage is everyone's and not specifically his, and as a result he avoids whatever work he can. And when work done by many has been done badly, it is impossible to identify who was responsible. That is why ploughmen must be kept distinct from vintagers and vintagers from ploughmen and both from ordinary labourers. (7) You should also form groups of not more than ten men each – our ancestors called them *decuriae* and were very much in favour of them, since it is particularly easy to keep watch over this number of men, while a larger crowd can escape the control of the overseer as he leads the way. (8) So if you have a large estate, you must assign these groups to different sections of it, and the work must be distributed in such a way that the men will not be on their own or in pairs, since they cannot be supervised properly if they are scattered all over the place; and conversely they must not be in groups of more than ten, since individuals will not consider that the work has anything to do with them personally if they are part of a large crowd. This system will induce them to compete with each other, and also identify those who are lazy. When a job becomes more interesting because there is an element of competition, then it will seem to be fair that those who don't pull their weight should be punished, and no one will complain about it.

150. Varro, *Agriculture*, 2, 10

Some special problems arose as the result of using slaves as herdsmen or shepherds. This was a particularly undesirable occupation: not only was a herdsman exposed to the climate and the danger of attack by brigands and wild beasts, but he led a solitary life with long periods away from the centres of human activity and from his wife and home. Such a 'marginal' occupation tended to be left to low-status workers, and the Greeks too used slaves (see Sophocles, *Oedipus Tyrannus*, 1121ff.: AVN 78).

On the other hand, moving large herds of cattle from summer to winter pastures (transhumance) caused problems: while it was virtually impossible to supervise these slaves, they had to be physically strong and well armed to protect their flocks. In the second century BC, Italian ranching increased greatly in importance, partly because rich Romans leased estates confiscated from those Italian communities which had supported Hannibal (see No. **141** above), and partly because leather and other products were needed as military equipment in Rome's wars of expansion. It was not surprising that these herdsmen contributed to the de-stabilisation of Sicily (see No. **229**, Ch. 27) and Italy (see No. **228**), and continued to cause trouble later (No. **233**).

(1) **Atticus**: We still have to discuss in this section how many and what kinds of herdsmen we should have.

Cossinius: For larger stock you need older men, for smaller stock even boys will do; but with regard to both groups, those who work along the cattle trails must be stronger than those who can go back to the farm-building on the estate every day — which is of course why you will see young men out in the cattle pastures, while not just boys but even young girls will be looking after the animals on the farm. (2) Those who look after animals should be required to spend the whole day pasturing their flocks, and have all the flocks feed together; on the other hand, everyone is to spend the night with his own flock. They should all be under the charge of a single Chief Herdsman; he should preferably be older and also more experienced than the others, since they will be more willing to obey someone who is older and more experienced than they are. (3) But he must not be so much older as to be unable to put up with hard work as a result of the infirmity of age. For neither old men nor boys easily put up with the hardships of the cattle trails along steep and rugged mountain sides; those who look after herds have to suffer these hardships, especially if they are herds of cattle or goats, which prefer rocky and wooded pastures. You should choose men of powerful physique, fast-moving and nimble, who aren't clumsy when they move their limbs, and aren't just able to follow after the flock but also to defend it from predatory beasts or brigands, who can lift loads up onto the backs of the pack animals, are good at sprinting and at hitting their target. (4) Not every race is good at looking after herds; neither Bastulans nor Turdulans [Spanish tribes] are suitable, but Gauls are particularly good at it, especially with beasts of burden.

As regards purchasing slaves, there are six ways of obtaining legitimate ownership:

1. by legal inheritance;

2. by acquiring him according to the proper forms by mancipatory purchase (*mancipio*) from someone who is legally entitled to sell;

3. when someone who is entitled to surrender the slave legally surrenders him under the proper circumstances (*in iure cessio*);

4. as a result of unchallenged possession (*usucapio*);

5. if he has bought him at an auction of war booty 'under the crown' (*sub corona*);

6. finally, when he has bought him as part of a property, or at a sale by auction (*sectio*) of property, confiscated by the State.

(5) When these persons are sold it is usual for the slave's savings (*peculium*) to go with him unless expressly excluded; and there is a guarantee that he is healthy and free from responsibility for any thefts or liability for any damage; alternatively, if the transaction is not by mancipatory purchase, there is a guarantee of double the price paid, or of the simple purchase price if that is what has been agreed [see Nos. **104**–5 above].

During the day the herdsman of each particular herd should eat his meals alone, but all of those who are under one Chief Herdsman should eat their supper together in the evening. The Chief Herdsman has to make sure that all the equipment needed by the flocks and the herdsmen follows after them, especially the food for the men and vetinary supplies for the animals. The owners keep pack animals for this purpose — sometimes mares, sometimes any other animal which is able to carry a load on its back.

(6) With regard to the breeding of children among herdsmen: there is no problem about those who stay on the farm all the time, since they have a slave woman with them on the estate, and this satisfies the sexual needs of the herdsman. But many people have thought it a good idea that women should be sent along with those who look after the animals on the cattle trails and in wooded country, and protect themselves from the rain with hastily constructed shelters rather than farm buildings; these women should follow the herds, prepare the herdsmen's meals and keep them busy at their work. Such women must be physically strong and not unattractive . . .

Here Varro digresses on the physical strength of these ladies, particularly in Illyricum, compared with pampered Roman matrons. He also says the Chief Herdsman must know writing; and there are some statistics about the number of herdsmen needed for different kinds of stock: one per 80–100 sheep (flocks usually consist of 700–800, sometimes up to 1,000 head; the proportion of shepherds can be reduced with larger flocks), and two men for 50 mares.

151. Cato, *Agriculture*, 5

The manager was the key figure in maintaining productivity – especially if the landowner only rarely visited an estate: this was frequently the case at Rome, where the commitments of social and political life required his presence in the Forum.

Consequently, managers were treated as a special category of slave in theoretical analyses of household management as well as practical handbooks on agriculture. The earliest Latin one was written by Cato the Elder for the benefit of his son.

These will be the duties of the manager:
Let him keep strict discipline.
Let religious festivals be observed.
He must keep his hands off what doesn't belong to him, and look after what does properly.
He must sort out disputes amongst the slaves.
If anyone has done anything wrong, he must punish him fairly in proportion to the damage he has caused.
The slaves must not be badly treated or suffer from cold or hunger.
He must keep them hard at work to stop them getting involved in trouble or things that don't concern them.
If the manager doesn't want them to make trouble, they won't.

If he does let them make trouble, the master must not let him get away with it.

He must reward good work, so that the others have an incentive to work well too.

The manager must not be the kind of person who goes out a lot, he must always be sober, he must never go out to dinner.

He must keep the slaves at their work and make sure that the master's orders are put into effect.

He must not think that he is wiser than his master.

His master's friends he must consider his own friends.

He must listen to whoever he is ordered to listen to.

He must not get involved in any religious activities except those at the crossroads during the festival of the Compitalia, and those at the household hearth.

He must lend no one money without his master's orders; and he must insist on repayment of any money his master has lent.

He must lend no one any seed, fodder, barley, wine or oil.

He should have two or three neighbouring households from whom to borrow things he needs, or to lend to, and no one else.

He should frequently go through the accounts with his master.

He must not employ the same day or wage-labourers for more than a day at a time.

He should not want to buy anything without the master's knowledge, nor to keep anything secret from the master.

He should not have any favourites.

He should have no desire to consult diviners, augurs, fortune-tellers or astrologers.

He must not be sparing with seed-corn, for that leads to disaster.

He must take pains to know how to carry out every agricultural operation, and must do so frequently, but never to the extent of tiring himself out. If he does this, he will find out the intentions of the slaves, and they will be more willing to do their work.

If he does these things, he will be less keen to go out, his health will be better and he will sleep better.

He must be the first to get out of bed, and the last to go to bed. Before that he must see that the farm is shut up, that everyone is asleep in their proper place, and that the animals are provided with fodder.

152. *ILS* 7367

Virtually all the funerary inscriptions relating to slaves refer to those of the urban *familia*; of rural workers, only the managers generally had the means, the literacy and the motivation to perpetuate their memory.

There is one case from Teate Marrucinorum (Chieti near Pescara, on the east coast of Italy) of a rural slave gang honouring its manager.

> HIPPOCRATI PLAUTI VILIC. FAMILIA RUST.
> QUIBUS IMPERAVIT MODESTE.

To Hippocrates, manager of Plautus; the rural slaves, over whom he exercised authority with moderation.

153. *ILS* 7370

Sometimes a master or mistress would erect a monument at Rome to a good steward.

> To the Spirits of the Dead.
> To Sabinianus, a manager and a good and most faithful person.
> His mistress Memmia Juliana.

154. *ILS* 7372

An inscription from Atina in central Italy mentions the manageress as well.

Caius Obinius Epicadus, freedman of Caius, and Trebia Aprodisia, freedwoman of Caia, were managers here for fourteen years.

155. Cicero, *Verrines* 2, 3.50

The extent of dependence upon the *vilicus* is expressed by the nightmare of the 'bad steward' (so frequent in the parables of the New Testament). In his prosecution of Verres, Roman governor of Sicily, for corruption, Cicero exploits the jury's anxieties about their own managers by comparing Verres' sale of the rights to collect state taxes, to a *vilicus* who sells part of the estate and pretends to his master that this represents an increase in the income.

(119) When this was what actually happened [i.e. corruption] , do you dare state that you sold the 10 per cent tax at a high price — when it is clear that you sold the goods and fortunes of the farmers for your own profit instead of that of the Republic? It is as though some manager responsible for an estate which should have brought in an income of 10,000 Sesterces sent his master 20,000 rather than 10,000 by cutting

down and selling all the trees, removing the tiles, getting rid of all the equipment and stock — and pocketed an additional 100,000 Sesterces for himself. His master will at first be unaware of the damage he has suffered and will be pleased with his manager and delighted that the income from his farm has risen by such an extent; but afterwards, when he hears that all those things on which the cultivation and profits of a farm depend have been taken away and sold, he will inflict the most severe punishment on his manager and think that he has been extremely badly treated.

156. Achilles Tatius, *Leukippe and Kleitophon*, 5, 17

When a landowner was away abroad for a long time, the manager's opportunities for indulging in peculation and less sophisticated vices were virtually unlimited. The handbooks advised an immediate tour of inspection on the master's return (see Nos. **135, 149** and **202**). A Greek romance describes what a wealthy widow called Melite found her steward Sosthenes had been doing in her absence.

After a voyage of five more days, we landed at Ephesus. She owned a large house, one of the finest ones there, expensively equipped and with lots of slaves. She ordered a particularly splendid dinner to be prepared and said, 'Let us go and visit the fields in the meantime.' These were about half a mile from the city; so we climbed into a carriage and drove there. As soon as we got there, we were walking along the rows of flowers, when suddenly a woman bound with thick ropes and holding a pitchfork threw herself at our feet; her hair had been cut off, her body was unkempt and the tunic she was wearing was filthy. 'Pity me, Mistress.' she said, 'as one woman to another: I was born free, but now by Fortune's will I am a slave.' She fell silent, so Melite said, 'Get up woman. Tell me who you are, and where you are from, and who put those irons on you. For despite your misfortunes your appearance proclaims that you must be of good birth.'

'It's your slave, because I wouldn't be a slave to his bed. I'm Lakaina, a Thessalian by race. I lay this my fate before you in supplication. Free me from the disaster in which I find myself. Give me some protection until I can pay you two thousand — for that was what Sosthenes paid the pirates for me. I guarantee that I can get hold of it very quickly; if I can't, I shall serve you as a slave [until the debt is paid off]. You can see with how many stripes he has beaten me' — here she undid her tunic and showed how her back had been horribly scarred. I was very moved by this story; she reminded me a little of Leukippe.

Melite said, 'Don't worry, woman. We'll free you from these bonds and send you home without requiring any compensation. Let someone go and call Sosthenes to us.'

So she was immediately freed from her bonds, and he arrived in great confusion. Melite said to him: 'You evil man, which even of my most useless slaves have you ever seen degraded in this way by me? Who is this woman? Tell me, and don't you dare lie to me.'

'All I know, Mistress, is that a trader called Kallisthenes sold her to me; he said he had bought her from pirates, but that she was free. [We are told that this man was the 'regular' slave-trader (*emporos synēthēs*) of the pirates: 8, 16.7.] The trader said that her name was Lakaina.'

She demoted him on the spot from his position as manager, and gave the girl to the women who attended to her, telling them to give her a bath and dress her in fresh clothes and take her to the city. Then when she had made all the other arrangements regarding her fields, which was why she had gone there, she got back into the carriage with me, and we returned to the city and sat down to dinner.

157. Columella, 12,3

The manager's wife also had a role to play in ensuring that an estate produced a profitable income for its owner. Columella's account shows that when rural slaves fell ill, they were not always treated as harshly as Cato's statements (No. **202** below) might imply; it also illustrates the ideal that a farm should be as self-sufficient as possible (for example, as regards clothing).

(6) In rainy weather and at times when the woman cannot do any agricultural work in the open because of cold or frost, she is to occupy herself with woolwork. To enable her to get on with the job of spinning and weaving and to make the others do it as well, wool should be prepared and ready-carded. It will do no harm if clothing for herself and the overseers and the other senior slaves is made at home in order to reduce the owner's expenses. (7) What she must continually be careful about is to go round once the slaves have left the farmhouse and look for anyone who ought to be out working in the fields; and if she finds any malingerer inside, who has escaped the notice of her husband, as can happen, she must ask why he is not at work and find out whether he has stayed behind because he feels ill or because he is lazy. If she finds that this is the case, she must immediately take him to the hospital, even if he is only pretending to be ill; for it is worthwhile letting some-one exhausted by his work take a day or two off and look after him, rather than force him to work excessively so that he really does become ill.

(8) Finally, she ought to stay in any one place as little as possible; her job is not to sit still, but sometimes to go to the loom and teach the person working there any particular skill she has, or learn some such skill from someone who knows more than she does; sometimes she should go and see those who are preparing the slaves' food; she must make sure that the kitchens, the cowsheds and not least the pens are properly cleaned; she should occasionally go and open up the sickroom, even if there aren't any patients there, and clean it so that it is in an orderly and healthy state to receive anyone who may fall ill.

CHAPTER 8

SLAVES OWNED BY THE STATE

158. Aristotle, *Politics*, 4, 12

The right of ownership over a slave was not always vested in a single household. Chattel slaves could be shared between several persons, or owned by *publicani* (companies carrying out contracts on behalf of the Roman state), or by a whole political community. This should not be confused with the relationship of dependence between a serf population like the Spartan Helots and the community which dominated it.

If they could afford it, states and municipalities, like individuals, would buy slaves so that free men would not have to do unpleasant, low status jobs. In the course of his discussion of government, Aristotle first talks about the decision-making or 'deliberative' body, and then deals with the 'executive', the magistracies. He suggests that certain magistracies can be left out of his discussion because they are not 'political', like priests, the people who pay for choruses at festivals, heralds and ambassadors.

(3) Some positions of responsibility are political, whether the super-intendence is over the whole body of citizens, or limited to a particular activity (like that of a general over men while they are on campaign) or section of the population (like the controller of women or of children). Others are economic, for communities frequently elect officials to supervise the corn supply. Others are subordinate, and communities that are wealthy enough will appoint slaves to do these jobs.

159. Aristotle, *Politics*, 2, 4

A number of Greek communities owned slaves to do work of this kind; Xenophon had suggested that Athens should buy slaves to work the mines (No. 87). Some philosophers went further: if only men with leisure ought to be full citizens, then conversely all craftsmen's jobs should be reserved to slaves (see AVN 4 and 5 on the low status of craftsmen). Such a rational distinction between consumer citizens and producer slaves was never adopted in practice.

(13) Phaleas' constitutional proposals make it clear that he intends

154

his community to be a small one, since all the craftsmen are to be state-owned slaves and not to be included among the citizens. But if in fact there ought to be any state-owned slaves, they should be the ones who work in public services — as happens at Epidamnos, and as Diophantos once suggested for Athens.

160. Scholia to Aristophanes, *Acharnians*, 54

There were several reasons why slaves were thought particularly suitable for responsible jobs involving supervision over the activities of citizens. Not only does policing involve unsocial hours and inevitably result in friction and misunderstandings with the population at large, making it highly unpopular; there is also the danger that normal social obligations towards particular individuals will threaten the objectivity of the police and perhaps result in corruption. These problems were solved by giving the responsibility for law and order to slaves whose only loyalty was to their owner — whether a private landowner (for instance in Justinian's *Codex* 9, 12.10: 468 AD), a Roman emperor, or the state itself. During the second half of the fifth century BC, when Athens was particularly wealthy, policing was entrusted to a state-owned force of slaves from Scythia, called *toxotai* (archers) — a favourite source of amusement for comic dramatists (for instance Aristophanes, *Thesmophoriazusae*, 930–1125 and *Lysistrata*, 435–52).

The archers are public slaves on guard duty in the city; there are one thousand of them. They used to live in tents in the middle of the City Square, but later they moved to the Hill of Ares. They are also called 'Scythians' or 'Peusinians' — Peusis was a politician a long time ago and organised the force.

161. Aristotle, *Constitution of Athens*, 50.2 and 54.1

Other tasks which were particularly unpleasant and strenuous and might antagonise the public were also entrusted to slaves.

There are ten magistrates to control the city (*astynomoi*) ... They have to ensure that none of the refuse-collectors leave dung within ten stades [a mile and a quarter] of the town wall, and prevent building on public highways, and balconies from encroaching on them, and high-level water pipes from emptying onto the road, and windows from opening onto roads; and they also take up the bodies of any dead persons found in the roadway. They have public slaves to assist them.

The following officials are also elected by lot: five road-builders (*hodopoioi*), who have public slaves to help them and whose job it is to keep the roads in good condition.

162. The State Accountant: *IG* 2.1, No. 403

An inscription from the year 221/220 BC illustrates the important role of slaves as accountants of public expenditure at Athens. Since the citizen magistrates were replaced each year, these slaves were in a better position to understand the state's finances than anyone else. They were granted a daily allowance of three obols (*IG* 2.2, 1672.4f.; compare the allowance of two obols for a citizen, No. 85).

(line 36ff.) Those chosen are to write up the names of those who dedicated offerings in the Temple [of the Hero Healer], together with their weight, on a stone stele, and are to set it up in the Temple. They are to present an account of their financial operations. A public slave is to be selected to write a counter-copy [for the state record office, the Metroon], so that when these things happen, the Council and the People will be in a proper and religious relationship towards the gods. A propitiatory sacrifice worth 15 drachmae is to be made to the god. For the preparation of the Wine Festival for the Hero Healer, the following were chosen by show of hands: from the Athenian citizenry in general: Glauketes from Kephisos, Sygenes from Ikaros, Konon from Alopeke; from the Council of the Areopagus: Theognis from Kydathene; Khares from Aphidne. The state slave chosen by show of hands was: Demetrios.

163. Keepers of Weights and Measures: *IG* 2.1, No. 476

In about 102 BC, the Athenian elite abolished the traditional democratic constitution and replaced it by an oligarchical one drawn up in consultation with Roman politicians; one theory (for which there is no evidence) is that this reform was connected with the revolt of slave miners at Laureum mentioned by Athenaeus (No. 80,272f. above) and with Marcus Antonius' campaign against the Cilician pirates. Among the reforms of the new régime were enactments to ensure that there would be no tampering with weights and measures; the public slaves had a crucial responsibility in this, but they remained slaves, and were threatened with corporal punishment appropriate to their status.

(line 37ff.) In order that weights and measures should be maintained in the future, the person responsible for care of weights and measures,

Diodoros son of Theophilos from the Deme Halai, is to hand them over to the public slave in charge of the Council chamber, and to the slave at Peiraieus, and to the slave at Eleusis. These persons are to watch over them. They must provide equivalents of these weights and measures to the government officials and to all other persons who ask for them . . . and they must not carry anything out of the buildings provided, except for the lead or copper equivalents. But if they do this to any of the silver standards . . . those who preside over the Council and the General who is in command at the relevant time are to punish the slave in charge of the Council chamber by whipping and punishing him in accordance with what his wrongdoing deserves, and the superintendent in charge is to punish the slave at Peiraieus . . . and the Hierophant and those appointed in that particular year for overseeing the Mysteries are to punish the slave at Eleusis.

164. From the Archive of Lucius Caecilius Jucundus, No. 143: Bruns 157 B

In Italy, as in Greece, public slaves, as outsiders without obligations towards any particular citizen, were employed to keep reliable accounts. In 1875, an entire archive was found at Pompeii relating to the business dealings of a wealthy Pompeian who leased pasture land (archive Nos. 145 and 147) and slaves (No. 151) from the colony; in all cases written receipts were issued on behalf of the town council by one of the public slaves (for translations of other documents from the Jucundus archive, see L&R II, 86).

July 10th in the year when Gnaeus Pompeius Grosphus and Grosphus Pompeius Gavianus were the two Justices of the city.
I, Privatus, slave of the colonists of the Colony of Cornelian Venus at Pompeii [the formal title of the Roman settlement established at Pompeii by the Dictator Cornelius Sulla in *c*. 80 BC], state that I have received 1,651 Sesterces and five Asses as payment for the fulling tax for the year when Lucius Veranius Hypsaeus and Albucius Justus were the two Justices of the City.
Signed at Pompeii, consulship of Marcus Ostorius Scapula and Titus Sextius Africanus [59 AD].
Signatures: of Privatus, *c.c.v.c.ser.* ['slave of the colonists of the Colony of Cornelian Venus'] ;
of Gnaeus Pompeius Grosphus Gavianius;
of Marcus Vesonius Marcianus;
of Aulus Clodius Justus;
of Privatus, *c.c.v.c.s.*

165. Pliny, *Letters*, 10, 31 and 32

When Trajan sent Pliny to Bithynia as governor to investigate alleged malpractices in public life, he discovered that convicted criminals (*servi poenae*) were being employed as public slaves. The emperor's reply illustrates the comparatively high status which municipal slaves were thought to enjoy.

31: Pliny to Trajan.

(1) Since you have allowed me to consult you on those issues about which I am in doubt, you ought to demean yourself to listen to my problems, without prejudice to your superior position. (2) There are several cities, principally Nicomedia and Nicaea, where persons who have been condemned to a term of forced labour in the mines or to gladiatorial establishments or similar punishments, are performing the functions and carrying out the responsibilities of public slaves; like public slaves, they are even being given an annual stipend. Since I heard about this, I've been very hesitant about what I ought to do. (3) But I thought it excessively severe to force men, many of whom were now quite old after such a long time had gone by, and who – it was said – were living temperate and virtuous lives, to undergo the punishment they had originally been condemned to; on the other hand I didn't think it correct to retain in public services persons who had been convicted. I thought that maintaining them at community expense when they weren't working would be wasteful, but that stopping their maintenance might be a source of civil disorder. (4) So I had to leave the whole issue unresolved until I could consult you. It might occur to you to ask how it could come about that persons who had been condemned were released from their punishment; I investigated this question myself, but got no answer that I found satisfactory. The Decrees by which they had been punished were produced, but no written evidence was brought forward to prove that they had been released. (5) Some people did, however, come forward on their behalf and say that they had been freed on the orders of governors or their legates. The fact that it is unlikely that anyone would have dared to do this if no one had authorised it makes this testimony credible.

32: Trajan to Pliny.

(1) Let us remember that you were sent to Bithynia for the very reason that it was clear that a lot of things had to be put right there. The fact that persons who had been condemned to punishment have not just, as you write, been released from that punishment without authorisation, but have even reverted to the status of respected public servants, is something that particularly calls for correction.

(2) You should therefore hand over to the punishment to which they have been condemned those convicted within the last ten years and released without any satisfactory authorisation; if any elderly persons are found who were convicted more than ten years ago, let us allocate them to those jobs which are more in the nature of punishments; such people are normally employed in public baths, to clean the sewers and to maintain roads and streets.

166. *Codex* 7, 9.1

Like other slaves, those who were owned by Roman municipalities could be manumitted, sometimes when the slave bought a substitute to take over his job.

The August Emperor Gordian, to Epigonus.

If, when you were a municipal slave, you were manumitted by the city council, and also with the assent of the provincial governor, in the way laid down by the city charter and by imperial legislation, then you cannot be forced to submit a second time to the yoke of slavery which you escaped through your manumission, because the person whom you gave as your substitute (*vicarius*) has run away.

167. Frontinus, *The Aqueducts of Rome*, 2

One of the few systematic treatments of a particular sector of public administration in antiquity is Frontinus' work on Rome's aqueducts. It emerges that these were originally looked after by slaves owned by public contractors (*publicani*), but later the responsibility was transferred to slaves owned by the state and by the emperor: this reveals the peculiar status of dependants of the 'house of Caesar' (*domus Caesaris*) — in one sense chattel slaves belonging to a household like any other, but also agents of the government. We may also note how difficult it was for 'amateur' citizen administrators to supervise state-owned slaves effectively.

(96) I find that the responsibility for each of the aqueducts used to be let out to contractors, and the condition was imposed upon those who bought the contracts that they should keep a specified number of slave workmen on the aqueducts outside the city, and a certain number inside the city, and also that they should post up on the public notice-boards the names of those they were going to use in this capacity for each of the city regions. At times the responsibility for inspecting these

operations lay with the Censors and the Aediles, and sometimes it came within the Quaestors' sphere of competence.

Marcus Agrippa was the first person who was given responsibility for the water supply as a permanent office:

(98) He kept a special slave family for the water supply, which looked after the aqueducts, the distribution towers and the reservoirs. This slave family was inherited by Augustus, and he handed it over to the state.

(116) Before I go on to discuss the maintenance of the aqueducts, I ought to make some remarks about the slave family which exists for this purpose. There are in fact two families, one of which belongs to the state and the other to Caesar. The state one is the earlier one; I have already noted that it was left by Agrippa to Augustus and then passed over to the state. It has about 240 men. Caesar's family was set up by Claudius when he brought his aqueduct into the city, and it contains 460 men.

(117) Each slave gang is subdivided into different groups of specialists — managers, people to look after the distribution towers, inspectors, people to mend the pavements, plasterers and other craftsmen. Some of these have to be outside the city to deal with problems which are small scale but need immediate attention. Those men within the city who are stationed at the distribution towers and public buildings [baths and fountains] will — particularly when there are sudden emergencies — take whatever action they can to transfer additional supplies of water from several other city regions towards the one which needs them. These large numbers of operatives in the two slave families had tended to be diverted to work for private individuals as a result of corruption or of insufficient supervision, and I arranged to bring them back to a certain degree of discipline and to work for the community, by writing down on the previous day what each gang was going to do, and having what it had actually done on each particular day filed in the records.

(118) The rations [or wages: *commoda*] of the state slave gang are paid out of the state treasury; this expense is partially covered by the payments for private rental of water rights. These come in from places and buildings which are near aqueducts, distribution towers, fountains or reservoirs. This income of almost 250,000 Sesterces used to be lost or misappropriated, was recently diverted into Domitian's private funds, and has now been restored to the People as a result of the sense of justice of the Divine Emperor Nerva; and I myself took pains to draw up definite rules so that it should be quite clear which were the places which were subject to these water rates. Caesar's slave family gets its rations from the Imperial finance office, and that is where all the lead and all the expenses for the upkeep of the aqueducts and the

distribution towers and the reservoirs come from.

168. Claudius' Senate Recommendation (*Senatusconsultum Claudianum*): *Code of Theodosius*, 4, 12

The anomalous position of imperial slaves, called 'fiscal' because they were paid (or not: see No. 234 below) by the emperor's treasury rather than the state's, was recognised in legislation passed during the reign of Claudius which permitted them to marry citizen women, and gave their children the status of Latins; for any other slave, cohabitation with a citizen woman was a serious offence, and the woman and her children were reduced to slave status (see No. 176 below). Apart from formally recognising the privileged status of fiscal slaves, the law had the effect of extending the emperor's control, as patron, over the persons and property of their wives and children. Later emperors frequently reminded their subjects of the provisions of the *Senatusconsultum Claudianum*.

1. The August Emperor Constantine, to Probus.

If any free woman is forced against her will to be united to a man of servile status, either by a slave or by any other person whatsoever, then she is to be avenged by the proper severity of the laws.

(1) But if any woman should be forgetful of her own honourable status, she is to lose her freedom, and her children are to be the slaves of the owner of the slave with whom she has been living. This law is to be enforced retrospectively.

Dated 1 April 314.

3. The same August Emperor, to the People.

Ancient custom penalises free-born women who live with fiscal slaves, and no favour can be shown them on grounds of ignorance or youth; so we rule that the bonds of such a cohabitation ought to be avoided. But if a free-born woman does live together with a fiscal slave, in ignorance or even willingly, then she is not to lose her free-born status. Those children who are born of a father who is a fiscal slave and a mother who is free-born are to have an intermediate status, so that as the free children of a slave and the illegitimate children of a free woman, they are to be Latins. Thus although they are freed from the restrictions of slavery, they shall nevertheless be held liable to observe the obligations due to patrons.

(1) We wish this law to be observed with regard to fiscal slaves, to those born on the imperial patrimony and on emphyteutic estates [estates leased by the emperor], and to estates belonging to the emperor's private account.

(2) We do not intend to derogate anything from the traditional rights of the local authorities, and do not include slaves belonging to any city whatsoever under this law; we want the municipalities to hold their powers unimpaired, and unaffected by the force of the ancient interdict.
(3) If a silly mistake or simple ignorance or a lapse due to the frailty of youth leads anyone into the snares of such a cohabitation, she is to be excepted from this ordinance.
Dated 27 August 326 (?), Serdica (Sofia).

169. Pliny the Elder, *Natural History*, 12, 5

The advantages of being a dependant of the imperial household were such that people might join it voluntarily. Here Pliny ironically compares a freedman who had imported a special Cretan variety of plane-tree to Dionysos, who introduced the vine to Greece.

(12) An extremely wealthy eunuch of Thessalian origin, who was a freedman of Marcellus Aeserninus but had chosen to have himself enrolled among the freedmen of the emperor in order to become more influential, introduced this type of tree from there to his suburban estate in Italy during the reign of Claudius; he could justifiably be called a New Dionysius!

170. Statius, *Silvae*, 3, 3

Among the poems of the 'court poet' of Domitian is one praising a treasury official of the *domus Caesaris*, the freedman Claudius Etruscus. Poems or speeches praising someone (panegyrics) in the Greek and Roman world followed a set form: ancestry, place of origin, public career and private virtues. Statius deals with all four of these topics — even though, as a slave, Etruscus had no ancestry, and the poet has to apologise for his slave origin by comparing it to that of some divine exemplars.

Ancestry

(43) Admittedly your ancestry is not famous, most gentle father, and you have no family tree stretching back many generations; but your immense good fortune has made up for your ancestry and counters any criticism of your parentage. For you had no ordinary masters, but those to whom East and West alike do service. This is not something for you to be ashamed of — for what is there on earth or in heaven that does not have to obey; everything rules and is ruled in its turn. Every land

has its own particular kings; fortunate Rome administers the crowns of these kings; our Leaders have the responsibility to rule Rome; and control over them rests with the gods. But the divine powers themselves are controlled — the swift dance of the stars is enslaved, the moon in its course is a slave and the sun's orbit wouldn't bring down light so regularly except in obedience to command. Furthermore — if I may be allowed to compare ordinary examples to great — Hercules put up with the appalling conditions imposed by the barbarous king Eurystheus, and Apollo's pipe was not ashamed when the god served as a slave.

Birthplace

(59) You, however, did not come to Latium from some barbarous shore; your birthplace was Smyrna, and had the pleasant water of the river Meles to drink, and the shallows of the Hermes, into which Lydia's god, Bacchus, wades when he wants to replenish his horn of plenty with its golden silt.

Public Career

(63) There followed a brilliant career, and the esteem with which you were regarded increased as a result of the various positions of responsibility that you held in turn; it was your privilege always to walk in divine company, always to stay by the emperors' side and attend to the secret rites of the gods. Tiberius' court was the first to be open to you when a youthful beard was only just beginning to alter your appearance. It was then that freedom was offered to you — and your age ignored because of your great ability. The next heir of the Caesars, despite his cruelty and madness, did not dismiss you. It was then that you accompanied that tyrant — who terrorised his people, whose speech and appearance were so frightening — to the frosts of the far North, and put up with him like those who tame fierce and savage beasts and force them to let go of limbs they have taken in their jaws, jaws which have already tasted blood, and order them not to live by robbery.

But it was Claudius who deservedly gave you the most senior positions, before he left the world in his old age for the starry heavens, and left you to his great-nephew. Has any conscientious worshipper had the chance to serve as many temples or altars? Arcadian Mercury with his wings is Jupiter's messenger; Juno owns Iris, the rain-bringing daughter of Thaumas; Triton stands ready to obey Neptune's orders; but you have blamelessly and fittingly borne the various yokes of all these Leaders, and your little boat managed to ride safely on every ocean.

And then great Fortune came stepping into your obedient home with a wonderful radiance — to you alone was entrusted the administration of the imperial treasures, the revenues accruing from every people, the income of the whole wide world. All that Spain produces from its gold-bearing mines, the gleaming ore of Dalmatia, all that is harvested from Africa's corn fields and crushed on the threshing-floors of the torrid Nile; whatever divers have brought up from the depths of the Indian Ocean; the rich flocks of Galaesus [near Tarentum]; snow-white crystals, and wood from Marseilles; the glory of Indian ivory — all these are entrusted to your administration alone, what the North Wind and the wild East Wind and the cloud-bringing South Wind carry to Rome; it would be easier to count the drops of rain in winter or the leaves on the trees! How vigilant a man! What an able mind! How quick to estimate how much is needed by the Roman armies all over the world, how much by the tribes of citizens; the cost of upkeep of temples and of aqueducts, of the forts that protect our shores and the wide network of long-distance roads; the gold needed to make his master's high ceilings glitter, the amount of ore required to be melted down to make statues of the gods, the metal that has to rattle as it is turned into coin in the fires of Italian Moneta.

Private Virtues

(106) You had few opportunities for leisure, and all thought of pleasure was banished from your thoughts; you ate little, your attention to your work was never reduced by being drowned deep in wine. On the other hand, you enjoyed the pleasure of wedded life and bound yourself by a solemn marriage to father dependants (*clientes*) who would be loyal to their master. Who doesn't know about your much-respected Etrusca's high birth and beauty? . . .

171. *ILS* 1552

Like other freedmen, those of the emperor were keen to express the respectability they had acquired in the form of lavish funerary monuments; these inscriptions are our main source of information about the career structure of the household administration, and the extreme degree to which the specialisation of different functions was carried: thus there was a special keeper of the robes the emperor wore at triumphs.

The following inscriptions also illustrate how a freedman would free a slave woman in order to marry her (see Nos. 33 and 79 above); the *esprit de corps* within particular departments, so that one treasury official would set up a tombstone for a colleague (see No. 50), and two aqueduct managers would share a tomb; how a slave might own slaves himself (see No. 127 above); and that ex-slaves shared the Roman respect for the ideal of monogamous family life.

To the Spirits of the Dead.
To Titus Flavius Januarius, freedman of Augustus,
assistant at the office of the 5 per cent inheritance tax; who died aged 26.
Flavia Erotis set this up for her ex-owner and husband,
who well deserved it.

172. *ILS* 1556

To the Spirits of the Dead.
To Felix, freedman of Augustus; recorder of the 5 per cent inheritance tax for Nearer Spain. Hilarus, his fellow-freedman, registrar of the 5 per cent inheritance tax for the province of Lusitania [set this up].

173. *ILS* 1604

To Hierocles [slave] of Augustus, superintendent of Public Works; Eros his under-slave (*vicarius*) set this up.

174. *ILS* 1612

To the Spirits of the Dead.
Sabbio, slave of our Emperor, manager of the Claudian Aqueduct, made this for himself and for his wife Fabia Verecunda, with whom he lived most faithfully for twenty-four years, and for his freedmen and freedwomen, and for their under-slaves (*vicarii*), and for all their descendants.

The tomb is shared with Sporus and his dependants, also a *vilicus* of the Claudian Aqueduct.

175. *ILS* 1763

Marcus Cocceius Ambrosius, freedman of Augustus, keeper of the White Ceremonial Robe for Triumphs, made this for his wife Cocceia Nice, with whom he lived for forty-five years and eleven days without cause for complaint; and their son Rufinus, home-born slave (*verna*) of our Emperor, Assistant at the Record Office, for himself and for his freedmen and freedwomen and their descendants.

This tomb is not to pass to an heir outside the family.
16 feet across, 22 deep.

176. Tacitus, *Annals*, 12

Just as any other *paterfamilias* relied upon his freedmen procurators and slave *vilici*, so some early emperors, particularly Claudius, relied heavily upon their freedmen for advice, even on matters of public policy; since freedmen were outsiders who were not involved in the political rivalry of citizens, it was assumed that the advice they gave their patron would be objective. Only in the Flavian period were men of citizen status prepared to sacrifice their independence to join the imperial administration. The resentment felt by this later generation of imperial officials at the fact that their jobs had once been done by slaves is clearly expressed by Tacitus (and Pliny: *Letters*, 8, 6).

(53) Following these events, Claudius made a proposal to the Senate about the punishment of women who married slaves. It was enacted that those women who had succumbed to this dishonour without the knowledge of the slave's owner should be reduced to slave status, but if he had given his approval, to the status of freedwomen. The emperor made it known that his proposal had originated from Pallas; so the consul-elect Barea Soranus proposed that he should be awarded the rank of an honorary ex-praetor together with fifteen million Sesterces. Cornelius Scipio moved an amendment that he should be publicly thanked for allowing himself to be included amongst the emperor's servants and preferring the public good to his inherited nobility, since he was a descendant of the kings of Arcadia. Claudius stated that Pallas was happy just with the honour, and that he would continue to make do with his previous modest income. And so the Senate's decree was engraved publicly on a bronze tablet, praising for his old-fashioned frugality a freedman who owned three hundred million Sesterces. (54) But his brother, who was called Felix, showed no such restraint. He had already been appointed to govern Judaea and thought that with such influential connections he could commit any crime with impunity.

CHAPTER 9

THE TREATMENT OF SLAVES:
CRUELTY, EXPLOITATION AND PROTECTION

177. Lysias 4: *Speech about a Premeditated Wounding*

A result of the Greek and Roman tendency to see free men and slaves as distinct and exclusive status groups was that punishments prescribed by law for slaves were of a different degree of severity to those for free men (see No. 7 above).

One of the most horrifying aspects of this is the frequency of references to the interrogation of slaves under torture (see No. **54**, Ch. 16; Achilles Tatius, 8, 10.2). In this speech, an Athenian accused of wounding the joint owner of a slave concubine has no reservations about suggesting that she should be interrogated about the affray, and attacks his rival's qualms about torturing the girl he loves as absurd.

(12) So all these arguments and witnesses have shown you, Councillors, that there was no premeditation and that I have done nothing wrong. And I think that just as it would have been an indication that *he* was telling the truth if *I* had refused to accept an interrogation, so in the same way the fact that *he* didn't want the woman to be tortured to give evidence should be an indication that *I* am not lying, and his assertion that she is free should not be believed. I am just as much concerned in the question of whether she is free, since I paid half the money for her. (13) In fact he is lying, and not telling the truth at all. It would be monstrous if I could do what I wanted with her in order to ransom myself from the enemy, but now I cannot even ask her to tell the truth about the reasons why this trial has come about, although I am in danger of suffering the penalty of exile. On the contrary, it would be much more just to allow her to be interrogated in this case than to have her sold to provide money to ransom me back from the enemy, since there are other sources for obtaining money for a ransom if the enemy are prepared to accept one, but there is no other way of escaping private enemies — for they don't want money, but are trying to expel one from one's country. (14) So you should not listen to his plea that the woman should not be tortured, alleging that she is free; on the contrary, you should condemn him for fabricating baseless accusations, since his intention in refusing such a clear test was simply to deceive you. (15) You should not consider his challenge more worthy to be believed than ours, when he proposed that his own slaves should be interrogated under

torture. What they know is that we went to see him, and we all accept that − but the woman knows better than they whether we had been invited or not, and whether I was hit first, or struck him. (16) And if we had tortured his slaves, then because they are his property alone they would have been stupid enough to try to please him and tell lies about me. But the woman belonged to us in common, since we had both paid the same amount of money, and she knew that very well, since everything that has happened between us was because of her. (17) And no one will fail to notice that if she were interrogated under torture, it would put me at a disadvantage − yet I'm prepared to risk this; for she clearly cared a great deal more for him than for me, and she has associated herself with him in doing me wrong, but has never ever joined me to offend him. Yet I have turned to her for help, while he has not been prepared to trust her.

178. *Digest* **48, 18: 'Torturing Slaves'; 1: Ulpian, from** *The Responsibilities of Proconsuls*, **book 8**

The Romans were perfectly aware that torturing someone was a serious matter, and should only be used where it was necessary and might bring useful results.

Interrogation is the usual method to bring out the truth about a criminal accusation. But we must consider under what circumstances and to what extent this should be done. That one should not use torture as a first step, and that this is not the way to give an interrogation the element of certainty, was both decreed in a Constitution of the Divine Emperor Augustus, and is stated in a letter of the Divine Emperor Hadrian to Sennius Sabinus. (1) This is the text of the rescript:

> Torture against slaves should be employed as the last resort, at a point when someone is suspected of having committed the crime, and proof is not quite forthcoming from other arguments, so that it seems that the only step that is still missing is an admission by slaves.

179. Dio Cassius, 55, 5

There was no feeling that the occasions on which interrogation under torture was called for should be restricted: on the contrary, by late antiquity torture had been extended from slaves to all citizens except those of the highest status. One of the few restrictions was that slaves could not be called as witnesses against their own master without his permission — and from the time of Augustus, this law was frequently circumvented by means of a fictitious sale; and later it was abandoned in all cases involving treason (*CTh.* 9, 6; cf. No. **75**).

(4) Because it was not possible to order a slave to be tortured to give evidence against his own master, Augustus ordered that whenever the necessity for something like this should arise, the slave should be sold to the public treasury or to himself, so that he could be interrogated on the grounds that he was not the property of the accused. Some people expressed opposition to this, since the change of ownership was making the law meaningless, while others claimed that it was essential, since many people were organising plots both against the Emperor and against the authorities as a result of this provision.

180. *Digest* **29, 5: 'The Senate Recommendations Proposed by Silanus and Claudius; Those Whose Wills may not be Opened'; 1: Ulpian, from** *On the Edict*, **book 50**

Another requirement of Roman law, formulated in a Senate Recommendation of 10 AD, which strikes us as particularly inhumane, was that if an owner was killed, all the slaves within earshot at the time had to be interrogated under torture and executed. The Will of the murdered man (which might provide for some of these slaves to be given their freedom) could not be opened until the enquiry was complete. An example mentioned by the historian Tacitus illustrates the rule that slaves who failed to assist their masters should be executed (*Annals*, 14, 42 = L&R II, 68). The jurists explain the reasoning behind this law:

(1) Since no household could be safe if slaves were not forced by the threat of danger to their own lives to protect their masters against enemies both internal and external; therefore Senatorial Recommendations were introduced to require the interrogation by the State of the slaves of men who had been murdered.

Sections 1−16 deal with definitions of the persons included under the terms 'masters' and 'slaves'.

(17) Labeo states that the term 'those murdered' includes all those killed as the result of violence or bloodshed, as for example anyone who has been throttled, strangled, thrown down from a height, struck with a stick or stone, or killed by means of some other weapon. (18) But if anyone has been done away with by poison or some other method which kills a person secretly, then vengeance for his death is not the concern

of this Senate Recommendation. This is because slaves must be punished for every occasion on which they have not brought their master help when they could have helped him against violence, but did not do so; now what could they have done to hinder those who were attacking him by means of poison or in some other way? (19) The Senate Recommendation does of course apply if the poison was administered by force. (20) So whenever violence was used in a way which normally results in death, we must take it that the Senate Recommendation applies. (21) So what does happen when it is asserted that a master was killed by poison and not by violence? Will the crime go unpunished? Certainly not: even if Silanus' Senate Recommendation does not apply and there is no investigation and punishment of all those who were under the same roof at the same time, any who knew of the crime or were responsible for it will nevertheless be punished. But the heir may enter into the inheritance and have the Will opened even before the judicial investigation has taken place.

[*What happens if the master commits suicide?*]
(22) If anybody turns his hand against himself, then although Silanus' Senate Recommendation does not apply, yet his death will be avenged in such a way that if he did this in the sight of his slaves and they might have been able to stop him from destroying himself, they are to be punished, but if they were not able to do so, they are to be acquitted.

[*Which slaves are to be interrogated?*]
(27) Let us examine how the phrase 'under the same roof' is to be understood; does it mean within the same walls or within the same dwelling or the same room or the same household or the same gardens or the same estate? Sextus says that courts have frequently adjudicated that all those should be punished as being 'under the same roof' who were somewhere where they were able to hear their master's voice, though of course some people have a louder voice than others, and not everyone can hear equally well. (28) The Divine Emperor Hadrian seems to have written something very similar in the following rescript:

> On occasions when slaves are able to come to their master's assistance, they ought not to have more regard for their own safety than for that of their masters; and the fact that the slave girl who was sleeping in the same bedroom as her mistress would certainly have been able to come to her assistance – if not by using her body, then at least by shouting out, so as to be heard by anyone in the house or nearby – is proved by the very fact that she said that the murderer had threatened to kill her if she cried out. She therefore deserves to suffer the penalty of death, so that no other slaves may think that they should consider their own interests when their masters are in danger.

(29) This rescript has a number of implications: it does not pardon someone who was in the same room; it shows no mercy to someone who was afraid of being killed; and it shows that slaves must assist their masters even if just by shouting. (30) If someone is murdered while he is doing something on his country estate, it would be more than unjust if all the slaves who had been in that part of the world were to be interrogated and punished just because he happened to own a widely dispersed estate; it is enough if only those are interrogated who were with him when he is said to have been killed, and are suspected of having carried out the murder or having known about it. (31) If a master has been murdered while on a journey, those who were with him when he was killed or who had been with him but fled, are to be punished. But if there was no one who was with his master when he was killed, then these Senate Recommendations do not apply. (32) A male slave who is still a child and a slave girl who is not yet of an age to be married are not covered by these provisions; for allowances have to be made for youth.

181. Antiphon 5: *Death of Herodes*

Could owners execute their own slaves with complete impunity? The heirs of a murdered Athenian executed a slave who admitted complicity in the murder, before the slave's evidence had been heard by a court. The speaker attacks this, on the grounds that no one had the right to execute a slave without a trial — but this merely shows that at Athens sentence of death had to be carried out by the public executioners.

(47) What they did was to buy the slave who denounced the murderer and secretly kill him on their own initiative, without being authorised to do so by any vote on the part of the City, and in spite of the fact that he had not killed the murdered man himself. He should have been kept chained up, or given to some of my friends in return for a surety, or handed over to the State authorities so that there could be a vote on what was to happen to him. But instead you took it upon yourselves to find him guilty and execute him — not even the State can do that, punish someone with death without a formal decision by the Athenian community. So you are leaving the jury to be judges of whatever the slave may have asserted, but you appointed yourselves the judges of what he may have done. (48) And yet not even those who are caught in the act of murdering their owners may be executed by the owner's relatives: instead, they hand them over to the Authorities in accordance with your ancestral laws. And if a slave is allowed to testify against a free man in a case of murder, and an owner can initiate a prosecution

on behalf of his slave if he so wishes, and a jury's vote applies just as much to the man who kills a slave as to the man who kills a free man — then it would have been right for this slave to have been sent for trial and not to have been put to death by you uncondemned.

182. Isocrates, *Panathenaicus*

This attack on the way the Spartans treated their *Perioikoi*, allied communities subject to their political hegemony, implies that arbitrarily killing one's own slave was generally recognised to be an offence against the gods.

(181) Right from the start these men have suffered severely, and in the present situation they have served Sparta well; yet the Spartan *Ephors* [annual magistrates] are allowed to execute without trial as many of them as they wish. As far as the rest of the Greeks are concerned, it is not holy to pollute oneself by killing even the most useless of one's household slaves.

183. Demosthenes 21: *Against Meidias*

The existence of religious sanctions or even legal pronouncements against killing one's own slave does not imply mechanisms for making the owner answerable before a court of law. But democratic Athens was anxious that wealthy men should be restrained from behaving like tyrants: so any citizen had the right to initiate legal proceedings against those who did not treat their slaves humanely.

The Law proclaims: (47) If anyone humiliates (*hybrizēi*) anyone, whether they are free or slave, or commits any illegal act against any of these: let any Athenian who has the right to do so who wishes submit their names to the *Thesmothetai*.

184. Xenophon, *Memorabilia*, 2, 1

Xenophon's account of the conversations of Socrates shows that it was taken for granted that a master would punish a slave who failed in any way to do as his master wished. Socrates is conversing with the anarchist Aristippos, who claims that it is neither ruling others nor being a slave, but simply being independent, that brings one closest to happiness. Socrates points out that we unfortunately live in a real world in which the strong do everything they can to enslave the weak: why is Aristippos so confident that no one will try to enslave him?

(15) Is it because you would be thought the kind of slave who brings no master any profit? No one wants to keep in his household a man who does not want to do any work but enjoys an expensive lifestyle. (16) Let us consider how masters behave towards slaves of this sort. Is it not the case that they control any inclinations towards lechery by starving them? And stop them from stealing by locking up the places from which they might take things? Prevent them from running away by putting them in chains? Force the laziness out of them with beatings? Or what do you do when you find you have someone like that among your slaves?

(17) I inflict every kind of punishment upon him — said Aristippos — until I can force him to serve properly.

185. *Digest* 18, 1.42: Marcianus, from *Institutes*, book 1

At Rome, the heads of households had originally had the absolute right to punish their slaves, like their sons, with death (the *ius vitae necisque*: see Nos. **201,235**,Ch. 20). Under the Empire, the general tendency for the state to restrict or at least monitor the rights of a *paterfamilias* extended to the execution of slaves. This does not mean that slaves could not continue to be executed in the most brutal fashion, but at least they were protected from any arbitrary whim of their masters by the need to obtain a condemnation before a court.

Owners may not sell their slaves, albeit they are criminally inclined, in order to fight with wild beasts. Thus the rescripts of the Divine Brothers.

186. *Digest* 48, 8.11: Modestinus, from *Rules*, book 6

(1) When a slave has been given up to wild beasts, punishment applies not just to the person who sold him, but also the person who bought him.

(2) Following the *Lex Petronia* and the Senate Recommendations applying to that law, the rights of owners when they wanted to hand over their slaves to fight wild beasts were taken away from them; but if the slave has been brought before a Judge, and the owner's complaint is found to be justified, then he may be handed over for punishment.

187. *Code of Theodosius*, 9, 12.1: 'On Punishing Slaves'

The August Emperor Constantine, to Bassus.

If an owner has chastised a slave by beating him with sticks or whipping him or has put him into chains in order to keep him under guard, he should not stand in fear of any criminal accusation if the slave dies; and all statutes of limitations and legal interpretations are hereby set aside.
1. But he should not make excessive use of his rights; he will indeed be accused of homicide if he willingly

— kills him with a stroke of a cane or a stone;

— inflicts a lethal wound by using something which is definitely a weapon;

— orders him to be hung from a noose;

— gives the shocking command that he should be thrown down from a height;

— pours a poison into him;

— mangles his body with the punishments reserved to the State, viz. by having his sides torn apart by the claws of wild beasts; or applying fire to burn his body;

— or by forcing the man's weakened limbs, running with blood and gore, to give up their life spirit as the result of torture — a form of brutality appropriate to savage barbarians.
Rome, 11 May 319 AD.

188. *A comparison of Roman Law with that of Moses*, 2, 5.5

The best protection for a slave was the fact that since he was an article of property, anyone who hurt him was in effect harming his master, who could sue for compensation — though, as elsewhere (see No. 3 above), damage to a slave was considered to be worth only half as much as the same damage to a free man.

An action for damages may be based on common law (*legitima*) or on statute law (*honoraria*). According to common law derived from the *Twelve Tables:*

He who injures another is liable to a fine of 25 Sesterces. [The writer should have written 'Asses' rather than 'Sesterces', as is clear from a parallel quotation in Aulus Gellius' *Attic Nights*, 20, 1.12.]

This was an undifferentiated penalty; there were also specific ones such as:

If he has broken or bruised a bone, he must pay a fine of 300 Sesterces for a free man, and 150 for a slave.

189. *Digest* 47, 10.15: Ulpian, from *On the Edict*, book 57

The right of an owner to exact compensation if anyone harmed his slave was confirmed by the 'Praetor's Edict', the statement of the principles upon which they would execute justice which the new praetors announced each year when they entered office, and which was codified permanently by Hadrian (see also No. 11 above).

(34) The Praetor's Edict states: 'I will give judgement in the case of anyone who is alleged to have beaten someone else's slave, contrary to acceptable practice, or to have interrogated him under torture without his master's permission. And if he is alleged to have done anything else, I will also hear that case and give judgement.'
(35) If anyone injures a slave in such a way as to injure his owner, I interpret this to mean that the owner can institute an action for damages on his own behalf; but if he didn't do it in order to insult the slave's owner, the injury done to the slave himself ought not to be left unavenged by the Praetor, especially if it was done by beating or torture; for it is obvious that the condition of the slave too is affected by this . . .
(49) So the Praetor does not promise to give a judgement on any case of injury brought on a slave's behalf; he won't accept an action if he was struck only lightly, or insulted mildly, or slandered by some action or the publication of some verses. I think that the Praetor ought to extend his investigation to include the quality of the slave — for it makes a lot of difference what kind of slave he is, well behaved, an overseer (*ordinarius*), a manager; or on the other hand an ordinary common labourer or someone nondescript like that. Or what if he's been chained up or has a reputation for evil or disgraceful behaviour? The Praetor will therefore take into consideration both the injury which is alleged to have been committed and the standing of the slave against whom it is alleged to have been committed; and accordingly allow or reject the action.

190. Seneca, *Dialogue 5*: *On Anger*, 3, 40

The right to sue for damages done to a slave did not protect the slave against brutal or sadistic treatment by his own master. One of the most outrageous atrocities was condemned as an example of extreme ostentation by several writers (see Dio Cassius, 54, 23.1ff.: dated to 15 BC).

(2) Chiding a man when he is angry will only provoke him to still greater anger. You must approach him with all kinds of flattery, unless

you happen to have sufficient status to be able to crush his anger, as the Divine Augustus once did when he was having dinner with Vedius Pollio. One of the host's slaves had broken a crystal cup; Vedius ordered the man to be seized and executed in a particularly bizarre way, by being thrown as food to lampreys – he kept some huge ones in his fish pond. Who would say that he did this for any reason other than ostentation? It was an act of savagery. The boy escaped and fled to Caesar's feet for refuge – all he was going to ask for was to be allowed to die in some other way than as food for fishes. Caesar was horrified at this unprecedented cruelty, and ordered the slave to be set free, all the crystal cups to be smashed in his presence, and the fish pond to be filled in. That was the way in which a Caesar could reprove his friend; he put his powers to good use. 'You order men to be dragged from a dinner party, and torn to pieces as a new kind of punishment? Are a man's bowels to be ripped apart just because one of your cups has been broken? Are you going to indulge your own moods to the extent of ordering someone to be led to execution in the very presence of Caesar?' If a man has so much power that he can put a stop to an outburst of anger from a position of authority, he should repress it unreservedly and making no allowances – at least, if it is one of the kind I've just described: beastly, horrible and bloodthirsty, and unable to be cured except by fear of some greater power.

191. Apuleius, *Metamorphoses*, 9

This account of work in a flour mill is one of the most colourful descriptions of the degradation to which masters could subject their slaves – and through its influence on novels such as Flaubert's *Salammbô*, it has contributed to the popular modern picture of what life was like for a 'typical' victim of slavery. Nevertheless, it should not be forgotten that this was a work of fiction.

(12) I inspected the organisation of this highly undesirable mill with a certain degree of pleasure. The men there were indescribable – their entire skin was coloured black and blue with the weals left by whippings, and their scarred backs were shaded rather than covered by tunics which were patched and torn. Some of them wore no more than a tiny covering around their loins, but all were dressed in such a way that you could see through their rags. They had letters branded on their foreheads, their hair had been partially shaved off, and they had fetters on their feet. They were sallow and discoloured, and the smoky and steamy atmosphere had affected their eyelids and inflamed their eyes. Their bodies were a dirty white because of the dusty flour – like athletes who

get covered with fine sand when they fight.

192. Diodorus Siculus, 5, 36 and 38

One area in which slaves were systematically and brutally exploited was mining. It is worth remembering that conditions were bad for all miners, not just slaves: this did not prevent free men from earning their living in this way (see Xenophon on the mines of Attica, No. 87 above; Ps.-Demosthenes, 42.20; an inscription from Spain, the *Lex Metalli Vipascensis* = *ILS* 6891 and L&R II, 43, illustrates the conditions of such free miners). Under the Empire, the labour shortage was made up by condemning criminals to the mines: see No. 125. Callistus (No. 138 above) and many other Christians worked in the mines because they were criminals, not because they were slaves. But in the late Republic, Roman contractors (*publicani*) used slaves for mining under the most atrocious conditions, for example in Spain. The revulsion felt by Diodorus' source, the Stoic philosopher Posidonius, comes through clearly.

(36.3) Originally any private person without mining experience could come and find a place to work in these mines, and since the silver-bearing seams in the earth were conveniently sited and plentiful, they would go away with great fortunes. But later the Romans gained control of Spain, and now a large number of Italians have taken over the mines and accumulated vast riches as a result of their desire to make profits; what they did was buy a great number of slaves and hand them over to the men in charge of the mining operations . . .

(38.1) The men engaged in these mining operations produce unbelievably large revenues for their masters, but as a result of their underground excavations day and night they become physical wrecks, and because of their extremely bad conditions, the mortality rate is high; they are not allowed to give up working or have a rest, but are forced by the beatings of their supervisors to stay at their places and throw away their wretched lives as a result of these horrible hardships. Some of them survive to endure their misery for a long time because of their physical stamina or sheer will-power; but because of the extent of their suffering, they prefer dying to surviving.

193. Xenophon, *The Householder*, 9

Perhaps the most blatant result of the inhumanity of chattel slavery was that the marriages of slaves could not be recognised. An owner had the right and the power to prevent his slaves from forming lasting relationships. Only in the fourth century AD, influenced by Christian ideals of family life, did Constantine decree that when slaves were sold, then husband and wife, parents and children, had to be sold together (*CTh.* 2, 25.1 = L&R II, 140). Inscriptions from Roman family tombs such as that of the Statilii show that at least 24—40 per cent of slaves were married (and their marriages would become legally recognised once they were freed). But most of the evidence is highly circumstantial (see Nos. **124**; **148**, Ch. 5; **149**, Ch. 5; **150**, Ch. 6; **201**;**206**, Ch. 6).

(5) I also showed my wife the women's quarters, divided off from the men's quarters by a bolted door, so that nothing could be brought out of this part of the house that shouldn't be, and so that the slaves shouldn't have children without our approval. For good slaves are generally better disposed towards their masters if they have had children, but if the bad ones live together, it is much easier for them to cause trouble.

194. *Digest* 37, 14.7: Modestinus, from the single-volume work *Manumissions*

Despite the criticisms of satirists and moral philosophers, neither Greek nor Roman legislation would do anything in principle to limit an owner's rights regarding the sexual exploitation of the slaves he owned (see Nos. **235**, Ch. 5 and **240** below). However, in Roman law a vendor could impose certain conditions on subsequent owners (see No. **10**); and by upholding the right of a previous owner to insist that a slave woman he sells shall not be prostituted, Vespasian did give slaves some protection. But it was not until 428 AD that a Christian emperor decreed that any slave forced into prostitution by her master should automatically become free (*CTh.* 15, 8.2).

The Divine Emperor Vespasian promulgated a decree to the effect that, if any woman had been sold on condition that she should not be employed as a prostitute, and she had been so prostituted, then she should become free; and that if the buyer were later to sell her to someone else without imposing this condition, she should become free in accordance with the conditions of the original sale, and become the freed-woman of the person who had originally sold her.

195. Salvian, *The Governance of God*, 7, 4

For Christians, with their much clearer and stricter attitudes towards sexual morality, the implications of an owner's absolute powers over his slaves were extremely serious.

(17) I would say that [in southern Gaul] the lady of the household certainly did not maintain her power unchallenged, because a woman whose rights as a wife have not been kept safe and unchallenged has not kept her rights over the household safe either. When the head of the household behaves like the husband of the slave girls, his wife is not far removed from the status of a slave. And was there any wealthy Aquitanian who did not behave like that? Was there any whose promiscuous slave girls didn't have a right to look on him as their lover — or their husband? In the words of the prophet: 'They went after women, each whinnying like a stallion after the wife of his neighbour' (Jeremiah 5, 8) . . .
    (19) I must ask those who know about human nature what the morals of slaves will have been like under these circumstances, when the morals of the head of the household had sunk as low as that. How corrupted will the slaves have been, when their masters were so utterly corrupt . . . Now the master's position within his household is like that of the head to the body: his own lifestyle sets a standard of behaviour for everyone . . . (20) These masters didn't just provide a provocation to behave wickedly, but an unavoidable necessity, since slave women were forced to obey their immoral owners against their will; the lust of those in a position of authority left those subjected to them with no alternative. From this we can imagine how heinous this filthy uncleanness was, when women were not permitted by their shameless owners to be chaste, even if they had wanted to.

196. Seneca, *Dialogue 5*: *On Anger*, 3, 24

There is no reason to doubt that in antiquity, as now, many cases of ill-treatment of the weaker members of the household were the result of unintended emotional outbursts rather than systematic brutality. Seneca's diatribes on the importance of controlling anger illustrate the vulnerability of slaves to their master's moods.

(2) Why do I have to punish my slave with a whipping or imprisonment if he gives me a cheeky answer or disrespectful look or mutters something which I can't quite hear? Is my status so special that offending my ears should be a crime? There are many people who have forgiven defeated enemies — am I not to forgive someone for being lazy or careless or

talkative? If he's a child, his age should excuse him, if female, her sex, if he doesn't belong to me, his independence, and if he does belong to my household, the ties of family (*familiaritas*).

197. Seneca, *Dialogue 5*: *On Anger*, 3, 32

(1) In various situations, there are different reasons why we should control ourselves. We should be afraid of the consequences if we are angry with certain people; we should have too much respect to be angry with some people, too much disgust to be angry with others. No doubt we shall have performed a heroic action if we send some wretched little slave off to the prison house (*ergastulum*). Why on earth are we so anxious to have them flogged immediately, to have their legs broken on the spot? We do not abandon our rights by postponing the exercise of them.

198. Galen, *The Diseases of the Mind*, 4 (Kühn 5117)

Although a doctor found the frequency with which slaves were beaten under the influence of anger disturbing, he did not question a master's right to have a delinquent slave beaten or whipped.

If a man adheres to the practice of never striking any of his slaves with his hand, he will be less likely to succumb [to a fit of anger] later on, even in circumstances most likely to provoke anger. I used to recommend this behaviour even when I was a young man, and have maintained it throughout my life; my father trained me to behave in this way myself, and I have criticised many of my friends when I saw how they had bruised their hands by hitting their slaves on the mouth – I told them that they deserved to rupture themselves and die in a fit of anger, when it was open to them to preside over the administration of as many strokes of the rod or the whip as they wished a little later, and they could carry out such a punishment just as they wished.

There are other people who don't just hit their slaves, but kick them and gouge out their eyes and strike them with a pen if they happen to be holding one. I have seen someone strike his slave in the eye while under the influence of anger with one of the reeds we use to write with. The story is told that the Emperor Hadrian struck one of his attendants in the eye with a pen. When he realised that he had become blind in one eye as a result of this stroke, he called him to him and offered to let him ask him for any gift to make up for what he had suffered. When the victim remained silent, Hadrian again asked him to make a request of whatever he wanted. He declined to accept anything else, but asked for his eye back — for what gift could provide compensation for the loss of an eye?

199. *Codex* 3, 36.5

Outbursts of rage could lead to legal complications. In the early third century AD, a lady called Statilia asked the emperor whether she had to fulfil a clause in her husband's Will which had clearly been written while he was beside himself with anger at two of his slaves.

The August Emperor Alexander, to Statilia.

It lay within your husband's own power to alter the clause he put in his Will when he was angry at his slaves, that one of them should be kept chained up for ever, and the other sold so as to be taken abroad. Now if a desire to forgive did in fact assuage this displeasure (and although this may not be proved in writing, there is no reason why it should not be proved by other arguments, particularly if some later meritorious actions on the part of these slaves can be proved, so great that their master's anger was likely to be assuaged), then the arbitrator appointed to divide up the inheritance (*arbiter familiae erciscundae*) should follow the deceased's most recent wishes.

200. Xenophon, *Memorabilia*, 2, 10

If a slave-owner looked after his slaves well, it might be not because he saw them as human beings like himself, but because he wanted to preserve his property: to keep his slaves from dying was just like keeping them from running away, as is shown by Socrates' attempt to encourage Diodoros to make friends with someone, by pointing out how keen he would be not to lose a slave through flight or sickness.

(1) Tell me, Diodoros — said Socrates — if one of your slaves runs away, do you take steps to recover him?

Heavens! — he said — I even get others to help me by announcing that there will be a reward for his safe return.

And if one of your slaves is ill — said Socrates — you look after him and call in physicians to stop him from dying?

Most certainly.

And if one of your friends, who is much more useful than your slaves, is in danger of dying through poverty, do you not think it right to try and save him?

201. Plutarch, *Cato the Elder*

In his advice to his son on how to manage a farm, the elder Cato twice refers to sick slaves as unproductive and useless. Even in antiquity, Cato was seen as an example of a cruel master, and his attitude towards his slaves was considered inhumane.

(4.4) He says that he never once bought a slave for more than 1,500 drachmae, since he didn't want luxurious (*trypherōn*) or beautiful ones, but hard workers, like herdsmen or cattle-drovers; and he thought that when these got older, they should be got rid of and not fed when they were no longer useful . . .

(5.2) I myself regard someone who uses slaves like pack animals and drives them away and sells them when they get old as unbalanced, since he thinks that the only bond between people is their need. But we consider that humanity (*khrēstotēta*) goes much further than just strict justice.

(21.1) He acquired many dependants; he generally bought young prisoners of war who were still able to be trained and educated like puppies or foals. None of them was ever allowed to enter another household unless he had been sent by Cato or his wife; and if he was asked how Cato was getting on, the only answer he gave was that he didn't know. (2) A slave was supposed either to be engaged on some essential household job, or else to be asleep; Cato was very pleased with those who would sleep a great deal, since he considered them easier to control than those who were energetic, and thought that those who enjoyed sleep were in every respect more useful than those who did not. Since he thought that what made slaves most troublesome was their sexual needs, he allowed them to get together with the female slaves for a fixed price, but forbad any kind of association with another woman. (3) In his youth, when he was still poor and serving in the army, he never made any complaint about the way he was served, but said that it would be shameful to engage in a running battle with a slave about one's stomach. But later on, when he was richer, he gave dinner-parties for his friends and fellow magistrates; and immediately after the meal he used to whip any slaves who had imperfectly prepared or served anything. (4) He continually tried to arrange for his slaves to quarrel and argue, and was suspicious and scared if they agreed amongst themselves. He would try those who were accused of a crime which warranted the death penalty in the presence of all the other dependants, and have them killed if they were found guilty.

202. Cato, *Agriculture*, 2

When we look at the context of Cato's remarks, however, it appears that while they may be evidence for Cato's disdain for slaves as a class, he did not advocate a *system* of treatment: in one passage he is giving examples of the sorts of things a landowner can say to counter his *vilicus'* excuses for incompetent work, in the other he is making a general point that when a master visits his estate, he should give orders to sell all unnecessary equipment (see A.E. Astin, *Cato the Censor* (Oxford, 1978), Appendix 12; on tours of inspection, see Nos. **149** and **156** above).

(1) When the head of a household arrives at his estate, after he has prayed to the family god, he must go round his farm on a tour of inspection on the very same day, if that is possible; if not, then on the next day. When he has found out how his farm has been cultivated and which jobs have been done and which have not been done, then on the next day after that he must call in his manager and ask him which are the jobs that have been done and which remain, and whether they were done on time, and whether what still has to be done can be done, and how much wine and grain and anything else has been produced. (2) When he has found this out, he must make a calculation of the labour and the time taken. If the work doesn't seem to him to be sufficient, and the manager starts to say how hard he tried, but the slaves weren't any good, and the weather was awful, and the slaves ran away, and he was required to carry out some public works, then when he has finished mentioning these and all sorts of other excuses, you must draw his attention to your calculation of the labour employed and time taken. (3) If he claims that it rained all the time, there are all sorts of jobs that can be done in rainy weather – washing wine-jars, coating them with pitch, cleaning the house, storing grain, shifting muck, digging a manure pit, cleaning seed, mending ropes or making new ones; the slaves ought to have been mending their patchwork cloaks and their hoods. (4) On festival days they would have been able to clean out old ditches, work on the public highway, prune back brambles, dig up the garden, clear a meadow, tie up bundles of sticks, remove thorns, grind barley and get on with cleaning. If he claims that the slaves have been ill, they needn't have been given such large rations. (5) When you have found out about all these things to your satisfaction, make sure that all the work that remains to be done will be carried out . . .

(7) The head of the household [on his tour of inspection] should examine his herds and arrange a sale; he should sell the oil if the price makes it worthwhile, and any wine and grain that is surplus to needs; he should sell any old oxen, cattle or sheep that are not up to standard, wool and hides, an old cart or old tools, an old slave, a sick slave — anything else that is surplus to requirements. The head of a household ought to sell, and not to buy.

203. Suetonius, *Claudius*, 25

It has been suggested that under the Emperor Claudius, the direction of Roman legislation became much more favourable towards slaves, possibly because his advisors included men who had once been slaves (see No. 176 above). In fact, Claudius himself was no more humane than other Romans: he exposed his daughter Claudia, alleging that he was not her father (Suetonius, *Claudius*, 27), and his judicial treatment of freedmen was by no means liberal (see No. 37 above). But he did hold that a slave's obligations towards his owner ceased if his owner no longer fulfilled his obligations towards him: that he gave such slaves the status of Junian Latins is confirmed by the *Digest* (40, 8.2). This is not evidence for a more humane attitude towards slaves, but rather for the ever increasing role of the emperor, who saw it as his duty to codify and enforce existing practice and convention.

(2) Certain individuals were leaving sick slaves and those worn out with age on the Island of Aesculapius because they thought they would not get better. Claudius decreed that all who had been abandoned in this way were to be free, and would not return under their master's authority if their health improved; and if anyone preferred to kill a slave rather than abandon him, he was to be liable to a charge of murder.

204. Dio Cassius, 60 (61), 29

Dio dates this legislation to the year 47 AD:

(7) Since many people didn't bother to give their slaves any treatment when they were sick, and even threw them out of the house, he decreed that any who survived after being treated in this way should be free.

205. Xenophon, *The Householder*, 13

Moral philosophers addressed themselves to codifying rules for the treatment of slaves (Plato, *Laws*, No. **80**, 264e above). Another of Socrates' pupils wrote a Socratic dialogue on household management, expressing his views on how a wealthy landowner should treat his wife and the other dependants within his household.

(9) It is possible to make human beings more ready to obey you simply by explaining to them the advantages of being obedient; but with slaves, the training considered to be appropriate to wild beasts is a particularly useful way of instilling obedience. You will achieve the greatest success with them by allowing them as much food as they want. Those who are ambitious by nature will also be motivated by praise (for there are some people who are as naturally keen for praise as others are for food and drink). (10) These are the things I teach those whom I wish to appoint as managers, since I believe that by doing so I can make them more honest persons, and I give them the following advantages: I don't make the cloaks and shoes which I have to provide for my workers all alike, but some worse and others of better quality, so that I can reward the better worker with better clothing and shoes, and give the worse to the man who is worse. (11) I think it is very demoralising for good slaves, Socrates, if they see that all the work is being done by them, while those who don't want to do any work or take any necessary risks get just as much as they do. (12) I myself think that better slaves should not be treated in the same way as worse ones, and I praise my managers when I see that they have given the best things to those who deserve them most, and if I see that someone has been treated too favourably as a result of flattery or some other unproductive favour, I don't let that pass, Socrates, but punish the man, and try to show him that this sort of thing isn't to his advantage [as a manager] either.

206. Aristotle, *The Householder*, 1, 5

A treatise ascribed to Aristotle but more probably the work of one of his pupils (perhaps his successor as head of the Athenian Academy, Theophrastus), contains ideas very similar to those of Plato and Xenophon, and later Varro (No. **148** above). The writer recommends that slaves should be told that they will be given their freedom after a stated number of years; and be allowed to raise a family — as 'hostages' to make it less likely that they will want to run away, and also so that the slaves who will replace them when they are freed will be *oikogeneis* ('house born'), real members of the family and not outsiders bought for money.

(1) The principal and most essential form of property is that which is best and most central to managing a household: the human being. So the first thing to do is acquire good slaves. There are two categories of slaves: overseer and labourer. Since we can see that it is upbringing that gives young people their particular character, it is essential to educate any slaves we have bought if we intend to give them that kind of work which is appropriate to free persons [i.e. supervisory functions].

(2) In our dealings with slaves, we should not let them be insolent towards us nor allow them free rein. Those whose position is nearer to that of free men should be treated with respect, those who are labourers given more food. Since the consumption of wine makes free men behave insolently too (and in many cultures even free men abstain from it — like the Carthaginians when they go campaigning), it is clear that wine should never, or only very rarely, be given to slaves.

(3) There are three things [that concern slaves]: work, punishment and food. Having food but no work and no punishment makes a slave insolent; giving him work and punishment without food is an act of violence and debilitates him. The alternative is to give him work to do together with sufficient food. One cannot manage someone without rewarding them, and food is a slave's reward. Slaves, just like other human beings, become worse when better behaviour brings no benefits, and there are no prizes for virtue and vice. (4) Consequently we ought to keep a watch over how our slaves behave, and make our distributions and apportion privileges according to desert, whether it is a matter of food or clothes or free time or punishment. In word and deed we must adopt the authority of a doctor when he issues his prescriptions — noting the difference that, unlike medicine, food has to be taken continuously.

(5) The races best suited for work are those which are neither extremely cowardly nor extremely courageous, since both of these are likely to cause trouble. Those who are too easily cowed cannot persevere with their work, while those who have too much courage are difficult to control.

(6) It is essential that each slave should have a clearly defined goal (*telos*). It is both just and advantageous to offer freedom as a prize — when the prize, and the period of time in which it can be attained, are clearly defined, this will make them work willingly. We should also let them have children to serve as hostages; and, as is customary in cities, we should not buy slaves of the same ethnic origins. We should also organise sacrifices and holidays, for the sake of the slaves rather than the free men — for free men get more of the things for the sake of which these practices have been instituted.

207. *Pseudo-Phocylides*

In the collections of maxims and moral advice which were popular in antiquity, particularly for teaching children to read and write, no great attention is devoted to slaves.

One corpus of such literature is known as *Pseudo-Phocylides*; it is not certain who compiled these 230 lines of moral advice, but it was certainly not the archaic Greek poet Phocylides. The evidence suggests that the author may have been a Hellenistic Jew. Only five lines concern themselves with the relationship between a master and his slave, and this is in fact the very last section of the poem: here, as in other respects, mere status leaves slaves with the last place. (There is one other reference to slaves: line 181 tells you not to have sex with any of your father's concubines, but that is a matter of respecting your father, not the slaves.)

Provide your servant (*therapōn*) with the share of food that he is owed.
Give a slave his rations (*takta*) so that he may respect you.
Do not brand your servant (*therapōn*) with marks that insult him.
Do not do a slave (*doulon*) harm by criticising him to his master.
Accept the advice even of a slave (*oiketēs*) if he is wise.

208. Cicero, *On Duties*, 1, 13

Stoic philosophers insisted that masters had an obligation to treat their slaves properly, just as they would treat free workmen whom they had contracted to hire for life; this goes back to Chrysippus (*c.* 280–207 BC; see No. **239**, 22.1 below and Athenaeus, 276b) and Cleanthes (331–232 BC), who was said by Seneca (*Letters*, 44.3) to have worked as a hired water-carrier.

One of the earliest written occurrences in Latin is in Cicero's handbook on proper behaviour, written for the benefit of his son.

(41) Let us also remember that we must behave justly even towards the lowest kinds of people. The most inferior status and fate is that of slaves. Those who tell us to use them in the same way as if they were hired workmen don't give us bad advice — we must insist that they do their work, but grant them what is just.

CHAPTER 10

RESISTANCE

209. Pliny, *Letters*, 3, 14

When a slave owner found it impossible to live with one of his slaves, there was a straightforward solution – he could sell the slave, or in the last resort have him executed.

In theory, it was unthinkable that a slave should have any such remedy (recognition of a slave's right to appeal against ill treatment by taking asylum at a shrine side-stepped the issue of the master's absolute power over his property). Thus the slaves' ways of exerting pressure on their owners to treat them properly were extra-legal: one was the threat of murdering a bad master. It would be misleading to assume that there was a constant state of 'class warfare' betweeen slaves and citizens within the same household (as there was between the Helots and the citizens of Sparta). Nevertheless, the possibility of being murdered by one's slaves was taken seriously: 'Citizens act as unpaid bodyguards for one another against slaves, and they act as bodyguards against criminals to prevent any citizen from dying a violent death' (Xenophon, *Hiero*, 4.3).

Roman legislation required the interrogation under torture of all those of a man's slaves who had been within earshot when he was killed (No. **180** above). Pliny draws a pessimistic conclusion from one such case.

(1) The horrible fate which the ex-Praetor Larcius Macedo suffered at the hands of his slaves deserves to be mentioned in something more than just a letter. He was an insolent and brutal master who didn't care to remember that his father had himself been a slave – or perhaps he remembered it all too well.

(2) He was having a bath in his villa at Formiae. Suddenly some of his slaves surrounded him; one of them grasped him by the throat, another hit him in the face, another in the chest and stomach, another (what an unpleasant thing to mention!) in the groin. When they saw that he had lost consciousness, they threw him onto the boiling hot bath-floor to see if he was still alive. He lay there without moving – either he felt nothing or he pretended to feel nothing: so that he made them believe that he was in fact dead. (3) At this point they carried him out as though he had fainted as a result of the heat; some of his

more faithful slaves took over, and his concubines appeared, with a lot of noise and wailing. The effect was that he was aroused by their shouting and recovered because of the fresh air, and showed that he was still alive by opening his eyes and moving some part of his body; it was now safe for him to do this. (4) The slaves all fled; most of them have been arrested and the rest are being sought. He himself was kept alive with great difficulty for a few days and then died; he had the consolation that while still alive he was avenged in the way victims of murder usually are.

(5) So you see how exposed we are to all sorts of danger, insult and humiliation. And it is not the case that anyone can feel himself secure because he is indulgent and mild — masters aren't killed with a just cause (*iudicio*), but as the result of sheer criminality.

210. *ILS* 3001

Belief in the efficacy of magic was universal among all classes in antiquity. Its use was particularly widespread among powerless and socially inferior groups, as a way of expressing resentment against a superior who they felt had wronged them; it was also much less likely to be detected than murder.

Many curse tablets (*tabulae defixionum*) were placed on tombs; the victim was supposed to become as dead as the corpses in the tomb. An inscription from Tuder in central Italy records the discovery of an attempt by a public slave to use magic to do away with his superiors, the Town Council.

For the safety of the Colony and of the members of the Council and of the People of Tuder!
To Jupiter Greatest and Best, the Protector, the Preserver;
because by the force of his thunderbolt he destroyed the names of the members of the Council which had been placed on the tombs of the dead as an unspeakable act of horrid sorcery by a most evil public slave; and because he liberated the City and its citizens and freed them from fear of danger.
This vow is paid by Lucius Cancius Primigenius, freedman of Clemens, member of the College of Six, Priest of Augustus, Priest of the Flavian dynasty, the first man ever to be granted all these honours by the Council.

211. Thucydides, 7, 27

If the slave could not remove his master, he could remove himself by running away. The frequency of references to fugitive slaves shows how many were dissatisfied with the particular master they had to serve — it cannot prove any general resistance to slavery as an institution. Opportunities for flight were particularly good in times of war and insecurity (see Nos. 59–61 and 67–8 above). During the Peloponnesian war, many slaves made the most of the presence of a Spartan army encamped inside Attica at Decelea; large numbers were arrested by the Boeotians and resold very profitably (*Oxyrhynchus Historian*, 12.4).

(5) The Athenians suffered greatly; they were deprived of the use of the whole of their countryside; more than twenty thousand slaves deserted (and a substantial number of these were craftsmen); and they lost all their herds and draught animals.

212. *Digest* 11, 4.1: Ulpian, from *On the Edict*, book 1

In principle, running away was a very serious crime against property, and the Romans had carefully defined procedures to ensure the swift recovery of runaways.

Anyone who has hidden a runaway slave is guilty of theft.
(2) The Senate has decreed that no runaways must be allowed onto country estates or be sheltered by the estate managers or agents of the landowners, and has laid down a fine; but if anyone restores such runaways to their owners within twenty days or brings them before the authorities, their previous behaviour is to be overlooked.
(3) Any person whatsoever who apprehends a runaway slave has an obligation to produce him in public;
(4) and the authorities are very properly required to guard them carefully to prevent them from escaping.
(7) Carefully guarding them may even include chaining them up.
(8) They are kept under guard up to the time when they can be taken before the Prefect of the *Vigiles* [the police at Rome] or the provincial governor.
(9) Their names and distinguishing features and the names of the persons whom they may claim as their owners should be submitted to the authorities, so that the runaways can be more easily recognised and dealt with (the term 'distinguishing features' here includes scars); and this also applies if details are posted up in writing in a public place or building.

213. Paul, *Letter to Philemon*

When a runaway slave called Onesimos joined the circle of the Apostle Paul, awaiting trial at Rome, there could be no question of Paul's committing the crime of harbouring the fugitive. To reconcile the runaway Christian to his Christian master Philemon, Paul needs all the diplomatic finesse he can muster: in his letter, he tries to confuse the metaphorical enslavement of all Christians to God with the very real slave status of Onesimos: it should be remembered that Christ is 'master' in the sense of 'slave-owner'.

Paul, the captive of Jesus Christ, and his brother Timothy, to Philemon the fellow-worker whom we love, and to Apphia whom we love, and to our fellow-soldier Arkhippos, and to the community within their household: may you have favour and peace from God our Father and from the Master, Jesus Christ.

I thank my God, and always remember you in my prayers, when I hear about the love and faith that you have towards the Master Jesus and towards all the holy ones, that your sharing in the faith may become active in recognising all the good that is in us through Jesus Christ. We find much pleasure and consolation in your love, since the hearts of the holy ones are refreshed through you, my brother.

For this reason, although Christ gives me much freedom of speech to impose an obligation upon you, I prefer to appeal to your love. Senior as I am now, and now a captive for Jesus Christ, I, Paul, appeal to you concerning your child, whom I bore in my chains, Onesimos ['Useful'], whom you once found useless but who is now very useful to you and to me, and whom I have sent back to you; receive him as you would my own heart. I wanted to keep him with me so that he could serve me as your substitute in the chains of the Gospel. But I didn't want to do anything without your knowledge, so that if you performed a good deed, it should have been done freely and not under compulsion. I suppose that the reason why you were without him for a short time was to receive him back for all eternity – no longer as a slave, but as more than a slave, rather as a beloved brother, especially to me – and how much more so to you! – both in the flesh and in the Master. So if you consider me your associate, receive him as you would me. If he did you some wrong or owes you anything, put that down to my account. I, Paul, wrote this and signed it; I will pay you back. I'm not going to remind you that you are indebted to me for your own self. Indeed, my brother, I would like to exploit you for the Master's sake: for his sake, you must relieve my concern. I have written to you confident that you will be obedient, knowing that you will do even more than I ask of you. At the same time, you must prepare to receive me as your guest, since I hope that because of your prayers I will be able to return to you.

Epaphras, my fellow-prisoner in Christ Jesus, greets you, and Marcus, and Aristarkhos, and Demas and Luke, my fellow-workers. May the favour of our Master Jesus Christ be with your spirits. Amen.

Written to Philemon, from Rome, by the hand of Onesimos the house-slave.

214. Two Egyptian Fugitives: Bruns 159.3

When a slave ran away, his owner took the same steps to get him back as for any other valuable property that had been lost (see No. **200** above). An Egyptian papyrus document of 146 BC shows how a reward would be offered to the finder – the figures mentioned are in Egyptian copper coinage, worth between $\frac{1}{400}$ and $\frac{1}{600}$ of the silver equivalent.

A boy called Hermon has run away at Alexandria, age about 15, wearing a cloak and a belt. Anyone who brings him back will receive 2 [corrected to:] 3 talents; anyone who gives information that he is at a shrine, 1 [corrected to:] 2 talents; if he is with a man who can be trusted to accept a court ruling, 3 [corrected to:] 5 talents. Whoever wishes is to inform the governor's officials.

There is also another slave who has run away with him, Bion.

Whoever brings him back will receive the same as for the one specified above.

Inform the governor's officials about him as well.

215. Symmachus, *Letters*, 9, 140

A powerful political figure would try to bring pressure on the judicial officials to ensure that persons he claimed as runaway slaves would be returned to him (see Cicero, *Ad.Fam*. 5, 11 and 13, 77):

My first reason for writing is to express my respect for you by sending you my greetings. The second is to claim the benefit of your proven friendship towards me with a reasonable request. Several of the slaves in my household have disappeared as runaways, and are hiding in places which are under your authority. I ask you to listen to the evidence submitted by my agent and return these people to me; for it would be in accordance with your high character both to pay due regard to the links of friendship between us, and to deny any refuge to dishonest slaves.

216. Pliny the Elder, *Natural History*, 28, 3

Just how anxious slave-owners were about the possibility that fugitives might get away completely can be seen from the fact that they enrolled the help of the spirit world to stop them (as Octavian did to relieve anxieties about the number of runaways who were joining Sextus Pompeius: see No. 59 above).

(13) We still believe today that by their prayers our Vestal Virgins can make slaves who have run away but haven't yet got out of Rome stay where they are.

217. Aristotle, *Finance Management*, 2, 2

There was even one occasion on which a state insurance system arranged compensation for runaways.

(34) Antimenes of Rhodes was a distinguished officer [the manuscript text is obscure: possibly he was the official in charge of finances] of Alexander the Great's in Babylonia, and used the following methods to raise money ... One source of revenue was to tell anyone who wished to do so to register the slaves belonging to members of the Macedonian army at whatever value they thought appropriate, in return for the payment of a premium of eight drachmae per annum. If the slave ran away, the owner would be paid the value he had registered. A large number of slaves were registered in this way, and this brought in a considerable income. If any slave did run away, Antimenes ordered the governor of the [province] in which the army was stationed at the time to recover the slave or to pay his owner the registered value.

218. Petronius, *Satyricon*, 103

If a slave had shown a particular propensity for running away, the regular way to deter him from doing so again was to brand him on the forehead so that everyone would immediately recognise him as a fugitive. This appears to have been practised at Athens (Aristophanes, *Birds*, 760; Xenophon, *Poroi*, 4.21); it was not normal to brand slaves otherwise than as a particularly degrading punishment (Nos. 5, Ch. 13, 191, 207). In Petronius' novel, some of the characters paradoxically adopt this *notum fugitivorum epigramma* (recognised mark of runaways) as a disguise.

(103) Eumolpus: You must do as I tell you. The man I've hired, as you know from the way he uses the razor, is a barber. Let him shave not just your heads, but your eyebrows too, right away. Then I shall inscribe some neat lettering on your foreheads to make it look as though you had been branded as a punishment. So the lettering will mislead the suspicions of anyone on the look-out for you, and at the same time the marks of your punishment will disguise your faces.

219. *ILS* 8731

Christians objected to branding slaves on the face, since the face was made in the image of God. In 315 or 316 AD, Constantine decreed that branding as a state punishment should be carried out on the hands and legs instead (*CTh.* 9, 40.2). An alternative way to show that a slave was a fugitive was to make him wear a collar stating whose property he was (the earliest reference to this dates to the late second century BC: Lucilius 854 Marx). Many such collars contain explicitly Christian symbols; the following two are from Rome.

I have run away: hold me. You will get a gold *solidus* if you return me to my master Zoninus.

220. *ILS* 8726

I am called Januarius. I am the slave of Dexter, Recorder of the Senate, who lives in the Fifth Region, at the field of Macarius.

221. *ILS* 9454

The purpose of these collars was so universally understood that on one example, from Nîmes in southern Gaul, the Latin phrase *Tene me quia fugio* ('Arrest me since I am a fugitive') has been abbreviated:

T. M. Q. F.

222. Euripides, *Suppliants*, 267

In theory, running away was a crime which deserved no mercy; but in practice there had to be scope for compromise. One way out was for the slave to appeal to a god. While a master could not give way to his slave, there was no disgrace in giving way to a god — and it presented no threat to property rights or to slavery as an institution (for parallel mechanisms for the resolution of conflict within a family, see I.M. Lewis, *Ecstatic Religion*).

Much of the epigraphical evidence for asylum dates to the Hellenistic period. But it is clear that compromises of this kind had to be accepted in any ancient slave-owning society; fifth-century examples are attested for Egypt (Herodotus, 2, 113.2) and the temple of Poseidon at Tainaron in Laconia (*IG* 4.1, 1228−32).

A wild beast can run for refuge to the rocks, a slave to the altars of the gods, and a city can shelter from a storm under the protection of another city.

223. Aristophanes, *Horae*: fragment 567 Koerte

It is clear that if a runaway took refuge at a shrine, he did not cease to be a slave: he merely had an opportunity to find himself a different master, human or divine.

The best thing for me to do is to run to the Temple of Theseus for refuge and stay there until I manage to find someone to buy me.

224. Asylum at Andania: Dittenberger, *Sylloge* 2, No. 736

Since there was no failsafe way of stopping discontented slaves from running away, it was in the interests of slave-owners that there should be recognised rules about the circumstances under which running away was to be considered justified. The Chians made such an arrangement with the slave leader Drimakos (see No. **80**, 265f above). The procedure was specified in a law passed by the Messenians in about 91 BC relating to a shrine at Andania; the relevant passage follows a clause specifying the different punishments for free men and for slaves who cause an affray within the temple precinct.

[line 81]   Slaves may take refuge.
Slaves are to be allowed to flee to the Temple for refuge, according to

the area marked out by the priests. No one is to harbour any of these runaways or give them food or grant them any help. Anyone who acts contrary to what is written may be sued by the slave's master for twice the value of the slave, with an additional penalty of fifty drachmae. The priest is to make a ruling about any runaways who come from our own city; and all those whom he condemns are to be handed over to their owners. If he does not hand them over, the slave may go free from the master who owns him.

225. Achilles Tatius, *Leukippe and Kleitophon*, 7, 13

That such provisions were not exceptional is shown by their appearance in Greek romances of the Roman period.

(2) Since the Temple of Artemis was near the estate [at Ephesus], Leukippe ran there and held onto the shrine. In the past this temple could not be entered by free women, but was reserved for the use of men and unmarried girls; if any woman did go in, she was punished with death, unless she was a slave woman who had a complaint against her master. Such a woman was allowed to appeal to the goddess for refuge, and the magistrates decided between her and her master. If it turned out that the master had done nothing wrong, he took the slave back, but swore that he would not bear a grudge against her for having run away from him. If on the other hand the servant seemed to have a just cause for complaint, she stayed there as the goddess's slave.

226. Justinian, *Institutes*, 1, 8.2

Roman law came to recognise that a slave who appealed to the gods (or to the religious power residing in a statue of the emperor) had a right to have his complaints investigated (see No. **239**, Ch. 22.3 below) and to be sold to a new master if they were found to be justified. This right in no way threatened slavery as an institution, and such a slave could not be classified as a *fugitivus* and charged with the crime of running away from his owner.

At the present time no persons subject to our sovereignty may act against their slaves with excessive brutality or without having grounds recognised by the law. For in accordance with a Constitution of the Divine Emperor Antoninus Pius, anyone who kills his own slave without cause is ordered to be punished just as severely as someone who kills another's slave.

But even excessive severity on the part of owners is restricted by a Constitution of the same Emperor; for when he was asked by several provincial governors about those slaves who take refuge in a temple or at the statues of emperors, he declared that when the brutality of a master appears intolerable, they be forced to sell the slaves on favourable terms so that the price should go to the owners; this was a good decision, since it is in the common interest that no one should use his property badly. The following is the text of his rescript to Aelius Marcianus:

> The power of owners over their slaves ought to be absolute, and no man's rights should be impaired. But it is in the interest of owners that protection against brutality or starvation or intolerable injustice should not be denied to those who rightly appeal against them.
>
> You should therefore try the complaints of those slaves of Julius Sabinus who fled for refuge to the statue, and if your finding is that they have been treated more harshly than is proper, or that some disgraceful injustice has been done to them, then order them to be sold with the proviso that they should not return into the power of their present owner. And if Sabinus tries to evade the intent of my Constitution, let him know that when I find out I shall deal most severely with him.

The duty of the City Prefect to hear complaints of ill treatment by slaves is specified in *Digest* 1, 12.1.1 and 8; see *Digest* 40, 1.5 (No. **32** above) and also No. **5**, Ch. **53**.

CHAPTER 11

REBELLION

227. Livy, 32, 26

This account of one of the first slave insurrections for which the historical evidence is reliable (198 BC) shows just how unusual the conditions had to be for a rebellion to occur; there was a similar uprising two years later (Livy, 33, 36). Not only had the Second Carthaginian War (219–202 BC) left large concentrations of enemy prisoners within Italy, not yet properly integrated into their new households, but these had a common ethnic origin (see Plato and Aristotle's remarks: No. **206** above) and some of their Carthaginian officers were there to lead them.

(4) To make up for this unexpected peace on the Gallic front this year, there was a slave insurrection near Rome. Some Carthaginian hostages were being held at Setia. Since these were the sons of leading aristocrats, they had a large force of slaves with them, and their number was increased by various captive slaves of the same national origin who had been bought by the people of Setia themselves out of the booty from the recent war with Carthage. They organised a conspiracy: they sent out some of their number first to recruit support amongst those in the rural territory of Setia, then among the slaves near Norba and Cerceii. Everything was already ready: they decided to attack the population while it was watching the games which were being put on at Setia in a few days' time. When Setia was captured as a result of the slaughter and the suddenness of the revolt, they would take over Norba and Cerceii; the object would be to free any Carthaginian hostages and prisoners of war and get the slaves who were with them to join them. The City Praetor, L. Cornelius Lentulus, was informed of this dangerous plot at Rome; two slaves came to see him before daybreak and told him in due order all the things that had happened and were going to happen. The Praetor ordered the two slaves to be kept under guard at his home; then he summoned a meeting of the Senate and announced what the informers had told him. He was ordered to go and investigate and suppress the conspiracy; on his march he and his five legates made everyone they met working in the fields take the oath of military service, pick up their weapons and follow. With this emergency levy of about two thousand men he arrived at Setia without anyone knowing where he was going. He quickly arrested the leaders of the conspiracy, and there was a rush

of slaves fleeing from the town. He sent some men to follow them out into the countryside, and himself undertook an enquiry as a result of which about two thousand men were punished. The information was the praiseworthy work of two slaves and one free man: the Senate ordered him to be granted 100,000 pieces of heavy bronze, and the slaves 25,000 pieces of bronze and their freedom; their owners were paid the price for them out of public funds.

Not very long after this there came news that some slaves who were left over from this conspiracy were about to take over Praeneste. The Praetor L. Cornelius went there and punished about 500 men who were involved in this crime. The State was apprehensive about Carthaginian hostages and prisoners of war engaging in plots like this; so patrols were posted in the streets of Rome, and the lesser officials were ordered to patrol the streets and the prison authorities to keep a closer guard on the State prison.

The Praetor sent a circular around the Latin communities stating that hostages should be put under house arrest and be given no opportunity to go out in public, and that prisoners should be kept in chains of not less than ten pounds' weight, and should be guarded under circumstances no different to those of a public prison.

228. Livy, 39, 29

The increase in cattle-ranching in southern Italy led to particular problems in 185 BC (there is no reason to connect these herdsmen with the Bacchanalian cult which was suppressed at the same time — except that both were seen as threats to law and order).

(8) There was a major disturbance among the slaves in Apulia that year. The Praetor L. Postumius had Tarentum as his province, and he made a rigorous enquiry into a conspiracy amongst shepherds who were responsible for a collapse of law and order on the roads and State pasture land as a result of their banditry. He sentenced nearly seven thousand men; although many fled from the area, punishment was inflicted on many others . . .

229. Diodorus Siculus, 34, 2

Diodorus Siculus' account of the First Slave War (*c.* 135—132 BC) survives through a summary made by the ninth-century patriarch of Constantinople, Photius, and some passages excerpted by a tenth century Byzantine Emperor, Constantine VII. Diodorus' account itself depends to a great extent on the Stoic philosopher Posidonius, and Stoic attitudes can be seen in the anxiety to prove that the atrocities committed by these slaves were not due to natural viciousness, but the result of justified discontent.

The account of the background to the revolt stresses the unique problems created by the unprecedented numbers of slaves forcibly resettled in Italy and Sicily; we may also note the role of armed and unsupervised herdsmen, the influence over the Roman administration exercised by local elites (although Diodorus is wrong in saying that these landowners sat on the juries which tried Roman governors accused of corruption: equestrian juries were only set up by Gaius Gracchus in 122 BC); and the fact that in the absence of recognised leaders amongst the slaves, potential commanders had to be legitimated by an appeal to religion and miracle-working.

The Background to the Revolt

Constantine Porphyrogenitus, Excerpt 2 (1), pp. 302f. (25) Diodorus Siculus says that no civil conflict was ever so great as that of the slaves which took place in Sicily. Many cities suffered terrible catastrophes in the course of this conflict, and countless men, women and children experienced the greatest misfortunes, and there was a danger that the whole island might come under the control of the runaways. The only standard they set themselves for the exercise of their power was that it should cause the maximum harm to the free population. For most people these occurrences were surprising and unexpected; but for anyone able to judge things realistically they didn't appear to arise without due cause. (26) Because of the extreme prosperity of the people who enjoyed the natural products of this very great island, almost everyone as he got richer adopted first a luxurious, and then an arrogant and provocative pattern of behaviour. As a result of these developments, slaves were coming to be treated worse and worse, and were correspondingly more and more alienated from their owners. When a suitable opportunity occurred, this hatred broke out into the open. Consequently, many tens of thousands of slaves rallied together to destroy their masters without any need for incitement. Something similar also happened in Asia Minor during these years, when Aristonikos laid claim to a kingdom which didn't belong to him and the slaves co-operated with him because of the ill treatment that they had received from their masters, involving many cities in terrible disasters. (27) . . . that in the same way all the men who owned a lot of land bought up entire consignments of slaves to work their farms . . . some were bound with chains, some were worn out by the hard work they were given to do; they branded all of them with humiliating brand-marks. As a result such a huge number of slaves flooded the whole of Sicily that those who heard it thought it exaggerated and unbelievable. The Sicilians who controlled all this wealth were competing in arrogance, greed and injustice with the Italians. Those Italians who owned a lot of slaves had accustomed their herdsmen to irresponsible behaviour to such an extent that instead of providing them with rations they encouraged them to rob. (28) This freedom was given to men who because of their physical power were able to put into practice anything they planned to do, men who because of underemployment and leisure could make the most of their opportunities, men who because of their lack of food were forced into risky undertakings; and this soon led to an increase in the crime-rate. They started by killing people who were travelling alone or in pairs in particularly out-of-the-way places. Then they got together in groups and attacked the farms of the weak by night, plundering their property and killing those who resisted. (29) They became more and more bold, and Sicily was no longer passable for travellers at night. It ceased to be safe for those who had been living in the countryside to stay there; every place was affected by violence and robbery and murder of every kind. But because the herdsmen were used to living out in the open and were equipped like soldiers, they were (not surprisingly) full of courage and arrogance. They carried around clubs and spears and hefty sticks and wore the skins of wolves or wild boars, so their appearance was frightening and in itself not much less than a provocation to violence. (30) A pack of trusty hounds accompanied each of them, and the great amount of milk and meat which was available for consumption dehumanised their minds as well as their bodies. So the whole country was, as it were, occupied by scattered groups of soldiers, since under their owners' maladministration these dangerous slaves had been armed. (31) The governors did try to control the fury of the slaves, but because they didn't dare to punish them because of the power and importance of their masters, they were forced to overlook the fact that the province was being plundered. This was because most of the landlords had the status of Roman equestrians, and since they provided the juries when provincial governors were accused of anything, they were greatly feared by those who held these offices.

Photius, Bibliotheca, p. 384. (4) The slaves were exhausted by the hardships they had to put up with, and humiliated by beatings which were often quite unjustified. They could not take any more. They got together when they had the chance and talked about revolting and in the end they put their plan into effect. (5) Antigenes of Enna owned a house-slave who was a Syrian by race, from Apamea. This man was something of a magician and wonder-worker. He pretended that he could foretell the future by means of commands that came to him from the gods when he was asleep, and because he was so good at this he managed to deceive a lot of people. He went on from there and didn't just prophesy on the basis of dreams, but even pretended to have visions of the gods while awake and hear from them what was going to happen. (6) Of the many fantasies he invented some happened to come true. Since no one refuted those that didn't, while those that did turn out true were widely acclaimed, his reputation increased enormously. In the end he would produce fire and flame from his mouth while in a trance, by means of a trick of some sort, and in this way produce inspired utterances about the future. (7) What he did was put some fire and the fuel needed to keep it going inside a walnut or something similar which had had holes bored into it at both ends; then he would put it into his mouth and breathe and thus produce sparks or even a flame. Before the revolt he said that the Syrian Goddess was appearing to him and promising him that he was going to be a king. He insisted on repeating this not just to others but even to his own master. (8) The thing was treated as a joke, and Antigenes, bewitched by his marvellous trick, introduced Eunous to his dinner guests (that was the wizard's name) and asked him all about his kingdom and what his policy would be towards each of the people present. He had no hesitation in explaining the details, stating that he would have a very moderate policy towards the owners of slaves and generally producing an amazingly entertaining story, so that the guests were amused and some of them would take considerable portions of food from the table and give them to him, asking that when he became king he should remember the favour they were doing him. (9) But indeed his magic-working had reserved a genuine kingship for him in the stars, and the favours received as a joke at these dinners were reciprocated under conditions which were serious indeed. The insurrection as a whole began like this.

The Course of the Revolt

Constantine Porphyrogenitus, Excerpt 2 (1), p. 304 .... (34) There was a citizen of Enna called Damophilos who was both extremely wealthy and extremely arrogant. He cultivated a huge area of land which he filled with herds of cattle owned by him and competed with the Italians living in Sicily not only as regards his luxurious lifestyle but also the number of his slaves and the harshness and inhumanity with which he treated them. He would proceed about the countryside accompanied by a retinue of expensive horses and four-wheeled carts and a paramilitary escort formed by his own slaves. In addition, he thought it very prestigious to have lots of beautiful boys and a crowd of uneducated hangers-on. (35) Both at Enna and in his country houses he insisted on displaying his great wealth of embossed silverware and purple carpets, and served huge meals which were provocative and more suitable for kings; in terms of the expense and waste he surpassed the luxuriousness of Orientals. So did his arrogance. Here was a man who was totally uneducated, in possession of power without responsibility together with vast wealth, and it first made him bored, then made him behave insolently towards others, and in the end destroyed him and brought horrible disasters upon his country.

(36) He bought large numbers of slaves and treated them in a humiliating way, marking with branding irons the bodies of men who had been of free birth in their own countries and experienced the misfortune of capture in war and enslavement. He bound some of them with chains and threw them into his prisons, and he appointed others as herdsmen without providing them with appropriate clothes or rations. (37) Because of his wilful and savage character, there wasn't a single day on which this same Damophilos didn't torture some of his slaves without just cause. His wife Metallis [*sic*; Photius calls her Megallis] took equal pleasure in these insolent punishments and treated her maids and those slaves who were under her jurisdiction with great brutality. The slaves developed the feelings of wild beasts towards their masters as a result of these humiliating punishments, and thought that nothing that could happen to them would be worse than the evil state they were in.

Constantine Porphyrogenitus, Excerpt 4, p. 384 .... (38) that Damophilos of Enna once refused to accept a request for clothes from some naked slaves who came up to him, but replied, 'Why ask me? The people who travel across the countryside don't go about naked — don't they provide a ready source of cloaks for those who need them?' He ordered the petitioners to be tied to pillars and beaten, and after this humiliation sent them away.

Constantine Porphyrogenitus, Excerpt 3, pp. 206–7. (24b) The slaves got together to consider rebellion and the murder of their master and mistress. They went to Eunous, who lived nearby, and asked him whether their plan had the approval of the gods. He made a show of being divinely inspired and asked them why they had come, and pronounced that the gods would grant them their revolt if they didn't delay but put their plans into effect immediately. For Fate had decreed that Enna, the citadel of the whole island, should be their State. When they heard this they assumed that the spirit world was behind them in their undertaking, and their emotions were so intent on rebellion that nothing could delay their plans. So they immediately set free those slaves who were chained up and got together those of the others who were living nearby. About four hundred of them assembled in a field near Enna. They made a solemn agreement amongst themselves and exchanged oaths on the strength of nocturnal sacrifices, and then armed themselves as well as the occasion permitted. They all seized the most effective weapon of all, fury, directed towards the destruction of the master and mistress who had humiliated them. Eunous led them. Shouting to each other in encouragement they broke into the city about the middle of the night and killed many people.

Photius, Bibliotheca, pp. 384–6. (11) Eunous was leading them and working the miracle of the flames of fire to encourage them. They broke into the houses and committed much bloodshed; not even babes in arms were spared — (12) they tore them from the breast and dashed them against the ground. I can't say how they humiliated and outraged the women, even in the sight of their husbands. A large number of slaves from inside the city joined them; they first did their worst to their masters and then turned to the slaughter of others. (13) When Eunous' group heard that Damophilos was staying in an orchard near the city together with his wife, they sent some of their number to drag him and his wife away from there, with their hands tied behind their backs; they had to put up with all sorts of insults along the way.

Constantine Porphyrogenitus, Excerpt 2 (1), p. 305. ... (39) that in Sicily, Damophilos had a grown-up but unmarried daughter, who had an extremely decent and humane character. She always used to be kind and comfort anyone her parents had whipped and help those slaves who had been chained up, and because she was so nice, she was extraordinarily popular with everybody. At this moment her previous kindness brought her unexpected help in the shape of those she had been kind to: not only did no one dare to lay a finger on the girl to humiliate her, but they all made sure that her virginity would remain untouched. They selected some suitable men from amongst themselves, including her particular friend Hermias, and escorted her to some relatives at Catania.

Constantine Porphyrogenitus, Excerpt 4, p. 384. ... (40) that the rebellious slaves were furious at all their masters' household; their insolence and desire for revenge were implacable; yet it was clear that it was not because of any natural savagery, but because of the humiliation that they had previously had to endure, that they went mad, and turned on those who had previously wronged them to punish them.

... that human nature is its own teacher even among slaves when it comes to a just repayment either of favour or of revenge.

Photius, Bibliotheca, p. 385f. (14) As I said, those who had been sent to get Damophilos and Megallis dragged them into the city and brought them to the theatre, where the mass of insurgents had gathered together.

Damophilos made an attempt to trick them into keeping him safe and was winning over many of the crowd with what he was saying. Hermias and Zeuxis hated him bitterly; they called him a deceiver, and instead of waiting for the formality of conviction by the People, one of them pushed a sword into his chest, the other struck his neck with an axe. Next, Eunous was elected king. This was not because he was particularly courageous or able as a commander, but simply because of his wonder-working and because he had started the revolt off, and also because his name seemed to symbolise that he would be well disposed towards those who would be subject to him.

Photius, Bibliotheca, p. 386 . . . . (24) that the rebel King Eunous called himself Antiokhos and the mass of the rebels Syrians . . .

. . . (15) Established as lord of the rebels in all matters, he summoned an assembly and killed off the people from Enna who had been captured, except for those who were skilled at making weapons; he forced these to carry out their work in chains. He gave Megallis to the female slaves to treat as they saw fit; they tortured her and threw her over a cliff. He personally killed his master and mistress, Antigenes and Python. (16) He put on a diadem and decked himself out as a king in every other respect, proclaimed the woman who was living with him, who came from the same city as he in Syria, as his Queen, and made those men who seemed to be particularly intelligent his councillors: one of them, a man who was exceptional both in planning and in action, was a man of Achaean origin who was also called Akhaios.

Constantine Porphyrogenitus, Excerpt 4, p. 384 . . . . (42) that King Antiokhos' advisor Akhaios wasn't pleased at the things the slaves had done and criticised the adventures they had dared to undertake and told them very boldly that they would swiftly be punished. Instead of having him executed for speaking so freely, Eunous gave him his master's house as a present and made him his advisor as well.

Constantine Porphyrogenitus, Excerpt 2 (1), p. 305 . . . . (43) that there was also another insurrection by runaway slaves who concentrated in considerable numbers. There was a Cilician from the area of the Taurus mountains called Kleon, who was used to living as a bandit from childhood and had become a herder of horses in Sicily, but continued to commit highway robbery and murder of every kind. When he heard about Eunous' progress and the successes of the slaves with him, he revolted, persuaded some nearby slaves to share his madness and overran the city of Akragas and the countryside round about.

Photius, Bibliotheca, p. 386. (17) Everyone had high hopes that the rival groups of slaves would start fighting amongst themselves so that by destroying each other the rebels would rid Sicily of the revolt. But they unexpectedly combined; at a bare word from Eunous, Kleon placed himself under his command and behaved towards him as a general would towards his king. He had a personal following of about five thousand soldiers. This happened about thirty days after the insurrection.

(18) Soon after, the rebels fought against Lucius Hypsaeus, who had been sent out from Rome as governor and had eight thousand soldiers from Sicily itself. They had twenty thousand troops, and were victorious. In a short time they managed to concentrate a force of up to two hundred thousand, and they were successful in many battles against the Romans and were rarely beaten. (19) When news of this got around, a conspiracy of a hundred and fifty slaves was hatched at Rome, one of over a thousand in Attica, and others at Delos and in many other places. But in each place the authorities of the local communities quickly suppressed the insurrection by acting swiftly and inflicting harsh punishments; so they restrained anybody who was on the point of revolting. But in Sicily the situation continued to deteriorate.

Constantine Porphyrogenitus, Excerpt 4, pp. 384f. (46) Eunous stationed his forces out of range of their missiles and directed insults at the Romans – it was not they, he pointed out, but the Romans who were runaways: runaways from danger. From some distance away, he put on a show of mimes for those in the city, in which the slaves performed the story of how they had revolted from their own particular masters, reproaching them for the arrogance and inordinate pride which was now leading them to their destruction. . . . (48) When the people of Sicily suffered from many serious difficulties, the citizen masses not only failed to sympathise with them, but on the contrary rejoiced because they were jealous at inequalities of wealth and differences in lifestyle. Their jealousy turned from the dumb grief it had previously been into open joy when they saw how the good fortune [of the wealthy] had been changed into a condition which would previously have been treated with utter contempt by the same people. What was most terrifying was that the insurgents were intelligent enough to think about the future and didn't set fire to farm buildings or destroy the equipment they contained or the harvests which had been stored there, and didn't touch any of the people working in agriculture; but the free masses, because of their jealousy, would go out into the countryside on the pretext of attacking the runaways and plunder the property there, and even burn down the farms.

Photius, Bibliotheca, p. 386. (20) Cities and their entire populations were captured and many armies were destroyed by the insurgents, until the Roman governor Rupilius recaptured Taormina for the Romans. He had besieged it so effectively that conditions of unspeakable and extreme hunger had been forced upon the insurgents — so that they began by eating their children, then their womenfolk, and in the end they didn't even hesitate to eat each other.

Constantine Porphyrogenitus, Excerpt 4, p. 387. . . . (Ch. 9.1) There was no respite from their pains for those who ate the sacred fish. For the spirit world ensured that all those who had been so stupid received no help — as though as a convenient example to everyone else. These people have suffered criticism by historians equal to the punishment they received from the gods, and thus obtained the reputation they deserved.

Photius, Bibliotheca, p. 386. (20) This was the occasion when he captured Kleon's brother Komanos as he was trying to flee from the besieged city. (21) In the end the Syrian Serapion betrayed the citadel and the governor was able to bring under his control all the runaways in the city. He tortured them and then threw them over a cliff. From there he went on to Enna, which he besieged in the same way; he forced the rebels to see that their hopes had come to a dead end. Their commander Kleon came out of the city and fought heroically with a few men until the Romans were able to display his corpse covered with wounds. This city too they captured through treachery, since it couldn't be taken by even the most powerful army. (22) Eunous took his bodyguard of a thousand men and fled in a cowardly fashion to a region where there were lots of cliffs. But the men with him realised that they could not avoid their fate, since the governor Rupilius [MS : Routilios] was already driving towards them, and they beheaded each other with their swords. The wonder-worker Eunous, the king who had fled through cowardice, was dragged out from the caves where he was hiding with four attendants — a cook, a baker, the man who massaged him in the bath and a fourth who used to entertain him when he was drinking. (23) He was put under guard; his body was eaten up by a mass of lice, and he ended his days at Morgantine in a manner appropriate to his villainy. Afterwards, Rupilius [MS : Routilios] marched across the whole of Sicily with a few selected soldiers and freed it from every trace of brigandage sooner than anyone expected.

230. Diodorus Siculus, 36

The information for the Second Slave War comes from the same sources as that for the First. We may note that the account illustrates the difficulties of finding leaders for such revolts. Potential leaders might be members of the citizen elite whose debts made them revolutionaries (Ch. 2.2–6) or estate managers (*epitropoi*) like Athenion (Ch. 5), whom slaves had been used to obeying. Otherwise a candidate with some divine associations had to be found.

Nerva's assizes illustrate how the Roman legal principle that a free man could not be enslaved against his will could not be maintained against the vested interests of slave owners; and how the failure of the authorities to show the flexibility required by convention led directly to armed resistance. The story of Caius Titinius is an example of the lack of co-operation between slave and free outlaws. We may also note that some slaves preferred to be promised their freedom by their masters than by their fellow-slaves (Ch. 4.8).

From Photius, Bibliotheca, pp. 386–90: The Preliminaries

(Ch. 1) Diodorus states that at Rome, at the same time as Marius had defeated the African kings Bocchus and Jugurtha in a great battle and destroyed many tens of thousands of Africans, and then later got hold of Jugurtha and brought him there as a prisoner after Bocchus had captured him to obtain pardon for having entered the war against them, the Romans were seriously demoralised because they had suffered some major disasters in the war against the Cimbri in Gaul. At exactly this time some people arrived from Sicily and told them about an uprising by many tens of thousands of slaves. When this was announced the whole Roman State found itself in a serious crisis, because nearly sixty thousand of the levies raised to fight the Cimbri in Gaul had been killed, and there was no means of finding any regular troops for an expedition.

(Ch. 2.1) There had been several short-lived and insignificant uprisings in Italy prior to the slave revolt in Sicily — as if God were giving advance warning of the scale of the coming rebellion there.

The first was near Nuceria, where thirty slaves organised a conspiracy and were quickly punished; the second was near Capua where two hundred slaves rebelled and were soon suppressed. (2) The third was quite extraordinary. Titus Vettius [MS : Manouitios] was a Roman of equestrian status and the son of a very wealthy father. He fell in love with an extremely attractive slave girl belonging to someone else. He made love to her and became extraordinarily infatuated with her; he bought her free for seven Attic talents (so much power did his madness have over him — and so reluctant was the girl's owner to sell her); a date was set for him to pay off the debt, since he was given credit because of his father's property. But when the day came he hadn't the means to pay and he was given the thirty days' grace allowed by law. (3) But

most of his soldiers had been disbanded. (2) But he set off with the troops that he did have with him, crossed the river Alba and marched past the rebels, who were positioned on the mountain called Kaprianos, and got to the city of Heraklea. Because the governor hadn't attacked them, they broadcast stories of his cowardice and incited a vast number of slaves to join them. Many came flooding in to join them and equipped themselves for battle as well as they could; in the first seven days they armed more than eight hundred, and soon there were no less than two thousand. (3) When the governor at Heraklea heard about how their numbers were increasing, he chose Marcus Titinius as commander and gave him six hundred soldiers from the garrison at Enna. He met the rebels in battle, but since they were superior to him both in numbers and because of the difficult terrain, he and his army were turned back, many of them were killed, and the rest saved themselves with great difficulty by dropping their weapons and fleeing. The rebels had won a victory and a large supply of weapons as well, and were greatly encouraged in their operations. The slaves were all ecstatic about revolting. (4) Many were deserting their masters every day. They were enjoying a quick and extraordinary increase in their numbers, so that after a couple of days there were more than six thousand of them. At this point they gathered together in a formal assembly, and when the proposal was put to them, the first thing they did was to elect someone called Salvius to be their king. He was thought to know all about divination and played ecstatic music on the flute at festivals for women. His policy as king was to avoid cities because he thought that they were sinful centres of luxury and dissipation. He divided the rebels into three groups and appointed a corresponding number of commanders for these sections: he ordered all three to march across the country and meet up at the same time and place. (5) Because they had sufficient supplies of animals of all sorts, including horses, as a result of their raids, more than two thousand cavalry were equipped in a short space of time, and not less than twenty thousand foot-soldiers, and they were already reliable because of their military training. So they suddenly attacked the well-defended city of Morgantine vigorously and without let-up. (6) The governor set off to come to the aid of the city, marching overnight. He had about ten thousand Italian and Sicilian troops with him. When he found that the rebels were busy with the siege, he attacked their encampment. He found that there weren't many guards but a lot of women they had taken prisoner and all sorts of other booty, and he easily captured the camp and plundered it. Then he moved on to Morgantine, (7) where he was suddenly attacked by the rebels, who held a superior position and set upon him with such force that they immediately gained the initiative and the governor's men turned and fled. The king of the rebels then made an announcement to the effect that they should not kill anyone who threw down their weapons, and most of them threw them away and fled. In this way Salvius showed himself a better general than his opponents and recovered his encampment, won a famous victory and got control of a large quantity of weapons. (8) Because of his humane proclamation, not more than six hundred of the Italians and Sicilians died in the battle, while about four thousand were captured. As a result of this victory, many more came to join Salvius, and his army doubled in size. He was in command of the countryside, and made a second attempt to capture Morgantine. He issued a proclamation giving all the slaves in the city their freedom. But the slave-owners made a counter-offer promising them the same thing if they supported them, and they preferred to get their freedom from their own masters. So they fought hard and repulsed the siege. But later the governor declared their manumission null and void and thus made most of them go over to the rebels.

Athenion

(Ch. 5.1) In the territory belonging to the people of Egesta and Lilybaion, and also that of other cities nearby, there was a revolutionary epidemic among the mass of the slaves. Their leader was a man of unusual courage, of Cilician origin, called Athenion. Since he was the estate manager of two extremely wealthy brothers and also highly skilled in astrology, he was able to convince first of all those slaves who were under his authority and then those on neighbouring estates. As a result he managed to get together more than a thousand in five days, (2) and was chosen king by them and wore a diadem. But the arrangements he made were the opposite of those of all the other rebels, for he didn't accept anyone who revolted, but selected the best of them to be soldiers and forced the rest to remain at their previous jobs and each give their attention to their own particular tasks and duties. Consequently, they were able to provide him with plenty of food for the soldiers. (3) He also claimed that the gods had promised him through the stars that he would be king over the whole of Sicily, and for that reason they had to spare the land and all the animals and crops they found on it as if they were his own private property. Finally, he had got together over ten thousand men, and risked an attack on the impregnable city of Lilybaion. When he failed to achieve anything he went away from the city, saying that the gods had ordered him to do this, since they would suffer a disaster if they continued with the siege. (4) As he was preparing the retreat from the city, some people arrived by sea bringing auxiliaries from Mauretania on board their ships; they had been sent to help the people of Lilybaion and were under a commander called Gomon. He and his supporters made a surprise attack on Athenion's followers by night as they were marching away, and they killed many of them and wounded several others before returning to the city. As a result the insurgents were amazed at his astrological powers of prediction.

(Ch. 6.1) There was confusion and 'an Iliad of disasters' throughout Sicily. Not just slaves but also those free men who were propertyless were indulging in looting and illegality of every kind, and in order to avoid any news of their frenzied behaviour being reported, they mercilessly murdered anyone they met, whether slave or free. As a result all the people who lived in the cities regarded the property they had inside the walls as just about their own, while what was outside was no longer theirs and belonged to any bandit who was able to control it by force. And many other horrible atrocities were committed throughout Sicily by all sorts of people.

King Tryphon

(Ch. 7.1) After the siege of Morgantine, Salvius overran the countryside as far as the plain of Leontinoi and there assembled the whole of his army, which was not less than thirty thousand picked men. He sacrificed to the heroes called the Palikoi and dedicated to them a toga of marine purple in thanksgiving for his victory. Then he proclaimed himself king and was addressed as Tryphon by the rebels. (2) He wanted to get hold of Triokala and fit it out as his palace; and he sent a message to Athenion, summoning him to him in the way a king summons his general. Everyone assumed that Athenion would fight for the leadership, and that the war would easily be brought to an end because of the rivalry between the rebels. But as though it was intending to increase the forces of the runaways, Fortune brought it about that their leaders were of one mind. Tryphon immediately marched to Triokala with his army, and Athenion came as well, with three thousand of his followers, obeying Tryphon as a general obeys his king. He sent away the rest of his army to overrun the countryside and incite the slaves to join the rebellion. After this, Tryphon had Athenion put under guard, since he suspected that he would attack him if a suitable opportunity arose. He equipped the fortress, which was naturally strong, with all sorts of defences to strengthen it even further. (3) They say that it is called Triokala because it has three great advantages, the first that it has plenty of flowing water which is unusually sweet; the second is that the countryside round about is rich in vines and rich in olives, and amazingly easy to cultivate; the third is its unparalleled strength, since it consists of a huge rock which it is impossible to capture. He surrounded it with a city wall eight stades [about a mile] long, dug a deep ditch around it, filled it with a plentiful supply of all the necessities of life, and used it as his residence. He also fitted out a royal palace and a public square which could hold a large number of people. (4) He selected sufficient men of outstanding intelligence whom he appointed as advisors and used as his council. For official audiences he also put on a purple-bordered *tebenna* [the Roman magistrates' robe of state] and a tunic with a wide border, and he had lictors with *fasces* to walk in front of him, and had all the other things that constitute and symbolise the office of a king.

The Roman Response

(Ch. 8.1) The Roman Senate voted to send Lucius Licinius Lucullus out against the rebels; his army consisted of fourteen thousand Romans and Italians, eight hundred Bithynians, Thessalians and Acarnanians, six hundred Lucanians under the command of Kleptios (an experienced commander who was well known for his bravery) and six hundred others, so that the grand total was † seventeen thousand. With these he occupied Sicily. (2) Tryphon abandoned his suspicions against Athenion and made plans for the war against the Romans. He preferred to fight it out at Triokala, but Athenion's advice was that they should not shut themselves up for a siege but fight it out in the open country. This was the opinion that prevailed, and so they moved their encampment nearer to Skirthaia. They were no fewer than forty thousand of them. The Roman encampment was twelve stades [1½ miles] away from them. (3) At first there was a constant exchange of missiles at long range. Then the two armies took positions facing each other and the battle shifted this way and that. Many men fell on both sides. Athenion had two hundred cavalry fighting with him, and victoriously filled the whole of the area around him with corpses. But then he was wounded in both knees, and when he was wounded a third time he was unable to continue the fight any longer. As a result the runaways' morale collapsed and they turned to flee. (4) Athenion was assumed to be dead and avoided capture, and by thus pretending to have died he managed to save himself when night fell. The Romans had won a splendid victory, since Tryphon's followers were fleeing, and he with them. Many were cut down in the rout and in the end no less than twenty thousand were killed; the rest fled to Triokala under cover of darkness. If the Roman commander had pursued them, it would have been easy to destroy these as well.

(5) The slave army was now in such desperation that they even discussed whether to flee back to their owners and surrender themselves to them. However, the view which prevailed was that of those who had decided to fight on until death and not betray themselves to their enemies. After nine days, the general arrived to besiege Triokala. He killed some of the enemy and lost some of his own men, and then retired defeated; whereupon the insurgents recovered their morale. Either through incompetence or bribery, the general failed to accomplish any of the things that were required, and later he was accused and punished

for this by the Romans.

(Ch. 9.1) Nor did Gaius Servilius, who was sent out as Lucullus' successor, do anything worth remembering; which is why he was later condemned to exile, like Lucullus. Tryphon died, and Athenion succeeded him as ruler and besieged various cities and fearlessly overran the whole of the countryside and became master of many people; Servilius took no measures to prevent him.

(Ch. 10.1) When the period of a year had gone by, Gaius Marius was chosen to be consul at Rome for the fifth time together with †Gaius Aquillius. Of the two, Aquillius was sent out to command against the insurgents, and because of his personal bravery he managed to defeat them in a glorious battle. He made for the rebel king Athenion and fought a heroic duel with him; he killed him, but was himself wounded in the head and needed medical treatment. Then he campaigned against the remaining rebels, of whom there were ten thousand. Although they didn't wait for him to come but fled to their strongholds, Aquillius didn't desist from doing everything to besiege them and bring them under control. (2) There were still a thousand left under the command of Satyros, and at first he planned to overcome them by force of arms, but then they sent envoys to him and surrendered. He didn't punish them immediately but sent them to Rome and forced them to fight the wild beasts. (3) Some writers state that they ended their lives in a particularly glorious way; instead of fighting the animals, they killed each other at the public altars, and Satyros himself killed the last man, and then heroically committed suicide after all the others. The slave war in Sicily lasted for about four years and came to this dramatic conclusion.

231. Plutarch, *Crassus*

Spartacus' slave rebellion (73–71 BC) has become a symbol of 'proletarian' resistance to oppression (as in Arthur Koestler's novel *The Gladiators*). The leaders were Celts, Germans and Thracians, and unlike the Sicilian slaves their objective (insofar as it was not simply to plunder Italy) was not to set up a Hellenistic monarchy, but to return to their tribal homelands.

Plutarch's and Appian's accounts again stress the responsibility of slave-owners who behaved brutally for alienating their slaves, and also the religious legitimation which was required for a leader. We may also note that the Romans' contempt for men on no other grounds than that they were slaves was a major reason for their failure to recognise the seriousness of the revolt.

(Ch. 8.1) The rebellion of the gladiators and their devastation of Italy, which many writers call Spartacus' war, began for the following reason. A man called 'Lentlos Batiatos' was keeping some gladiators at Capua. Many of them were Celts and Thracians; they were forcibly kept imprisoned to fight as gladiators, not because they had done anything wrong, but because of the wickedness of the man who had bought them. (2) Two hundred of them decided to run away, but someone informed against them, and seventy-eight of them who found out about this and escaped before anything could happen to them snatched up some axes and spits from a kitchen somewhere and got away. On their way they happened to come across some carts carrying gladiators' armour to another city, and they took the armour and armed themselves with it. The first of these was Spartacus, a Thracian from a nomadic tribe who was not only very brave and physically powerful, but also more intelligent and more humane than one would expect of someone whom Chance had made a slave, and he was far more like a Greek than was normal for his race. (3) The story goes that when he was first brought to Rome to be sold, a snake appeared and wound itself round his face as he was asleep, and his wife, who came from the same tribe as Spartacus and was a prophetess and initiated into the ecstatic cult of Dionysos, stated that it signified that a great and fearful power would accompany him to a lucky conclusion. This woman was living with him at the time and ran away with him. (Ch. 9.1) First of all they fought off some men who came out from Capua, and got hold of a lot of military weapons. They threw away the gladiatorial weapons as dishonourable and barbarous and were delighted to be able to take these in exchange. Next the Praetor Clodius was sent out from Rome with three thousand men, and besieged them on a mountain. There was only one narrow and difficult way up this mountain, which Clodius had guarded; (2) everywhere else there were sheer cliffs which offered no foothold. There was a lot of wild vine growing at the top, and they cut some useful pieces from the branches out of which they wove sufficiently strong ladders which when they were fixed to the top were long enough to stretch all the way along the cliff face to the plain below. All except one of them got down safely by means of these ladders. The last man stayed to look after the weapons, and when they had got to the bottom he threw the weapons down, and when he had thrown them all down he got down to safety himself.

(3) The Romans weren't aware of any of this. For this reason the fugitives were able to surround them and throw them into confusion with a sudden attack, and when they fled they captured their camp. Many of the herdsmen and shepherds who worked in the area also joined them; these were powerful and athletic types, some of whom they armed, while they used others as scouts and light troops.

(4) The second general to be sent out against them was Publius Varinus. First, they engaged and put to flight his legate Furius, who had two thousand soldiers with him. Next, Spartacus kept under observation this man's colleague and co-commander Cossinius who had been sent out with a large force, and very nearly captured him as he was taking a bath near Salinae. (5) He just got away with great difficulty, and Spartacus got hold of his equipment then and there, and then following hard on his heels captured his camp, inflicting heavy casualties, including Cossinius himself. He survived many other battles against the Roman general himself, and in the end captured his lictors and his horse, and was already powerful and feared. But he considered what the most likely outcome would be, and didn't suppose that he could break the power of the Romans. Consequently, he led his army towards the Alps, thinking that they ought to cross over them and go to their own home-lands, some to Thrace and some to Gaul. (6) But because they were powerful in terms of numbers and overconfident, they wouldn't obey him, but marched all over Italy causing much devastation.

The Senate was now no longer so much concerned at the humiliation and disgrace that the revolt represented, but rather at the panic and danger it was causing. They sent out both the Consuls, as though to one of the more difficult and greater wars. (7) Of these, Gellius suddenly attacked the German contingent, which had separated off from Spartacus' own followers because of its arrogant over-confidence, and he destroyed it utterly. Lentulus surrounded Spartacus with a large army, but Spartacus moved against him, joined battle, defeated his legates and captured all his equipment. Cassius, the governor of Cisalpine Gaul, met him with ten thousand men as he was pushing his way forward towards the Alps; there was a battle, he was defeated, and only got away himself with difficulty after losing many of his men.

(Ch. 10.1) When the Senate heard about all this it became extremely annoyed and ordered the Consuls to retire from the conflict and appointed Crassus to take command of the war. Many of the most notable people at Rome served with him as a result of his high reputation and connections. He himself stayed behind to protect Picenum, so that he could meet Spartacus as he was moving in that direction; and he sent his legate Mummius with two legions round behind him, telling him to follow the enemy's rear but not to offer battle or even to fight from a distance. (2) But at the first promising occasion, Mummius gave battle and was defeated; casualties were heavy and many could only save themselves by running away without their weapons. Crassus gave Mummius himself an extremely bitter reception, and when he rearmed the soldiers, he required a solemn undertaking from them that they would look after their weapons. He divided the first five hundred, who had shown the greatest cowardice, into fifty groups of ten and executed one man chosen by lot from each group. He was reintroducing an ancestral punishment for soldiers which had not been inflicted for some time. (3) It is a great disgrace to die in this way, and many frightening and atrocious things are done during the execution while everyone is watching.

He punished his men in this way, and then he led them against the enemy. But Spartacus retreated towards the sea by way of Lucania. He met some Cilician pirates at the Straits of Messina and decided to go to Sicily and rekindle the flames of the slave war there, which had been put out not long before and only needed a little extra fuel; he planned to ferry two thousand men across to the island. (4) The Cilicians made an agreement and received some presents from him, but then they deceived him and sailed away. So he marched away from the sea again and encamped in the Reggio peninsula. When Crassus arrived he saw what particular course of action the geographical circumstances required, and decided to cut the peninsula off with a wall; this would give his soldiers something to occupy their time, and at the same time deprive the enemy of their supplies.

(5) It was a vast and difficult job, but contrary to expectation he managed to get it finished in a very short time, digging a three-hundred-stade-long ditch across the isthmus from sea to sea; it was fifteen feet wide and of equal depth. Behind the ditch he put a wall which was remarkably high and strong. (6) At first Spartacus wasn't very worried about these operations and scoffed at them. But then he couldn't obtain any more plunder; and when he wanted to get out he realised that he was cut off and that it wasn't possible for him to get any more plunder within the territory of the peninsula. So he waited for a stormy winter night on which it snowed and then poured earth and wood and tree-branches into a small section of the ditch so that a third of his army got across.

(Ch. 11.1) This made Crassus worried that it might occur to Spartacus to march on Rome; but he was cheered by the news that many of Spartacus' men had had an argument with him and left him — they had set up camp by themselves on the edge of the Lucanian marshes (the water in these marshes is said to change periodically from fresh to salty and undrinkable). Crassus attacked them and drove them away from the marshes, but he couldn't give chase and kill them because Spartacus suddenly appeared and stopped the rout.

(2) Crassus had previously written to the Senate that they should recall Lucullus from Thrace and Pompey from Iberia. He now regretted this, and did everything he could to get the war over before they arrived. He knew that any success would bring glory to whoever had arrived to assist him, and not to himself. Consequently, he decided he would first attack those who had left Spartacus and were fighting by themselves

under the command of Caius Cannicius and Castus. He sent six thousand men to occupy a certain hill before they got there, and ordered them to make sure that the operation remained unobserved. (3) The soldiers covered up their helmets and tried to keep out of sight, but they were seen by two women who were offering a sacrifice on behalf of the enemy, and would have found themselves in a dangerous situation if Crassus hadn't appeared quickly to give battle. This was the most hard-fought battle of all. He killed twelve thousand three hundred, and only found two of them with wounds on their backs: all the others had died standing in their ranks and fighting the Romans.

(4) After the defeat of these men, Spartacus retreated to the Peteline mountains [near Petelia in eastern Bruttium]. One of Crassus' legates called Quintus, and his Quaestor Scrophas, followed within striking distance. Spartacus turned to face them and the Romans were completely routed and only just managed to drag the wounded Quaestor away to safety. This success destroyed Spartacus, since it made the runaways totally overconfident. (5) They refused to avoid battle any longer and wouldn't obey their commanders, but surrounded them with weapons in their hands as they were already marching away and forced them to lead them back again through Lucania in the direction of the Romans. Crassus' objectives were identical, since he had already heard that Pompey was on his way. There were already a lot of people canvassing support for Pompey's candidature as the man who had won this war — he just had to come and fight, and the war would be over. So Crassus was keen to bring the struggle to an end; he encamped next to the enemy and dug a trench: the slaves came up to the trench and attacked his men as they were working. (6) More and more men on both sides joined in the fighting, and Spartacus saw that he had no option but to bring up his whole army in battle order.

First of all his horse was brought forward and he drew his sword and said that if he won he could have many fine horses of the enemy's, but if he was defeated he wouldn't need a horse. So he killed his horse. Then he pushed his way through all the weapons and the wounds towards Crassus himself; he couldn't get at Crassus, but he did kill two centurions who attacked him together.

(7) In the end the men with him turned and fled, and he stood all alone surrounded by great numbers of enemies and was killed while resisting. Fortune had been kind to Crassus; he had been an excellent general; he had risked his own life in the course of the fighting. Nevertheless, his success brought more prestige to Pompey — for the fugitives ran into Pompey's army and were destroyed, so that he could even write to the Senate that while Crassus had defeated the runaways in pitched battle, it was he who had torn up the roots of the rebellion.

(8) Thus Pompey was able to celebrate a famous triumph over

Sertorius and Spain, while Crassus didn't even try to request a major triumph, and it was thought dishonourable and demeaning for him to celebrate the minor triumph called the ovation for winning a war over slaves.

232. Appian, *Roman Civil Wars*, 1, 14

(116) At this time there were in Italy some gladiators who were being trained to appear in spectacles at Capua. A Thracian called Spartacus, who had fought in the Roman army but was among the gladiators as the result of capture in war and sale, had persuaded about seventy of them to gamble for their freedom rather than be put on show at a public spectacle. Together with them he overcame the guards and escaped. He armed them with wooden stakes and swords which belonged to some people they met on the road, and fled to Mount Vesuvius. There he received lots of runaway slaves as well as some free persons from the countryside, and plundered the area round about. He chose the gladiators Oenomaus and Crixus to be his lieutenants. He soon collected lots of supporters, since he divided up the booty absolutely equally.

The first person to be sent out against him was Varinius Glabrus, and after him Publius Valerius: they didn't command regular armies, but all the men they could levy immediately along their route of march — for the Romans didn't yet look upon this operation as a war, but rather as a police action against bandits — and when they engaged Spartacus, they were beaten. Spartacus himself even made off with Varinius' horse — so close was the Roman general himself to being captured by a gladiator.

After this even more people were keen to join Spartacus, and his army already totalled 70,000; he had weapons made and collected supplies. The Romans sent out both Consuls with two legions. (117) Crixus, leading thirty thousand men, was defeated by one of the Consuls near Mount Garganos: he and two-thirds of his army were destroyed. Spartacus headed on through the Apennine mountains towards the Alps and the Celtic lands beyond the Alps, but one of the Consuls got ahead of him to cut off his escape route while the other followed on his rear. Spartacus turned upon each of them and defeated each section in turn. So they retreated from him in great confusion, and he sacrificed three hundred Roman prisoners of war in honour of Crixus, and then marched on Rome with 120,000 infantry. He had burnt any equipment he didn't need and killed all the prisoners and slaughtered the pack animals so that his army would not be impeded in any way. Many deserters from the Roman side approached him, but he refused to accept them. When the Consuls again offered battle in the territory of Picenum, there was another major encounter and again a major Roman defeat.

He abandoned his march on Rome since he didn't think that he was powerful enough for that yet and his army as a whole was not yet properly armed — for not a single city had co-operated with him: they were all slaves and deserters and generally an indiscriminate rabble. He occupied the mountains overlooking Thurii and the city itself. He forbade merchants from importing any gold or silver, and his own men from possessing any; but they bought lots of iron and brass and didn't do anything to harm the people who traded in these metals. In this way they came to be well supplied with a lot of war material, and they went out on frequent plundering expeditions. When they again faced the Romans in battle, they again defeated them and returned loaded with booty. (118) At first the Romans had laughed off and scorned this war because it was only against gladiators, but it was now in its third year and causing them much concern. At the election of a new set of magistrates, no one was keen to announce himself as a candidate until Licinius Crassus, who was distinguished among the Romans both for his ancestry and for his wealth, accepted the command and marched against Spartacus with six new legions; when he reached the front he also took over the two legions commanded by the Consuls. He executed one man chosen by lot out of every ten of them because they had allowed themselves to be defeated so often. Some think that it wasn't this that happened, but that he engaged Spartacus with the whole of his army, and that the whole army was defeated, and he drew lots for one in ten of all of them and executed about four thousand, undeterred by the vastness of the number. Whatever he did had the effect of demonstrating to them that they had more to fear from Crassus than from a defeat at the hands of the enemy, and the result was that he immediately defeated ten thousand of Spartacus' supporters who were encamped by themselves, killed two-thirds of them and then contemptuously marched against Spartacus himself. He won a glorious victory over him and chased him towards the sea (Spartacus was hoping to sail over to Sicily); he caught him and hemmed him in with a ditch, wall and palisade.

(119) Spartacus tried to break out in the direction of Samnium, but Crassus killed about six thousand of his men in the morning and about the same number in the afternoon, while only three Roman soldiers lost their lives and seven were wounded. This shows the extent of the total change in the Romans' morale as a result of their punishment. Spartacus was waiting for some cavalry to join him from somewhere and no longer went out to battle with his whole army: instead he inflicted a lot of damage on particular sections of the surrounding army with sudden and continual attacks; by throwing bundles of wood into the

ditch and setting them on fire he made it impossible for them to get on with the work. He had a Roman prisoner crucified in the area between the two armies to give his own side an idea of what they were likely to suffer if they didn't win. When they heard about the circumvallation at Rome, and thought it disgraceful if this war against gladiators were to go on any longer, they appointed Pompey, who had just returned from Spain, to participate in the campaign: they thought that further operations against Spartacus would still be serious and large scale.

(120) Because of this appointment, Crassus was keen to get to grips with Spartacus any way he could, so that the glory for the war wouldn't go to Pompey: Spartacus himself wanted to resolve things before Pompey's arrival, and he suggested that Crassus might come to an agreement with him. When this idea was rejected, he decided to risk battle, and since his cavalry had now appeared, he broke through the circumvallation with the whole of his army and fled towards Brundisium, with Crassus in pursuit. When Spartacus learned that Lucullus too had arrived at Brundisium, fresh from a victory over Mithridates, he realised that the whole thing was hopeless and engaged Crassus with his entire army, which was considerable even at this stage. With so many tens of thousands of desperate men, there was a long and hard-fought battle; Spartacus was wounded in the thigh by a spear and fell onto his knees; he held his shield out in front of him and resisted those who attacked him until he was surrounded himself and fell together with a great crowd of people around him. The rest of his army broke ranks, and there was much slaughter; so many were killed that it was impossible to count them. About one thousand Romans died; Spartacus' corpse could not be found. A lot of people fled from the battle up into the mountains, and Crassus went after them. They divided themselves into four sections and continued to resist until all of them had been destroyed, except for six thousand who were captured and crucified along the length of the road from Capua to Rome.

233. Tacitus, *Annals*, 4

The suppression of piracy and the cessation of major wars of expansion under the Empire removed the conditions which had made the great slave wars possible. Nevertheless, minor revolts continued to occur: in this conspiracy of 24 AD, we recognise some of the usual features — leadership provided by a disgruntled free man, the role of unsupervised herdsmen and the terror of the slave-owning elite.

(27) During the same summer, a chance event suppressed the beginnings

of a slave war in Italy. The person responsible for the unrest was Titus Curtisius, who had once served in the Praetorian guard. He was inciting the wild rural slaves who worked in the far-flung cattle pastures to seize their freedom, first by means of secret meetings at Brundisium and neighbouring settlements, then by openly distributing pamphlets. But, as though by a gift of the gods, three ships from the navy, whose job it was to assist those who sailed the seas thereabouts, happened to turn up, and the Quaestor whose traditional sphere of authority was controlling the cattle trails, Cutius Lupus, was also in the area. He organised the men from the ships and suppressed the revolt just as it was about to break out. A military tribune, Staius, was quickly sent out by the emperor with a strong force, and took the leader and those most closely involved in the plot to Rome. Rome was already in a state of terror because the great number of domestic slaves was increasing beyond counting, while the free population was declining all the time.

234. Dio Cassius, 77, 10

Under Septimius Severus (in 206–7 AD), Italy was terrorised by a brigand chief called Felix Bulla; it is not certain whether he was a slave or not, and not all rebellions which exploited the discontent of slaves can properly be described as slave rebellions. Bulla's activities show that irresponsible treatment continued to lead to violent resistance, even among the dependants of the *domus Caesaris*.

(1) During this same period, an Italian called Bulla got together a robber band of six hundred men and devastated Italy for two years, despite the presence of the emperors and of all their soldiers . . . (5) Later on, he got up onto a platform and put on the dress of a Roman magistrate, summoned the centurion [whom he had just captured], shaved his head and said, 'Tell your masters that you must look after your slaves if they aren't to become robbers.' For most of the supporters he had came from the imperial household, and some of them had been paid erratically, and others had not been paid at all.

CHAPTER 12

THE TRUE FREEDOM OF THE SPIRIT:
STOICS AND CHRISTIANS

235. Dio Chrysostom, 15: *Slavery and Freedom*

Already some of the earliest Greeks to interest themselves in philosophical problems, the Sophists, had speculated about whether social
inferiority implied moral inferiority, and about the circumstances under
which slavery might be held to be justified. Aristotle developed the
theory of 'natural slavery' which implied that, for their own good,
inferior barbarians ought to become the slaves of superior Hellenes (see
No. 2 above; a racial theory which did not correspond to Greek practice,
and was quite inappropriate at Rome, where slavery functioned precisely
as a way of making outsiders part of society). In the Hellenistic period,
the Stoic solution was that a person's moral status depended upon his
soul, and the question of what social status he had was unconnected
and unimportant.

This view was frequently advocated by the popular philosophers of
the Roman period. The following lecture by Dio of Prusa shows that
'slave' was a standard term of abuse to ordinary Greeks (1); it illustrates
the prejudice that while Greeks who fell into slavery retained their
natural freedom, barbarians were naturally slaves, so that when they
happened to become slaves, they merely got what they deserved (16);
it draws an analogy between the dependent status of slaves and that of
children (18–20); and it ends with the moralising conclusion that
while the application of the word 'slave' to members of a particular
status group is vacuous, moral inferiority is indeed a form of slavery.

(1) Just now I heard some people arguing about a case of freedom or
slavery – not in the law court or the town square (*agora*), but at home,
where there are no time-limits on the length of speeches. Each of the
two men had several supporters there. I think that what had happened
was that they had already been arguing on opposite sides about some
other issues, and that one of them felt that he was losing the argument
and couldn't do anything about it, so that as so often happens he
became abusive and started to reproach his opponent on the grounds
that he was not a free man. But he responded by smiling sweetly and
saying:

(2) **Slave:** What's your evidence? Are you able to say who is a slave
and who is free?

Citizen: Of course I am. At least I know that I am a free man myself and so are all these people, whereas you do not share in freedom.

This made some of the people who were there laugh. But it didn't have the effect of shaming the other man into silence: on the contrary, just as fighting-cocks become excited and aggressive when they are struck, the insult made him excited and aggressive, and he asked him what was the basis of his knowledge about his own status and his opponent's.

(3) **Citizen:** Because I know that my father is as Athenian as anyone, and yours is someone's house-slave (he mentioned the name).

Slave: So what prevents me from rubbing myself down with oil in the Kynosarges, where the bastards go? I might have a free mother — perhaps even an Athenian mother — as well as the father whom you mention. After all, many Athenian women have become pregnant by foreigners or slaves, because of the absence or unavailability of citizens, some without knowing the man's status and others quite aware of it. Of the persons born as a result, none is a slave — they're just non-Athenians.

(4) **Citizen:** But I know that your mother too was a slave, in the same household as your father.

Slave: Very well; do you know who your mother is?

Citizen: Of course I do. An Athenian, daughter of Athenians, who brought her husband a substantial dowry.

Slave: And you would be able to state on oath that you are the son of the man she claims is your father? Telemakhos didn't dare to insist that Penelope, daughter of Ikarios, was telling the truth when she said Odysseus was his father, and she was an exceptionally modest lady. But it looks as though you wouldn't just take an oath about yourself and your mother if you were asked to, but even about who made some slave woman pregnant — like the woman you say is my mother. (5) Do you think it is impossible for such a woman to become pregnant by some free man or other, or perhaps by her owner? Don't many Athenians have sex with their slave women, some of them secretly and some even openly? They're not all superior to Herakles, who didn't think it beneath him to make love to Iardanos' slave-girl, from whom the kings of Sardis were descended. (6) I suppose you don't believe that Klytaimnestra, the daughter of Tyndareus and wife of Agamemnon, lived with her husband but also made love with Aigistheus while he was away, and that Atreus' wife Aerope had intercourse with Thyestes, and that both in the past and in the present many other women married to famous and wealthy husbands have had sexual relations with other men and sometimes had children by them. But the slave woman you mention was so utterly faithful to her own husband that she never had sex with any other man. (7) And as regards yourself and me, you insist that both of us are the sons of the person believed to be and referred to as our mother. But one could mention many Athenians, including some very famous ones, who were later shown to have been smuggled in secretly from outside and brought up although they were the sons of neither the father nor the mother to whom they were said to belong. You can see cases like this being acted out and narrated every time you go to a performance of comedy or tragedy – yet, nevertheless, you are absolutely certain that you know how and from whom you and I were born. (8) Don't you know that the law allows a man to be accused of slander if he insults someone without having clear evidence for the things he says?

Citizen: Well, I do know that free women often smuggle in children which aren't their own when they don't have any children themselves because they can't become pregnant, since every woman wants to keep her husband and her home, and at the same time there is no shortage of money for bringing up children. But the opposite happens with slaves – some of them kill their children before they are born, and some afterwards if they can avoid detection; sometimes their husbands even connive at it – they don't want the additional problem of having to look after a child when things are difficult enough for slaves as it is.

(9) Slave: That's quite true, but there are exceptions – like the slave woman who belonged to Oineos, the bastard son of Pandion. Oineos' herdsman at Eleutherai, and the herdsman's wife, not only didn't abandon their own children, but even took in and brought up as their own other children they found in the road, although they had no idea whose they were; and even afterwards they weren't willing to admit that these were not their own children. But perhaps you would have slandered Zethos and Amphion before it became known who they were, and sworn on oath that the sons of Zeus were slaves?

(10) The other man gave a hollow laugh.

Citizen: You're appealing to the tragedians for your evidence?

Slave: The Greeks believe them. Whatever heroic characters play-wrights depict, they sacrifice to them as heroes, and one can see the shrines which have been built for them. And you should also please remember Priam's Phrygian slave woman, who looked after Alexander on Mount Ida as though he were her own son: she took him from her husband the herdsman, and didn't mind bringing up the child. They say that Telephos, the son of Auge and Herakles, wasn't brought up by a woman but by a hind. Do you think a hind is more likely to pity a child and look after it than a human being who happens to be a slave woman?

(11) Now if I did agree with you that those whom you mentioned really were my parents, how in the name of the gods do you know for certain that they were really of slave status? Or are you absolutely sure

that you know who their parents were, and ready to swear about each of them that they too had two slaves as their parents, and similarly with their parents in turn, and so on for all of them right to the beginning of the line? For clearly, if a single one of these ancestors is free-born, it is no longer properly possible to consider his descendants to be slaves. And it is not conceivable, my friend, that from generation unto generation (as they say) there should be any descent group in which there were not both unlimited numbers of free men and just as many who were slaves — as well as tyrants and kings, slaves who had been chained up and slaves who had been branded and traders and craftsmen and all other types of men there are, sharing all kinds of jobs and lifestyles, successes and failures. (12) Surely you know that poets trace the ancestry of so-called heroes right back to the gods in order to place the figure in question above criticism? Most of them are said to be descended from Zeus, in order to avoid having kings and the founders of cities and the heroes after whom they are named finding themselves in situations which are commonly regarded as bringing disgrace. But what if that is what human affairs are really like — as we and others wiser than ourselves assert? Then your descent can bring you no greater share in real freedom than to anyone supposed to be a plain slave, nor can it bring me any greater share in slavery. Unless you manage to trace your ancestry back to Zeus or Poseidon or Apollo, of course.

(13) **Citizen**: Look, let's forget all about family and ancestors, since you think one can't make any firm statements about it. Perhaps the circumstances of your birth will be found to have been like those of Amphion and Zethos, or Priam's son Alexander. But we all know that you yourself are in a condition of slavery.

Slave: Come, come: do you think that everyone who is in a condition of slavery is a real slave? Aren't there many men who are of free status who are held in a state of slavery unjustly? Some of them have appealed to a court of law and proved that they were free; others continue to put up with it till the end because they have no incontrovertible proof of their freedom, or because their so-called masters treat them humanely. (14) Think of Eumaios, son of Ktesios and grandson of Hormenos; he was the son of a man who was undeniably free and wealthy, but served Odysseus and Laertes as a slave in Ithaka. He had many opportunities to sail off home if he had wanted to, but he never thought it worthwhile. What about the many Athenians who were taken prisoner in Sicily — they served as slaves in Sicily and in the Peloponnese, although they were of free status. The same is true of those who were made prisoners in many other battles — some just for a short time until they found someone to ransom them, others until their deaths. (15) Then there was the occasion after the battle in which the Athenians were defeated at Akanthos, when Kallias' son was believed to have been in Thrace for a long time as a slave, so that when he later escaped and returned, he started an argument about Kallias' estate and caused the next-of-kin a lot of trouble. I think myself that he was an imposter — he wasn't Kallias' son, but his groom, who looked very like the young man (he in fact died in the battle). He also spoke correct Greek and knew how to read and write.

But tens of thousands of others have suffered this misfortune. (16) I guess that at this very moment many of the people serving as slaves right here are free men. After all, when an Athenian is taken prisoner in war and shipped off to Persia or Thrace or Sicily and sold there, we don't say that such a free man is now a slave. On the other hand if some Thracian or Persian is brought here (and not simply one whose parents are ordinary free men, but even the son of a noble or king), we don't accept that he is free any longer. (17) Now at Athens and in many other communities there is a law which prevents anyone who really (*physei*) is a slave from ever attaining the status of a citizen. But no one would have denied citizenship to Kallias' son if he had in fact survived the battle, been captured, taken to Thrace, kept there for many years and frequently beaten. So there are occasions on which the law says that those unjustly in a state of servitude have not become slaves. (18) Now what on earth is it that you see me do or suffer that makes you say that you are certain I am a slave?

Citizen: You are fed by your master, you accompany him about and you do what he tells you: and if you don't, you are beaten.

Slave: Then you have proved that sons too are their fathers' slaves. Many poor men are attended by their sons when they go out to the gymnasium, or at dinners; and they are all fed by their fathers and often beaten by them, and they do whatever their fathers tell them to do. (19) Though as regards obeying and being beaten, you will argue that the pupils of schoolteachers are their slaves, and that teachers of gymnastics are the owners of their pupils, or anyone else who teaches anything. They all give them instructions and beat them if they don't obey.

Citizen: No doubt. But teachers of gymnastics and others can't chain their pupils up or sell them or send them to work in the tread-mill. Masters are allowed to do all these things.

(20) **Slave**: Perhaps you don't know that in many well-governed communities, fathers are permitted to do all the things you mention to their sons — chain them up, if they wish, and sell them, and something even more extreme than that: they are allowed to kill them without a trial and without stating their reason. But that doesn't go any further towards making them their fathers' slaves rather than their sons. And if I did indeed serve as a slave, and was truly a slave from the beginning, then why shouldn't I now be as free as anyone else; and conversely,

even if you are the son of people who are undeniably free, why shouldn't you be utterly and completely a slave?

(21) **Citizen**: I just can't see how I am to turn into a slave when I am actually free. But it is quite possible for you to become free, if your master manumits you.

Slave: But my dear friend, can no one become free even if his master doesn't manumit him?

Citizen: How on earth could he?

Slave: The way after the battle of Chaeronea the Athenians voted that the slaves who had fought together with them should be free; if the war had continued and Philip hadn't made peace so soon, many if not all the Athenians' slaves would have received their freedom, though they wouldn't have been manumitted by their own masters [see No. **89** above].

Citizen: I accept that, the community can make you free by a public act.

(22) **Slave**: Well now: you don't think I could free myself?

Citizen: If you got the money from somewhere and paid your master.

Slave: I don't mean that way; I mean the way Cyrus set free not just himself, but the whole of Persia, a huge number of people, without paying any money or being manumitted by his master. As you know, Cyrus was the †lamp-maker† of Astyages, and when he had the power and thought it opportune, he not only became free, but king over the whole of Asia at the same time.

Citizen: I take your point. Now how do you think I could become a slave?

(23) **Slave**: The way tens of thousands of people who are free sell themselves to become slaves in accordance with written contracts — and the terms are sometimes not at all moderate, but very exacting indeed.

The people who were present had accepted the drift of the argument so far, because they thought that it wasn't serious but rather a kind of logical exercise. But then they objected that it seemed absurd if every piece of evidence by which one could distinguish a slave from a free man were to be disallowed, and clever arguments could be set up to counter every single point. (24) So they moved away from the question of whether this particular man was really a slave, and considered instead what a slave actually is. They thought that if someone has full rights of ownership over someone so that he is able to do whatever he wants with him, just as with any other piece of property or livestock, then that person is correctly described as the slave of the man who owns him.

The man who had spoken in the argument about slavery again raised an objection: what did 'full rights of ownership' mean? (25) After all, there were many people who seemed to have owned a house or an estate or a horse or an ox for a long period of time, and some of them had even inherited them from their parents, but they had no legal right to them. In the same way, a man or woman might be owned unjustly. There are several ways in which people come to possess slaves, just like other property: they can get them from someone else either as a gift or as an inheritance or by purchase, or they can have them right from the moment when they are born (these they call 'home-bred' slaves); and the third way of obtaining possession is by taking a prisoner in warfare or in a pirate raid and keeping him in servitude as a result; that, I suppose, is the earliest way of all. For the first people to be slaves can't have been descended from slaves, but will have been overpowered in a war or a raid, and forced to serve their captors as slaves. (26) So the morality of this most ancient method, from which all the others are derived, is extremely dubious and can't really be defended at all. As soon as these people have the opportunity to run away, there is nothing to stop them from being free again, since they were not legitimately enslaved; and therefore they cannot have been real slaves at any time. Sometimes they haven't just escaped from slavery themselves, but enslaved their masters in their turn – so, at the throw of a dice (as the saying goes), the whole situation was reversed.

One of those present suggested that these people themselves could no doubt not be called slaves, but that the name could properly be used of their children and the second and third generations after them.

(27) **Slave:** But how? If it is being captured that makes a man a slave, then shouldn't this be applied to those who are captured themselves much more than to the descendants? If it is not that but birth which is the criterion, then it is clear that since those who were captured were free men, their children could not be slaves either. Look at the example of the Messenians: after an interval of how many years was it that they got back both their freedom and their country? (28) After the Thebans had defeated the Spartans at Leuktra, they marched into the Peloponnese together with their allies and forced the Spartans to give up Messenia; they resettled all the people who were descended from those Messenians who had previously been the Spartans' slaves and were called Helots [369 BC]. No one says that the Thebans did this unjustly, but rather with great honour, and great justice. So if that method of getting possession of a slave from which all the others originated is unjust, then none of the others are likely to be either, and the word 'slave' cannot properly be used at all. (29) But perhaps the term 'slave' wasn't originally used like this – for a man for whose body money has been paid, or who is born from so-called slaves, as most people think; rather, for a servile and illiberal disposition. For we will all agree that many so-called slaves have the character of free men, while many free

men have very servile characters. It's like the terms 'noble' and 'well-born': people first used them to refer to those who were well-born in terms of virtue, without making any detailed examination of who their parents were. But later those with inherited wealth and status were called 'well-born' by some people. (30) There is clear evidence for this — for the old meaning of the word is still used for cocks, or horses, or hounds, just as it used to be for men. If you see a horse which is proud and restless and a keen runner, you don't ask whether its ancestors came from Arcadia or Media or Thessaly: you judge the horse itself and call it 'well-bred'. And if those who know about hounds see one which is swift and keen and good at tracking, they won't ask whether the breed is Carian or Spartan or anything else, they'll call it a 'noble' hound. The same is true of fighting-cocks and other animals.

(31) Clearly the same applies to human beings: if a man is well-born in terms of virtue, then he ought to be called 'noble', even if no one knows who his parents or ancestors were.

And it is not possible for anyone to be noble without being well-born, or to be well-born without being free. After all, if it were normal to use the words 'freedom' and 'slavery' for horses, cocks or hounds, we wouldn't make any distinction between those which are 'noble' and those which are 'free', or between those which are 'servile' and those which are 'low-born'. (32) Similarly it isn't right to distinguish between men who are 'noble and well-born' and men who are 'free'; the same people must be both. Nor should some people be called 'common and base' and a different group 'slaves'.

So our argument leads us to the conclusion that it is not the philosophers who have changed the meanings of these words, but the foolish majority of mankind, in their ignorance.

236. Horace, *Satires*, 2, 7.75–94

According to traditional Roman morality, it was necessary to prove that you were a good man (your *virtus*) through your own actions; inherited status did not suffice in itself. Hence the Romans found it easy to accept Stoic ideas about the importance of spiritual freedom. Here Horace shows that a good slave can have more 'freedom' than a bad master — but we should note that at the end of the poem he betrays his irritation at his slave's preaching: 'If you don't get out of here quickly, you'll be assigned to my Sabine farm as the ninth labourer' (117f.).

Are you my owner — you, who submit to orders from so many powerful forces and persons? You, who would not be freed from fear and dread if you were touched three or even four times by the

Praetor's rod? Furthermore (and this should have just as much force as what I have just been saying): whether the man subject to a slave is called a substitute (according to your usage) or a fellow-slave — what am I with respect to you? Why, you who order me around are some other person's wretched slave, moved about like a puppet whose strings are pulled by someone else.

Is anyone free then? The Wise Man, who is in full command over himself, who is not afraid of poverty or death or imprisonment, who has the courage to defy his desires and scorn public respect, who is complete in himself and polished and rounded off so that nothing outside him can stick to the smooth surface, against whom Fortune's onslaught always fails. Are you able to identify any one of these characteristics as your own? Some woman asks you for five talents; she annoys you, throws you out, pours cold water over you, summons you back. Tear this shameful halter from your neck: come on, say, 'I am free, I am free.' You can't do it; your mind is oppressed by a master who is not gentle, but goads you with sharp pricks until you are exhausted, and drives you on in spite of your resistance.

237. Seneca, *Dialogue 9: The Tranquillity of the Mind*, 10.3

The Stoic belief that all men are subject to a capricious Fortune was one reason for dismissing status distinctions as comparatively less important than moral freedom. It also paved the way for the Christian's subjection of all men to a rather more benevolent Godhead.

We are all fettered to Fortune. For some, the chain is made of gold, and is loose; for others it is tight and filthy — but what difference does that make? All of us are surrounded by the same kind of captivity, and even those who hold others bound are in bonds themselves, unless you happen to think that the handcuff the guard wears on his left wrist hurts less than the prisoner's. Public offices hold one man captive, wealth another; some are disadvantaged by high birth, some by humble birth; some have to put up with other people's commands, some with their own. Some have to stay in one place because they've been exiled, others because they've been appointed to a priesthood — all life is slavery.

[The *Flamen Dialis*, the priest of the state cult of Jupiter, was not allowed to spend more than three nights in succession outside the boundary of the city of Rome.]

238. Seneca, *Letters*, 47

The most famous plea that slaves were human beings who should be treated accordingly, with the greatest influence on Renaissance humanists, occurs in the *Moral Letters* of Seneca. But it is primarily a rhetorical exercise, and Seneca is much more interested in writing exciting Latin than in improving the conditions of his readers' slaves.

(1) It gave me great pleasure to learn from those who had been to see you that you live on terms of familiarity with your slaves. This is appropriate to your wisdom and scholarship.

'These people are slaves.' No: they are human beings.

'These people are slaves.' No: they are those with whom you share your roof.

'These people are slaves.' No: when you consider how much power Chance can exert over you both, they are fellow-slaves.

'These people are slaves.' No: when you consider how much Chance can exert over you both, they are fellow-slaves.

(2) That's why I find it ludicrous that there should be people who think it shameful to have dinner with their slave — what reason is there for this attitude, except for the arrogant social convention that when a master dines, he should have a crowd of slaves standing all around him? While he eats more than he can hold down, and burdens his stomach, bloated by his excessive greed and no longer capable of fulfilling the functions of a stomach, so that he vomits it all out with greater labour than that with which he swallowed it — (3) meanwhile his wretched slaves aren't even allowed to move their lips in order to speak. Every sound is suppressed by the threat of a beating; and not even unintentional noises like coughing, sneezing or hiccups are exempted from chastisement. If the silence is disturbed by any sound, it must be atoned for by a dire punishment. Throughout the night they stand there hungry and silent. (4) That's how it comes about that those who aren't allowed to talk in the presence of their master will tell tales about him behind his back. But those slaves who were allowed to talk not just in their master's presence, but actually with their master, were ready to offer their neck on his behalf, and to turn aside onto their own head danger that was threatening him: they talked when they served dinner, but kept quiet when they were being tortured. (5) Then there is that proverb which originates from the same arrogant attitude, that we have as many enemies as we have slaves. They aren't our enemies unless we make them so. I shan't mention some other cruel and inhumane ways in which we would be maltreating them even if they were dumb beasts instead of human beings — when, for instance, we lie down to dine, and someone has to clear up the vomit, while another stands at the

bottom of the couch to remove the leavings of the drunken guests. (6) There is someone whose task it is to carve expensive fowl. He guides his well-trained hand around the bird's breast and rump as he carves it up; he has no personal motive for doing this whatsoever. What a wretch, to live for no other purpose than to carve up fattened birds skilfully — unless the man who teaches someone this skill because it is going to give him pleasure is more to be pitied than the slave who has no choice but to learn it! (7) Another pours the wine; he is dressed like a woman and has great difficulty in not betraying his age. (8) Another, whose job it is to assess the behaviour of the guests, stands there uneasily and checks who is sufficiently unrestrained with regard to his appetite or his tongue to be invited back tomorrow. There are those who prepare the menu and know their master's taste with utter precision, so that they can judge what sorts of things have the right savour to wake him up, the appearance to give him pleasure, the novelty to put him back on his feet when he feels sick; what he finds boring because he has had too much of it, what he craves for on any particular day. He cannot bear to eat with these people, and considers that it detracts from his prestige if he has to touch the same table as his slave. Heavens above — how many owners does he have out of that lot? (9) I saw Callistus' one-time master stand at the door and be left to wait while others were asked inside — the man who had written out the advertisement for him and had put him up for sale amongst a group of particularly worthless slaves. That slave had been put in the first batch of ten at the sale (where all the auctioneer cares about is testing his voice), and he paid his master back what he deserved: he in his turn turned him away, he too did not consider him worthy to be in his house. His master sold Callistus: and how much Callistus cost his master! (10) You must think carefully about the fact that the man whom you call your slave is born from the same seed, enjoys the same sky, breathes like you, dies like you! You are as able to recognise a free man in him as he to recognise a slave in you. After the destruction of Varus' army, Chance pulled down many men of respectable birth who were expecting to attain senatorial rank as the result of a military career; it made one of them a shepherd, another a door-keeper. Will you be contemptuous of a man whose status is one which you may yourself be reduced to — for all that you're contemptuous of it?

(11) I don't want to let myself go on this vast topic, and give you a homily on how to treat slaves: we behave towards them in a proud, cruel and insulting fashion. The sum of what I wish to preach is this: treat those whose status is inferior to your own in the same manner as you would wish your own superior to treat you. Each time you remember how much you are entitled to do to your slave, you must remember also just how much your own master is entitled to do to you. (12) 'But I don't have any master,' you object. The world is still

young: perhaps there will come a time when you do have one. Don't you know how old Hecuba was when she began to serve as a slave, or Croesus, or the mother of Darius, or Plato or Diogenes? (13) Be forgiving towards your slave, even courteous, let him take part in your conversations, and when you discuss important family issues, and when you have dinner. At this point all those who go in for luxurious living will scream at me: 'There's no more undignified and degrading way to behave than that.' Yet I'll catch these very same people kissing the hand of someone else's slave as a mark of respect. (14) Can't you even see this, that our ancestors took away from slave-owners any grounds for others to suspect them of insulting behaviour, and from slaves any grounds for feeling that they were being treated in an insulting fashion? They gave the owner the title 'Head of the household', and the slaves 'Members of the household' — that's the term which is still used in mimes. They instituted a religious festival [the Saturnalia], not so that masters should eat with their slaves on that day only, but so that they should always do so. They allowed masters to have a position of respect and to administer justice within the household; they thought that the household was a state in miniature.

(15) 'What's your conclusion? Do you want me to invite all my slaves to eat with me?' Not more so than that you should invite all your children. You would be mistaken if you thought that I was going to ignore some just because they do low-status work, which is what you consider that of mule-drovers or cowherds to be. I'm not going to assess them according to their jobs, but according to their moral character. Everyone makes his own moral character: jobs are assigned by Chance. You must invite some people to dine with you because they deserve it, and others so that they may deserve it in future. If there is anything slavish in such people because of their unpleasant jobs, then association with men of free birth will drive it out of them. (16) My dear Lucilius, you mustn't look for friends only in the Forum and in the Council chamber; if you look carefully, you'll find them in your own home too. Good wood often warps if no craftsman uses it: test it, see if you can use it. Just as a man who doesn't look at a horse he's going to buy but at the saddle and bridle instead is a fool, so someone who assesses a person by his clothes or social rank — which is wrapped round us just like our clothes — is an utter idiot. (17) 'The man is a slave.' Perhaps he is free in his heart. 'The man is a slave.' Is that going to harm him? Show me who isn't a slave: some are slaves to sex, others to money, some to social prestige, all are slaves to hope and fear. I'll give you some examples: the man of consular rank who acts as the slave of some old woman [because he wants a legacy from her]; the rich man who's after a young slave girl; I'll show you some young men from the best families who have made themselves the property of popular

actors – and no kind of slavery is more dishonourable than that which is entered into voluntarily. So there can be no reason why you should let these high-principled people stop you from showing yourself to your slaves as a pleasant person and not as their proud superior. Let them respect you rather than fear you. (18) I suppose that someone will say that what I'm now doing is inciting slaves to put on the cap of freedom, dethroning masters from their superior position because I said 'Let them respect their master instead of fearing him'. 'What you must mean is this,' they'll say: 'They should respect us in the same way as clients do, as dependants who call on us to pay their respects as a sign of their humble status.' Anyone who's going to say that, will have forgotten that what is enough for a god isn't too little for slave-owners. Whoever is respected, is loved too: and love cannot be mixed up with fear. (19) So I think that you are absolutely right that you don't want to be feared by your slaves, and that when you punish them, you do so with words: beatings are for punishing dumb animals. Not everything that displeases us also does us harm. Our luxury has made us so mad that we are angry at anything that doesn't correspond exactly to our whim. (20) We are putting on the attitudes of tyrants – for they too have fits of anger, as though someone was doing them harm, and quite forget both their own position of power, and the powerlessness of others: yet the superiority of their rank makes them absolutely proof against any danger of being harmed. It isn't that they don't know this, but rather that by complaining they can find an opportunity to do harm themselves: they find that they are hurt in order to hurt others. (21) I don't want to keep you any longer: I know that I don't have to preach to you. Among the other advantages of good manners is this: that they satisfy their own demands, and thus remain constant. Bad manners are fickle and ever-changing – not improving, just changing into something else.

239. Seneca, *On Benefits*, 3, 17

Examples of loyal slaves were important evidence in favour of the Stoic proposition that slaves were moral agents who deserved to be treated humanely. When historians or rhetoricians recounted the story of the Roman civil wars, it was paradoxical that slaves and freedmen should sometimes have remained more faithful to their masters and patrons than sons to their fathers (see Velleius Paterculus, 2, 67; Appian, *Roman Civil Wars*, 4, 43.179–48.208; and Valerius Maximus, 6, 8). Seneca argues that people who have natural or social obligations towards one another – like sons towards their fathers – can nevertheless confer benefits which are beyond the call of duty. To prove that this may be so for sons, Seneca shows that it is even possible for the lowest form of human being, the slave — for according to Stoic doctrine (see Epictetus, 4.1) it is only the slave's body that is owned by his master, while the soul may remain free, and thus able to behave virtuously — for example, by conferring benefits.

(3) He who is glad that he has been done a good turn will experience that same pleasure all the time, and he will be happy because he considers, not the thing he has received, but the mind of the person from whom he received it. A good turn continually pleases a person who is grateful, but pleases an ungrateful person only once [i.e. at the moment when it is performed]. (4) How can you make a comparison between these two different types — one is worried and uneasy, as men who fraudulently deny their debts tend to be; he does not respect his parents as he ought, nor his tutor or his schoolteachers. But the other is cheerful and happy as he looks out for a chance to repay his gratitude, and he experiences great joy from this very feeling. He isn't wondering how he can possibly escape his obligations, but in what way he can repay more fully and more richly not just his parents and friends, but also persons of lower social status than himself. For even if he has been done a good turn by his slave, he does does not consider from whom, but what it was that he received.

(Ch. 18.1) Yet there are some people, like Hecaton, who question whether a slave is able to do his master a good turn. Now some philosophers make the following distinction: some things are benefits, some things are obligations, some things are services rendered; a benefit is the sort of thing that an outsider might bestow (an outsider is defined as someone who without blame might have done nothing); obligations are proper to a son or wife, or to those persons whom ties of kinship encourage and oblige to assist you; while services are rendered by a slave, whose status places him in a position where nothing that he might do would give him a claim upon his superior.

(2) But anyone who denies that a slave may sometimes do his master a good turn is ignorant of human law — for what is crucial is the intention of whoever confers the benefit, not his status. Virtue's door is barred to no man. It is open to everyone, it admits everyone, it invites everyone inside, whether they are free-born or freedmen or slaves or kings or exiles; it does not select on grounds of family or wealth; Virtue is satisfied with man just as he is. What security could we find against sudden disasters, what great prize would there be for our souls to strive for, if a clear-cut example of virtuous behaviour could be made void by the fortuitous rank of the doer? (3) If what a slave does for his owner is not a benefit, then nor is what anyone does for their king, or what a soldier does for his commander — for if one only has *obligations* towards superiors, then it makes no difference what the nature of those bonds of authority may be. If a slave can't

have a benefit ascribed to him because he cannot escape and is afraid of extreme punishments, then the same objection holds for anyone with a king or a military commander over him, since these persons have the same rights over him even if under a different label. But people *can* bestow benefits upon their kings and their commanders; so it follows that they can also do so for their owners. (4) It is within a slave's power to be just, to be courageous, to be great-hearted; it follows that it is also within his power to confer a benefit, since this too is an essential element of a virtuous character. Indeed, slaves can bestow benefits upon their masters so obviously that the benefit they gave was often their masters' very survival.

(Ch. 19.1) It cannot be doubted that it is within a slave's power to bestow a benefit on anybody at random – so why shouldn't he be able to do the same for his owner? 'Because,' runs the objection, 'if he gives his master money, he cannot thereby become his creditor. Otherwise he would be putting his master under an obligation towards him every day – he accompanies him on his journeys, looks after him when ill, works hard to cultivate his farm; but all these actions, which would be called benefits if they were to be performed by an outsider, are services when they are performed by a slave. For a benefit is something which someone has done who was entitled to choose *not* to do it. But a slave does not have the power to refuse; thus he does not give, he merely obeys – nor has he any right to claim that he has done something when he was in no position *not* to do it.'

(2) Even if I accept these premisses, I shall win my argument, and raise slaves up to a position where in many respects they shall be free men. First of all, tell me this: if I can show you someone who fights to protect his master without any regard for himself, and when pierced through with wounds nevertheless sheds the last drops of blood in his veins, who tries by means of the delay caused by his own death to allow his owner time to escape – are you going to deny that this man conferred a benefit, just because he happens to be a slave? (3) If I can show you someone whom none of a tyrant's promises could entice to betray his owner's secrets, who was terrified by no threats and vanquished by no tortures, so that he confounded the suspicions of the investigating judge to the full extent that he could, and paid for his loyalty with his life – are you going to deny that this man conferred a benefit upon his owner, just because he happens to be a slave? (4) Consider this: isn't an example of virtuous behaviour in a slave greater to the extent that it is rarer, and something that deserves even more gratitude, for the following reason: that even though authority is disliked, and the constraints of necessity are hard to bear, love for his master has nevertheless overcome the general resentment at serving as a slave in this one particular person. So the act has not ceased to be a benefit because it was performed by a

slave: on the contrary, it has become a greater benefit, because not even his status as a slave was able to deter him from it. (Ch. 20.1) Anyone who thinks that slavery permeates the whole of a man's character, is wrong. The better part of him escapes. Bodies are under an obligation to the owners to whom they are assigned; the mind however is subject to its own authority, which is so free and unrestrained that it cannot even be held within this prison within which it is enclosed, and prevented from using its natural energy to perform great deeds and escape into the heavens as a companion to the gods. (2) So it is just the body which Chance hands over to the owner; that is what he buys and sells – the bit within cannot be given into ownership. Whatever comes from that interior part, is free. And indeed we cannot order our slaves to do everything, and they aren't obliged to obey us in everything – they wouldn't obey orders contrary to the interests of the State, and they wouldn't become accomplices in any criminal undertaking.

(Ch. 21.1) There are certain actions which the law neither requires nor forbids; it is in this area that the slave finds the opportunity to confer a benefit. So long as he does the things which are normally required of a slave, he performs a service; but when he does more than a slave has to do, it becomes a benefit – when it has shifted into the sphere which we associate with friendship, it ceases to be called a service. (2) Now there are certain things which an owner has a responsibility to provide for his slave, like food and clothing allowances; no one has ever called these things benefits. But if a master has been kind to his slave, given him a liberal education, taught him those skills which free-born men are taught – that is a benefit. And conversely the same can happen on the slave's part. Whatever there is that exceeds the prescribed obligations of a slave and is performed freely, and not as the result of a command, is a benefit, so long as it is of such magnitude that it would have been described as such if it had been performed by some other person.

(Ch. 22.1) According to Chrysippus, a slave is a worker whom we have hired for life. In just the same way as a hired worker confers a benefit if he does more than his contract has committed him to do, so also with a slave. When he overcomes the limitations of his status by showing goodwill towards his master, and surpasses what his master has a right to expect by daring to do something noble which would bring honour even to those born into some higher rank, we are confronted with a benefit performed within the household community.

(2) Surely you can't think it fair that those people with whom we are angry when they do less than they should, shouldn't deserve our gratitude when they do more than is required or is normal? Let me tell you the circumstances under which an action is not a benefit: when one could have said, 'It makes no difference whether he wanted to do it

or not.' But if he did something which he was entitled to refuse, then the fact that he wanted to do it ought to be praised.

(3) A benefit and an injury are polar opposites; a man who can receive an injury from his master can also confer a benefit upon him. But there are persons appointed to investigate injuries inflicted upon slaves by their masters, whose duty it is to restrain sadism and sexual passion and meanness in providing slaves with the necessities of life. [This was the responsibility of the City Prefect at Rome, and of the governors in the provinces: see Nos. 32 and 226 above.] So we must conclude that this is not a question of an *owner* obtaining a benefit from a *slave*, but rather of one human being obtaining a benefit from another human being.

(4) To sum up: the slave did everything that lay within his power: he conferred a benefit upon his owner — it lies within *your* power not to accept a benefit coming from a slave. But who is so great that Chance may not force him to turn for help even to those of the lowest social status?

(Ch. 23.1) I shall now relate many different examples of such benefits, some of them quite contradictory. One man gave his owner his life, another helped him to die; one saved him when he was in danger of death, and — as though that instance wasn't impressive enough — another saved him by dying himself; one assisted his master's suicide, another frustrated it.

(2) In the eighteenth book of his *Annals*, Claudius Quadrigarius tells how, when Grumentum was being besieged and had reached a state of utter desperation, two fugitive slaves crossed over and gave assistance to the enemy. Later, when the victorious army was running amock throughout the captured city, these two ran on ahead by a route that was well known to them to the house in which they had served as slaves, and pushed their mistress along in front of them; when anyone asked who she was, they proclaimed that she was their mistress and had treated them most cruelly, and that she was being led off to be punished by them. They brought her outside the city walls and hid her very carefully until the enemy's anger had cooled down; afterwards, when the soldiers had had their fill of slaughter and soon conducted themselves like civilised Romans once again, they too returned to their normal behaviour and gave their mistress back her freedom. (3) She manumitted them both on the spot and didn't think it degrading to have received her life from people over whom she had had the power of life and death. Indeed, she might rather have congratulated herself on the fact that if she had been saved by someone else, the gift would have been a matter of ordinary and unexceptional mercy, but since she had been saved in this way, the story made her famous, and she became an example to Rome as well as Grumentum. (4) When everyone was

looking after their own interests, in the middle of the enormous confusion of the city's capture, they all deserted her except for these two deserters; and they, in order to show what the reason for that first desertion had been, transferred their loyalty from the victors to their prisoner by pretending to be killers. The greatest thing about the good deed that they did was that they thought that it was worth pretending to kill their mistress, in order to stop her from really being killed. Believe me, to do something noble at the cost of being thought a criminal is not typical of a humble, let alone a servile, spirit.

(5) Vettius, the leader of the Marsians, was being taken to the Roman commander; his slave snatched a sword from the very same soldier by whom he was being dragged along, and first of all killed his master and then said, 'Now it is time for me to look after my own interests – I have already set my master free'; and so he killed himself with a single blow. Give me a more glorious instance of a slave saving his master!

(Ch. 24.1) Caesar was besieging Corfinium, and Domitius was blockaded inside; he ordered a physician who was a slave of his to give him some poison. When he saw how reluctant he was, he said, 'What are you hesitating for, as though this is something entirely within your power. I ask for death, and I am armed.' He promised to do as he had been told and prepared a harmless drink for him to take; when this had put him to sleep, the slave went to Domitius' son and said, 'Order me to be kept under guard until you can tell from the outcome whether or not I have given your father poison.' Domitius lived, and in due course was granted his life by Caesar; but his slave had granted him his life first.

(Ch. 25.1) During the Civil War, there was a slave who hid his master, and put on his rings and his clothes, and went to meet the police and told them that he had no wish to impede them from carrying out their commands, and then offered them his neck. What a man he proved himself to be – ready to die for his owner at a time when it was a sign of unusual loyalty not to want one's master's death: to be seen to be forgiving when everything in the political world was heartless, and to be trustworthy when the political world was utterly without faith. Or to desire death as the prize for being loyal, at a time when enormous rewards were being offered for treachery.

(Ch. 26.1) I cannot pass over some instances from our own era. In the reign of Tiberius, the rage for prosecutions was so widespread, and indeed almost universal, that it did more harm to a city at peace than all the civil wars put together. The mutterings of drunkards were eagerly taken up, everything you did was dangerous, including harmless jokes. Nothing was safe. Anything was an excuse for atrocities. No one asked what was the fate of the accused, since there could be only one outcome.

(2) A man of praetorian rank called Paulus was at a dinner wearing a ring with a large gem engraved with a portrait of Tiberius Caesar. It would be stupid for me to try to find a euphemism for saying that he made use of a chamber-pot. Immediately this action was noticed by Maro, one of the notorious informers of the period, and immediately also a slave of the man for whom this trap had been set removed the ring from his drunken master's finger. When Maro appealed to the diners as witnesses that the Emperor's image had been polluted, and was already drawing up a formal indictment, the slave showed them the ring on his own hand. Anyone who dismisses this man as a mere slave will also say that Maro was an ideal dinner companion.

(Ch. 27.1) In the times of the Divine Augustus, a man's words were not yet so dangerous, but they could cause trouble. At a dinner, a man of senatorial rank called Rufus had prayed that Caesar would not return safely from the journey that he was planning – for, he added, all the bulls and calves that were going to be sacrificed in thanksgiving for his return were praying for the same thing. There were some who listened carefully to these words. As soon as it was dawn, the slave who had been standing at the bottom of his couch during the dinner told him what he had said during the meal while he was drunk, and urged him to be the first to tell Caesar and be his own accuser. (2) He accepted this advice and went to meet Caesar as he was on his way down to the Forum. He swore tht he hadn't known what he was thinking the previous day, and prayed that it would recoil upon himself and upon his own children, and asked the emperor to forgive him and restore him to favour. (3) When the emperor had said that he would do so, he said, 'No one will believe that you have taken me back into your favour unless you give me something as a present,' and he asked for a sum of money which would not have been rejected as mean even by a close friend; and he got it. The emperor commented that, 'For the sake of my own purse I shall have to take care never to be angry with you in future!' (4) The emperor acted honourably in pardoning him, and in being so liberal as well as forgiving. Of course, anyone who hears about this example has to praise the emperor, but only after he has first praised the slave. It goes without saying that the slave who did this was granted his freedom. But it wasn't for free: the money which the emperor had paid out represented the cost of his manumission.

(Ch. 28.1) After all these many examples, can it still be doubted that an owner can sometimes be done a good turn by his slave? Why should a man's status diminish the value of his action, instead of the action raising the man's status? Everyone is made up of the same elements and comes from the same origin; no one is more honourable than another, unless his mind is more upright and better suited to good habits. (2) Aren't those people who display the masks of their ancestors in their halls and place long lists of the names of their families with all the complicated branchings of family trees in the porches of their houses, merely well-known rather than truly noble? The same universe is everybody's parent; from it everyone can trace their ancestry, whether through high or low estate. Don't be deceived by people who when they find famous names missing when they make up their list of ancestors, fill in the space by inserting the name of a god. (3) You should not look down on any man, even if the names of his ancestors are forgotten and Chance has given him little help. Whether your ancestors include freedmen or slaves or foreigners, you should show some pride and ignore anything dishonourable in your immediate background; for right at the beginning of the line, great nobility awaits you. (4) Why does our pride lead us to such stupidity that we think it beneath us to accept benefits from slaves, so that we are obsessed by their rank and ignore their merits? Are you going to call another man a slave when you are yourself enslaved — to sex or food or a prostitute, if not to prostitutes in general as their common property? (5) You are going to call another man a slave? Where are those bearers taking you in that plush litter? And those attendants in the funny raincoats, dressed up to look like soldiers — where are they going to take you? To some slave door-keeper's door, to the gardens owned by some slave who doesn't even have a prescribed series of duties to perform. And then you deny that you can be done a good turn by your own slave, when you think you've been done a good turn when someone else's slave deigns to give you a formal greeting! (6) What sort of contradiction is this? At one and the same time you look down on slaves, and try to win their favour; when you are inside your own house, you behave arrogantly and despotically, when you are outside, you behave humbly, and allow yourself to be despised to the same extent as you yourself despise others.

240. Aulus Gellius, *Attic Nights*, 2, 18

Another powerful argument to convince intellectuals that some men of slave status were actually as truly noble as any free citizen, was that some philosophers had been slaves.

Phaedon of Elis was one of those who followed Socrates, and he was a very close friend of Socrates and of Plato. Plato used his name for the title of that wonderful book about the immortality of the soul. This Phaedon was a slave of excellent [literally 'a free man's'] physical appearance and character; some writers state that as a boy he had been forced into prostitution by his owner, who ran a brothel. Cebes, who belonged to Socrates' circle, is said to have bought him at Socrates' suggestion, and have given him a philosophical education. He later became a famous philosopher, and his extremely well-written essays about Socrates can still be read.

There were quite a few other slaves who later became famous philosophers. One of them was Menippus, whose writings Marcus Varro imitated in the *Satires*, which some people entitle *Cynic* but he himself called *Menippean*. And there was also Pompylus, the slave of Theophrastus the Peripatetic, and a slave of Zeno the Stoic who was called Persaeus, and of Epicurus, whose name was Mys; they were all considerable philosophers.

Diogenes the Cynic also served as a slave for a time; but he had been sold into slavery although of free birth. When Xeniades the Corinthian wanted to buy him, he was asked whether there was any skill that he had learnt, and Diogenes replied, 'I know how to rule free men.' Xeniades was so impressed by his reply that he bought him, gave him his freedom, and put him in charge of his children, saying, 'Take my children and rule them.'

The memory of the noble philosopher Epictetus, since he was also a slave, is so fresh in our minds that I do not have to write about it as though it were something which has been forgotten.

241. St Theodoret of Cyrrhus' commentary on St Paul's *First Letter to the Corinthians*, 7.21–3

The idea that a person's legal status affected only his body, so that quite different criteria had to be applied to see whether his soul – and therefore his *real* character – was slave or free, could be accepted and developed without difficulty by Christians. The abolition of slavery as an institution did not occur to them, and would not have interested them: the liberation of every man's soul did. (The evidence for the hypothesis that early Christian communities contained an above-average proportion of slaves is slight, and statements ascribing abolitionist tendencies to heretical groups like the *circumcelliones* in North Africa merely show that this was one of the most terrible crimes an opponent could be accused of.) St Paul had returned the fugitive slave Onesimos to his owner (No. 213 above), and in his *First Letter to the Corinthians*, he tells slaves to obey their masters and not run away.

At the same time, the terminology of slave-ownership was metaphorically applied to salvation: the word *Redemption* means buying a slave his freedom, as this fifth-century Syrian bishop's commentary on St Paul makes clear.

(21) 'Are you who have been called by Christ a slave? It shouldn't concern you; even if you are able to gain manumission, you should accept your slave status all the more.' — God's Grace recognises no difference between being a slave and being a master. So you should not try to escape from your status as a slave on the grounds that it is degrading for the Christian Faith. And even if it is possible for you to win manumission, you must stay and be a slave, and await the reward you will obtain for this. This is hyperbole, but it is not pointless: he is telling you not to use religion as a pretext for running away from slavery. And he also offers you quite a different consolation:

(22) 'The slave who has been called by Christ becomes Christ's freedman; and in the same way, the free man who has been called becomes Christ's slave.' — It is our custom to call someone who is an ex-slave a freedman; Paul applies this term to the slave who has been blessed by Faith. He calls the free man Christ's slave, and the slave his freedman, both in order to teach those who are free that they have a master, Christ, and similarly to teach slaves that they have attained true freedom. For no one is so truly free as he who has been set free from sin; and no one endures a slavery as grievous as that of the man subject to the slavery of the passions.

(23) 'You have been bought free for a price: do not become the slaves of human masters.' — This ruling does not contradict what he has just said: he is ordering us not to have the thoughts of a slave, whether we are labelled slaves or addressed as free men. And he has cleverly demonstrated that both slaves and their masters are actually fellow-slaves by saying that both categories 'have been bought free for a price': for the Master has redeemed you both for the price of his own blood.

242. Augustine, *Commentary on Psalm 99*, 7 (*PL* 37, 1275)

In a commentary on the Psalms, an African Latin bishop made use of the idea that just because a redeemed slave became a freedman, his obligations towards his *patronus* did not cease.

All slavery is filled with bitterness: all who are tied to slave status complain at having to serve. But you must not be afraid of the service of this Master: there will be no groaning, no grumbling, no dissatisfaction here. No one wishes to be sold away from this household, since it is so wonderful that we should all have been bought back ('redeemed'). It is a great joy, my brothers, to be a slave in this great household, even a slave with chains on his feet. You must not be afraid to trust your Master, chained slaves: blame your own deserts for your chains; have faith in your chains, if you want them to become like adornments. It was not without meaning, nor without listening to people, that the psalmist said: 'May the groaning of those who are in chains reach unto your presence' (78,11).

'Serve the Master in joy.' The master's slavery is free; slavery is free when it is charity, and not necessity, that enforces slavery. 'You, brothers, have been called to be freed,' said the Apostle; 'Only you must not let your freedom give an opportunity to the flesh; you must be slaves to one another, because of the charity given by the Holy Spirit' (*Galatians*, 5.13). Charity makes you a slave, after the truth has made you a free man. 'If you remain faithful to my Word,' said the Evangelist, 'You will really be my pupils; you will recognise the Truth, and the Truth will set you free' (*John*, 8.31f.). You are both a slave and a free man; you are a slave, because that is what you were made; but from that status you have become free, because you love Him who made you. Do not complain at having to serve; your complaints will not bring it about that you cease serving, but that you serve as a bad slave. You are the Master's slave, and the Master's freedman; you shouldn't want to be set free with the result that you leave the household of Him who set you free.

243. Macrobius, *Saturnalia*, 1, 10

One of the finest arguments in favour of treating slaves humanely was presented by a Roman pagan in the fifth century AD. Like Athenaeus' *Banqueting Sophists* (No. **80**), the *Saturnalia* is in the form of a banquet at which a number of well-read members of elite society discuss a whole series of different problems with reference to Latin (and occasionally Greek) literature. The dinner party is so called because it takes place during the religious festival with which slaves were specially associated (see Dionysius of Halicarnassus, 4, 14.4). An unwelcome guest bearing the Christian name Evangelus (corresponding to Athenaeus' Cynic Kynoulkos) suggests that the participation of slaves degrades this pagan festival, and a leading representative of pagan culture, Vettius Agorius Praetextatus, replies with *exempla* taken from Livy and Aulus Gellius, and arguments from Seneca and other classical moralists.

Slavery did not, of course, disappear in the early Middle Ages, as is clear (for instance) from many of the early lives of Saints; and we may wonder whether the Christian or pagan contemporaries of these philosophers treated their slaves any better than their ancestors had done.

(22) 'Philochorus says that it was Cecrops who first set up an altar in Attica to Saturnus and Ops, revering these two gods as Jupiter and

the Earth, and instituting the custom that when the crops and fruits
had been gathered in, the heads of households should all eat together
with the slaves with whom they had endured the hard labour of cultivating the land. For God is pleased at the respect shown to him by
slaves, and at contemplating their hard work. That is why, following
foreign tradition, we sacrifice to this god with head uncovered.

(23) I think that we have already shown clearly that the Saturnalia
used to be celebrated on just one day, December the nineteenth, but
was later extended to three; first when Caesar added one day to
December, and then as a result of Augustus' edict proclaiming that the
festival of the Saturnalia should last for three days, beginning on the
seventeenth and ending on the nineteenth, which was previously the
one single day on which they were held. In addition, the celebration of
the *Sigillaria* makes the period of public enjoyment and religious
activity last for seven whole days.'

(Ch. 11.1) At this point Evangelus interrupted and said, 'I can't
bear this parade of knowledge and display of rhetoric by Praetextatus
any longer. Just now he asserted that it was in honour of some god
that slaves feasted together with their masters, as though the gods care
about slaves, or any intelligent man would throw his home open to the
accusation of admitting such degrading company; and now he wants to
ascribe some religious function to the *Sigillaria*, an opportunity for
children who can't yet walk to play with clay masks. Just because he is
a recognised authority on ritual, he's smuggling in all sorts of super-
stitions. I suppose we're not allowed to disbelieve Praetextatus just
once in a while.'

(2) Everyone recoiled in horror at this, but Praetextatus himself
smiled.

'I'm quite happy that you should think me superstitious, and someone unworthy of belief, so long as I cannot give reasons to demonstrate
the truth of both of these statements of mine. Let's talk about slaves
first. Were you joking, or do you seriously think that there is a category
of human being which the immortal gods do not think worthy of their
care and providence? Or perhaps you won't recognise slaves as being
human at all? Now listen how angry heaven once was at the way a slave
was punished. (3) In 280 BC a man called Autronius Maximus had his
slave beaten and driven round the Circus with his head tied to the forked
stick (*patibulum*) before the start of the Games. Jupiter was so angry
at this that he ordered someone called Annius in a dream to announce
to the Senate that this deed of extreme cruelty did not please him.
(4) When Annius concealed the dream, an unexpected death carried off
his son, and when he was equally negligent regarding a second message
from Heaven, he himself was affected by a sudden physical infirmity. In
the end he was carried to the Senate in a litter, on the advice of a

meeting of his friends, and he gave them the message, and he had hardly finished speaking when his good health returned to him and he was able to leave the Senate house on his own two feet. (5) As a result of a Senate Recommendation and a law proposed by Maenius, one day was added to these Circus games in order to propitiate Jupiter; it is called *instauraticius*, not, as some think, because of the forked stick — in Greek, *apo tou staurou* ('from the cross'), but from the word "recovery"; according to Varro, *instaurare* means to make good as new. So you see how much the highest of the gods cares for a slave. But what is the origin of your vast and senseless contempt for slaves? As though they weren't created from, and nourished by, the same elements as you, and don't draw breath from the same origin?'

[There follows a long passage based directly on material taken from Seneca's 47th letter (Chs. 10ff.) on the idea that slaves are really fellow-slaves to Fortune, and ought to be treated as friends. Seneca's references to slaves who were ready to die for their masters leads Macrobius to cite some examples, probably taken from a first-century handbook of *exempla* like that of Valerius Maximus.]

(16) Do you want me to list the good qualities that have been proven to be in the heart of a slave? First of all there was the case of Urbinus; he had been ordered to be killed and was hiding on his estate at Reate. When his hiding-place was betrayed, one of his slaves put on his ring and clothes and, pretending to be his master, lay down in the bedroom which the people searching for him broke into; he offered his neck to the soldiers as they came in and received the stroke as though he were himself Urbinus. Later, after recovering his civic rights, Urbinus had a tomb made for him and added an inscription which referred to this great act of virtue.

(17) Demosthenes' freedman Aesopus knew that his patron had committed adultery with Julia. Despite being tortured at length, he steadfastly refused to betray his patron, until finally Demosthenes was confronted with the testimony of others who knew about it and admitted the crime himself.

(18) In case you may think that it is easy for a secret to be kept by just one person, Labienus' freedmen could be forced by no kind of torture to reveal where Labienus was hiding with their help.

No one should imagine that this kind of loyalty on the part of freedmen is due to their gratitude for having been granted their freedom, rather than to natural virtue; take the case of the goodwill a slave showed his master despite having himself been punished by that master. (19) Antius Restio was outlawed and fled, by night, unaccompanied; his other slaves set about plundering his property, but there was one slave who had been chained up and branded on the forehead;

after his master's condemnation, someone else took pity on him and set him free. He followed after his fugitive master and told him not to be afraid of him, since he knew that the degradation he had had to endure was due to Fortune and not to his master, and he hid him and looked after his needs. (20) Then, when he realised that the police agents were approaching, he throttled an old man who happened to be nearby, built a pyre and threw his body onto it. He set it on fire and went up to the people searching for Restio and told them that the proscribed man was paying the penalty he owed the slave, and was now suffering very much more severely than he had ever made the slave suffer. The story was believed and Restio was saved.

(21) After Caepio's criminal plot to kill Augustus had been detected and he had been condemned, a slave carried him down to the Tiber in a chest, took him to Ostia and brought him to his ancestral villa in Laurentine territory, travelling by night. Later he accompanied him on a journey by sea, was shipwrecked together with him, and secretly hid his master at Naples; when he was arrested by a centurion, he could not be induced to betray his master by bribes or threats.

(22) When Asinius Pollio was bringing heavy pressure to bear upon the people of Padua to supply him with money and weapons, and many owners went into hiding as a result, slaves who betrayed their masters were promised a reward in addition to their freedom. But we know that not one single slave was induced by the reward to betray his master.

(23) Now listen to this example not just of loyalty in a slave, but of an imaginative and inventive mind. When Grumentum was being besieged, some slaves left their mistress and went over to the enemy. Then when the city was captured, they attacked the house in accordance with a plan that they had agreed between them, dragged out their mistress with what appeared to be threats to punish her, and shouted to those they passed that at last they had an opportunity to punish their mistress for her cruelty. Pretending to drag her off to her death, they protected her with all due respect and loyalty.

(24) Consider that even nobility of character is to be found in this status group, preferring death to degradation. When Caius Vettius, the Pelignian from Italica, was arrested by his own troops in order to be handed over to Pompeius, his slave killed him and then committed suicide so as not to survive his master.

(25) When Caius Gracchus fled from the Aventine hill, his slave Euporus (or Philocrates, according to some sources), who had been an inseparable companion as long as there was some hope of getting to safety, and had protected him in any way he could, finally killed himself over Gracchus' dead body by ripping open his side with his own hand.

(26) After Africanus' father Publius Scipio had fought a battle

against Hannibal, his slave put the wounded man on a horse and brought him back to camp by himself; all the others had abandoned him.

(27) It may not be much to stand by a master who is alive; how do you reply to the fact that we find among slaves a desire to exact vengeance for their masters' deaths? When a slave of King Seleucus was serving the friend by whom his master had been killed, he stabbed him in the middle of the meal to avenge his master.

(28) In one and the same slave I can find two positive qualities which are highly esteemed even amongst the famous and noble: the ability to exercise power properly, and the great-mindedness to reject the exercise of power. (29) The Messenian Anaxilaus — the man who founded Messana in Sicily — was tyrant of Rhegium. He left two small children, and was satisfied to entrust them to the care of his slave Micythus. He was a conscientious guardian, and his rule was so mild that the people of Rhegium did not think it a disgrace to be ruled by a slave. When the boys had grown up, he gave them both their property and their kingdom, and he himself took a small travel allowance and went away; he spent his old age most peacefully at Olympia.

(30) There are many examples showing how useful slaves have been to their communities. In the Punic War, when there were no more men who could be enrolled, those slaves who promised that they would fight in place of their masters were given citizenship and called *volones*, because they offered to do this of their own accord.

(31) And when the Romans had been defeated at the battle of Cannae [see No. 58 above], eight thousand slaves were bought free and served as soldiers; although the Romans captured by Hannibal could have been ransomed at less cost, the Republic nevertheless preferred to rely on slaves during this crisis. And after news had been received of the disastrous defeat at Lake Trasimenus, freedmen were among those called up to serve.

(32) In the Social War, there is the famous example of the brave assistance given by twelve cohorts conscripted from freedmen. We are told that when Caius Caesar appointed men to take the places of those who had been lost, he even took slaves from his friends and made use of their courageous help.

Augustus Caesar levied several cohorts of freedmen for his German and Illyrian campaigns; he called them volunteers.

(33) You shouldn't imagine that such things only happen in our own Republic. When Zopyrion attacked the people of Borysthene, they freed their slaves, gave resident foreigners citizenship, remitted debts — and were thus able to repulse the enemy.

(34) When only fifteen hundred Spartans survived who were capable of bearing arms, the Spartan Cleomenes levied nine thousand warriors from manumitted slaves; and the Athenians also gave their slaves their

freedom when their state had no further manpower resources to fall back upon.

(35) Nor should you think that these virtues are to be found in slaves of the male sex only. There is an equally memorable action performed by slave women, and you won't easily find an example of a deed more useful to the State performed by any noblewoman.

(36) It is such a well-known fact that July 7th is the festival of slave women that the origin and reason for this celebration should not remain unknown either. On that day free women, together with their slaves, make a sacrifice to Juno Caprotina beneath a wild fig-tree; this commemorates the excellent courage shown by slave women in defence of the honour of the State. (37) After Rome had been captured and the Gallic revolt had subsided, the State was really in extreme straits, and the neighbouring tribes, looking for an opportunity to invade Roman territory, appointed Postumius Livius, the dictator of Fidenae, to command them; he sent orders to the Senate requiring them to hand over all mothers of families and unmarried girls if they wanted to keep what was left of their State. (38) The Senate's deliberations were uncertain and hesitant, but a slave girl called Tutela or Philotis promised that she would go across to the enemy with the other slave women, pretending to be their mistresses; and they dressed up as mothers and girls and marched over to the enemy with a lot of people following them in tears, to make it look as though they were grieving. (39) Livius divided them up around the camp, and they plied the men with lots of wine, pretending that it was a feast day for the Romans. When the men had all fallen asleep, they signalled to the Romans from a wild fig-tree that stood next to the camp. (40) A sudden attack resulted in victory; mindful of the benefit received, the Senate ordered all slave women to be manumitted, gave them a dowry from public funds, permitted them to wear the dress they had used on that occasion, renamed that day the 'Caprotine Nones' after the fig-tree from which the signal for the victory had been given, and decided that an annual sacrifice should be celebrated involving the sap which flows from a wild fig-tree, in memory of the deed which I have mentioned.

Macrobius goes on to show that slaves have risen to the heights of philosophy: his list is taken verbatim from the passage of Aulus Gellius (No. **240** above). The section on slaves concludes:

(46) There, I think, you have an argument for not looking down with contempt on slave status, since Jupiter himself showed interest in a slave, and there is evidence that many of them have been trustworthy, prudent, brave — and even philosophers.

SELECT BIBLIOGRAPHY

General

R.H. Barrow, *Slavery in the Roman Empire* (London, 1928)

M.I. Finley (ed.), *Slavery in Classical Antiquity* (Cambridge/New York, 1960)

K. Hopkins, *Conquerors and Slaves* (Cambridge, 1978)

A.H.M. Jones, 'Slavery in the Ancient World', *Economic History Review*, 9 (1956), 185–99

J. Vogt, *Ancient Slavery and the Ideal of Man* (English translation, Oxford, 1974)

W.L. Westermann, *The Slave Systems of Greek and Roman Antiquity* (Philadelphia, 1955); reviews by P.A. Brunt, *JRS*, 48 (1958), 164–70; G.E.M. de Ste Croix, *CR*, 1957, 54–9

On Egypt: I. Biezunska-Malowist, *L'esclavage dans l'Egypte greco-romaine*. I: *Periode ptolemaique*; II: *Periode romaine* (Wroclaw, 1974; 1977)

J.L. Watson (ed.), *Asian and African Systems of Slavery* (Oxford, 1980)

The proceedings of international conferences on ancient slavery have been published as *Actes du Colloque 1970/71/72/73 sur l'esclavage* (Paris, 1972; 1973; 1974; 1976 respectively)

Bibliographical

J. Vogt and N. Brockmeyer, *Bibliographie zur antiken Sklaverei* (Bochum, 1971)

J. Deininger, 'Neue Forschungen zur antiken Sklaverei (1970–1975)', *Historische Zeitschrift*, 222 (1976), 359–74

Arethusa 8: *Marxism and the Classics* (1975) includes articles by D. Konstan, G.E.M. de Ste Croix and others, with a bibliography

N. Brockmeyer, *Antike Sklaverei* (*Erträge der Forschung*, 116: Darmstadt, 1979)

On Chapter One

W. Kunkel, *An Introduction to Roman Legal and Constitutional History* (English translation J.M. Kelly, Oxford, 1973)

W. Ashley, *The Theory of Natural Slavery* (Indiana, 1941)

A.R.W. Harrison, *The Law of Athens*, I (Oxford, 1968), Ch. 6 (slavery) and 7 (freedmen)

G.E.R. Lloyd, *Polarity and Analogy* (Cambridge, 1966)

J.A. Crook, *Law and Life of Rome* (London, 1967)

W.W. Buckland, *The Roman Law of Slavery* (Cambridge, 1908)

R.F. Willetts, *Aristocratic Society in Ancient Crete* (London, 1955)
R. Schlaifer, 'Greek theories of slavery from Homer to Aristotle', *Harvard Studies in Classical Philology*, 47 (1936), 165–204
A.J. Raymer, 'Slavery: the Greco-Roman Defence', *Greece and Rome*, 10 (1940), 17–21
V. Cuffel, 'The Classical Greek Concept of Slavery', *Journal of the History of Ideas*, 27 (1966), 3, 323–42
W.L. Westermann, 'Enslaved Persons who are Free', *American Journal of Philology*, 59 (1938), 1–30

On Chapter Two

H. Michell, *Sparta* (1952), 75–92
P. Cartledge, *Sparta and Lakonia* (London, 1979), esp. Ch. 10 & App. 4
W.G. Forrest, *The Emergence of Greek Democracy* (London, 1966), Ch. 6
O. Murray, *Early Greece* (Glasgow, 1980), Ch. 11
M.I. Finley, 'The Servile Statuses of Ancient Greece', *Revue internationale des droits de l'antiquité*, 10 (1960), 165ff.
    'Between Slavery and Freedom', *Comparative Studies in Society and History*, 6 (1964), 233ff.; both articles reprinted in *Economy and Society of Ancient Greece* (ed. R.P. Saller and B.D. Shaw, London, 1981)
W.V. Harris, *War and Imperialism in Republican Rome 327–70 BC* (Oxford, 1978)
I. Mendelsohn, *Slavery in the Ancient Near East* (New York, 1949)
W.L. Westermann, *Slavery in Ptolemaic Egypt* (New York, 1929)
E.A. Thompson, 'Slavery in Early Germany', *Hermathena*, 89 (1957), 17–29

On Chapter Three

R.F. Willetts, 'Freedmen at Gortyna', *Classical Quarterly*, NS 4 (1954), 216–9
S. Treggiari, *Roman Freedmen during the Late Republic* (Oxford, 1969)
A.M. Duff, *Freedmen in the Early Roman Empire* (Oxford, 1928; reprint 1958)
L.R. Taylor, 'Freedmen and freeborn in the epitaphs of imperial Rome', *American Journal of Philology*, 82 (1961), 113–32
M.L. Gordon, 'The Freedman's Son in Municipal Life', *JRS*, 21 (1931), 65–77
G. Alföldi, 'Die Freilassung von Sklaven und die Struktur der Sklaverei in der römischen Kaiserzeit', *Rivista Storica dell' Antichità*, 2, (1972), 97–129
P. Veyne, 'Vie de Trimalcion', *Annales E.S.C.*, 16 (1961), 213–47

On Chapter Four

V. Ehrenberg, *The People of Aristophanes* (Oxford, 1951²), Ch. 7

W. Beare, 'Slave Costume in New Comedy', *Classical Quarterly*, 43 (1949), 30f

G.E. Duckworth, *The Nature of Roman Comedy* (Princeton, 1952)

G.R. Morrow, *Plato's Law of Slavery* (reprint New York, 1976)

P.W. Harsch, 'The Intriguing Slave in Greek Comedy', *Transactions of the American Philological Association*, 86 (1955), 135–42

G. Vlastos, 'Does Slavery exist in Plato's Republic?' *Classical Philology*, 63 (1968), 291–5

K.W. Welwei, *Unfreie im antiken Kriegsdienst* (Wiesbaden, 1974 & 1977)

J.M. Libowel, 'Galley Slaves in the Second Punic War', *Classical Philology*, 68 (1973), 16–19

R. Macmullen, 'Social Mobility and the Theodosian Code', *JRS*, 54 (1964), 49–53

J.A. Notopoulos, 'The Slaves at the Battle of Marathon', *American Journal of Philology*, 62 (1941), 352–4

F. Bömer, *Untersuchungen über die Religion der Sklaven in Griechenland und Rom* (4 vols., Mainz, 1957–63)

On Chapter Five

M.I. Finley, *The Ancient Economy* (London, 1973); review by M.W. Frederiksen, *JRS*, 65 (1975), 164ff

K. Polanyi, *Primitive, Archaic and Modern Economies* (ed. C. Dalton, New York, 1968)

K. Polanyi, *Trade and Market in the Early Empires* (Glencoe, 1957)

D. Konstan, 'Marxism and Roman Slavery', *Arethusa*, 8 (1975), 145–69

M.M. Austin & P. Vidal-Naquet, *Economic and Social History of Ancient Greece: An Introduction* (English edn, London, 1977)

W.L. Westermann, 'Athenaeus and the slaves at Athens', *Harvard Studies in Classical Philology*, Suppl. Vol. (1941), 451ff. (= *Slavery in Classical Antiquity*, ed. Finley, 73ff.)

A.W. Gomme, *The Population of Athens* (Oxford, 1933)

J. Vogt, *Ancient Slavery and the Ideal of Man* (Oxford, 1974), Ch. 2 (on Utopias)

J. Pečirka, 'The Crisis of the Athenian Polis', *Eirene*, 9 (1976), 5–29 (Marxist interpretation)

A.H.M. Jones, 'The Economic Basis of the Athenian Democracy', *Past and Present*, 1 (1952), 13–31

P.A. Brunt, *Italian Manpower 225 BC – AD 14* (Oxford, 1971)

R. Duncan-Jones, *The Economy of the Roman Empire: Quantitative Studies* (Cambridge, 1974), esp. Ch. 2 and Appendix 10

M.I. Finley, 'Was Greek Civilization based on Slave Labour?', *Historia*,
    8 (1959), 145–64
Ch. G. Starr, 'An Overdose of Slavery', *Journal of Economic History*,
    18 (1958), 17–32
A.M. Burford, 'The Economics of Temple-Building', *Proceedings of the
    Cambridge Philological Society*, NS 11 (1965), 21ff.
M.I. Finley, *Ancient Slavery and Modern Ideology* (London, 1980),
    Chs. 2 & 4

On Chapter Six

J.M. Crook, *Law and Life of Rome* (London, 1967), esp. Ch. 6 (on
    sales)
H.A. Ormerod, *Piracy in the Ancient World* (Oxford, 1924)
M.I. Finley, 'The Black Sea and Danubian Regions and the Slave Trade
    in Antiquity', *Klio*, 40 (1962), 51–9
D. Daube, 'Slave Catching', *Juridical Review*, 64 (1952), 12–28
M.I. Finley, *Aspects of Antiquity* (London, 1963), Ch. 13
J.F. Oates, 'A Rhodian Auction of a Slave-Girl', *Journal of Egyptian
    Archaeology*, 55 (1969), 191–210
K.R. Bradley, 'The Age at Time of Sale of Female Slaves', *Arethusa*,
    11, 1/2 (1978), 243 (argues that female slaves were bought primarily
    neither for their labour value, nor as status symbols, but for breeding:
    see reply by A. Dalby, 'On Female Slaves in Roman Egypt', *Arethusa*,
    12, 2 (1979), 255)

On Chapter Seven

C.A. Forbes, 'The Education and Training of Slaves', *Transactions of
    the American Philological Association*, 86 (1955), 321–60
S.L. Mohler, 'Slave Education in the Roman Empire', *Transactions of
    the American Philological Association*, 71 (1940), 262–80
S. Treggiari, 'Jobs in the Household of Livia', *Papers of the British
    School at Rome*, 43 (1975), 48–77
        'Jobs for Women', *American Journal of Ancient History*, 1
    (1976), 76–104
A.M. Burford, *Craftsmen in Greek and Roman Society* (London, 1977)
W.L. Westermann, 'Industrial Slavery', *Journal of Economic History*,
    2 (1942), 149ff.
T. Frank, *Economic Survey of Ancient Rome* (6 vols., Baltimore,
    1933–40)
M. Rostovtzeff, *Social and Economic History of the Hellenistic World*
    (3 vols., Oxford, 1941)
S. Lauffer, *Die Bergwerkssklaven von Laureion* (2 vols., Mainz, 1956)
O. Davies, *Roman Mines in Europe* (Oxford, 1935)
J.S. Richardson, 'The Spanish Mines and the Development of Provincial
    Taxation in the Second Century BC', *JRS*, 66 (1976), 139–52

M.H. Jameson, 'Agriculture and Slavery in Classical Athens', *Classical Journal*, 73 (1977/78), 122–45 (with Bibliography, esp. on the sociology of peasants)

C. Mossé, *The Ancient World at Work* (English translation, London, 1969)

W.E. Heitland, *Agricola* (Cambridge, 1921)

M. Weber, *Römische Agrargesellschaft* (Stuttgart, 1891; reprint Amsterdam, 1966)

M. Weber, *The Agrarian Sociology of Ancient Civilizations* (English translation, London, 1976)

P.A. Brunt, *Italian Manpower 225 BC – AD 14* (Oxford, 1971)

A.J. Toynbee, *Hannibal's Legacy* (Oxford, 1965)

M.I. Finley, 'Private Farm Tenancy in Italy before Diocletian', *Studies in Roman Property* (Cambridge, 1976), 103–21

R. Beare, 'Were Bailiffs ever free born?', *Classical Quarterly*, NS 28 (1978), 398–401

J.C. Fitzgibbon, 'Ergastula', *Classical News and Views* (Ottawa), 20 (1976), 55–9

P. Garnsey (ed.), *Non-slave Labour in Graeco-Roman Antiquity* (Cambridge, 1980)

On Chapter Eight

A.H.M. Jones, *The Greek City from Alexander to Justinian* (Oxford, 1940), Part IV

O. Jacob, *Les Esclaves Publics a Athènes* (Liège/Paris, 1928; reprint 1980)

F. Millar, *The Emperor in the Roman World* (London, 1977), esp. Chs. 3 and 5

P.R.C. Weaver, *Familia Caesaris* (Cambridge, 1972)

S.I. Oost, 'The Career of M. Antonius Pallas', *American Journal of Philology*, 79 (1958), 11ff.

J. Andreau, *Les Affaires de Monsieur Jucundus* (Rome, 1974)

N. Rouland, 'A propos des servi publici populi Romani', *Chiron*, 7 (1977), 262–78

On Chapter Nine

A.R.W. Harrison, *The Law of Athens*, I (Oxford, 1968), Ch. 6

G.R. Morrow, 'The Murder of Slaves in Attic Law', *Classical Philology* (1937), 210–27

A. Piganiol, 'Les Empereurs parlent aux esclaves', *Romanitas*, I (1958) 7ff.

H. Klees, *Herren und Sklaven* (Wiesbaden, 1975)

S. Treggiari, 'Family Life among the Staff of the Volusii', *Transactions of the American Philological Association*, 105 (1975), 393–401

On Chapter Ten

I.M. Lewis, *Ecstatic Religion* (Harmondsworth, 1971: contemporary parallels)

A. Audollent, *Defixionum Tabellae* (Paris, 1904)

P.R. Coleman-Norton, 'The Apostle Paul and the Roman Law of Slavery', *Studies in Honor of A.C. Johnson* (Princeton, 1951), 155–77

H. Bellen, *Studien zur Sklavenflucht im römischen Kaiserreich* (Wiesbaden, 1971)

M. Hadas, 'Vestal Virgins and runaway Slaves', *Classical World*, 24 (1931), 108

On Chapter Eleven

J. Vogt, *Ancient Slavery and the Ideal of Man* (Oxford, 1974), Chs. 3 & 4

A. Fuks, 'Slave War and Slave Troubles in Chios in the Third Century BC', *Athenaeum*, 46 (1968), 102–11

W.L. Westermann, 'Slave Maintenance and Slave Revolts', *Classical Philology*, 40 (1945), 1ff.

P. Green, 'The First Sicilian Slave War', *Past and Present*, 20 (1961), 10–29

W.G. Forrest & T. Stinton, 'The First Sicilian Slave War', *Past and Present*, 22 (1962), 87ff.

V. Vavrinek, 'Aristonicus of Pergamum', *Eirene*, 13 (1975), 109–29

Z. Rubensohn, 'Was the Bellum Spartacium a Slave Insurrection?', *Rivista di Filologia*, 99 (1971), 290ff.

B. Baldwin, 'Two Aspects of the Spartacus Slave Revolt', *Classical Journal*, 62 (1966), 289ff.

On Chapter Twelve

J. Vogt, *Ancient Slavery and the Ideal of Man* (Oxford, 1974), Chs. 7 & 8

H. Gülzow, *Christentum und Sklaverei* (Bonn, 1969)

S. Scott Bartchy, *First Century Slavery and I Corinthians 7:21* (Missoula, Mont., 1973)

M.T. Griffin, *Seneca: A Philosopher in Politics* (Oxford, 1976)

G.E.M. de Ste Croix, 'Early Christian Attitudes to Property and Slavery', *Church, Society and Politics*, ed. D. Baker (Oxford, 1975), 1–38

J.A.O. Larsen, 'Freedom and its Obstacles in Ancient Greece', *Classical Philology*, 57 (1962), 230–4

Some controversial questions connected with slavery are outside the scope of this selection. One is the extent to which slavery may have been responsible for technological stagnation in antiquity:

B. Farrington, *Head and Hand in Ancient Greece* (London, 1947)

E.R. Dodds, *The Ancient Concept of Progress* (Oxford, 1972)

L. Edelstein, *The Idea of Progress in Classical Antiquity* (Baltimore, 1968)

M.I. Finley, 'Technical Innovation', *Economic History Review*, 18 (1965), 29ff.

Lynn White Jr, *Medieval Technology and Social Change* (Oxford, 1962)

On the problem of the decline of slavery and the theory that it was replaced by 'feudalism':

A.H.M. Jones, 'The Roman Colonate', *Studies in Ancient Society* (ed. M.I. Finley, London, 1974), Ch. xiii

A.H.M. Jones, *The Later Roman Empire* (Oxford, 1964), Ch. 20, p. 795ff.

M. Bloch, 'Comment et Pourquoi Finit l'Esclavage Antique?', *Annales E.S.C.*, 2 (1947), 30–44 & 161–70

F.W. Walbank, *The Awful Revolution* (London, 1968)

P. Anderson, *Passages from Antiquity to Feudalism* (London, 1975)

M.I. Rostovtzeff, 'The Decay of the Ancient World and its Economic Explanations', *Economic History Review*, 2 (1930), 197–214

INDEX OF PASSAGES CITED

Literary Sources
PC = Penguin Classics (Harmondsworth)

Achilles Tatius, Leukippe and Kleitophon, probably second century AD; a Greek romance in which the narrator-hero K. is repeatedly parted from the heroine L. by pirates, shipwrecks, Egyptian robbers etc.; she ends up as a slave at Ephesus, where the two are united.
Tr.: S. Gaselee (Loeb, 1917).

5, 17.1–10	**156**
7, 10.5	**53**
7, 13.2f.	**225**

Aelian (Claudius Aelianus), *c.* AD 170–235; teacher of rhetoric from Praeneste (Palestrina) near Rome, influenced by Stoicism; wrote collections of moralising anecdotes about animals (*de natura animalium*) and on historical and ethnographic themes (*Varia Historia* – 'different stories').
Tr.: A.F. Scholfield (Loeb, 3 vols., 1958–9).

VH 2, 7	**120**

Aeschines (Aiskhinēs), *c.* 397–322 BC; Athenian politician who advocated a 'common peace' to cover all or most Greek states in order to counter Macedonian military intervention; accused by Demosthenes of having accepted bribes from Philip of Macedon, he retaliated by prosecuting Demosthenes' supporter Timarchus for being a notorious profligate (345 BC).
Tr.: C.D. Adams (Loeb, 1919).

1 (*in Timarch.*), 97	**91**

Anaxandrides, 4th century BC dramatist (Middle Comedy; ed. Edmonds, *Fragments of Attic Comedy*, 2, p. 46). **80, 263c**

Antiphanes, *c.* 408–*c.* 334 BC, Athenian dramatist (Middle Comedy; ed. Edmonds, *Fragments of Attic Comedy*, 2, p. 201). **80, 262c**

Antiphon, *c.* 480–411 BC, earliest Athenian orator.
Tr.: K.J. Maidment (Loeb 'Minor Attic Orators' I, 1941).

5 (*Death of Herodes*), 47f.	**181**

Appian (Appianos), from Alexandria, Roman citizen and imperial

Procurator under Antoninus Pius (mid-2nd century AD); wrote a series of histories of the wars the Romans had fought against different nations, including the Roman Civil Wars (books 12–17).
Tr.: H. White (Loeb, 4 vols. 1912–).

Bell. Civ. 1, 1.7	**141**
Bell. Civ. 1, 14.116–120	**232**
Bell. Civ. 2, 17.120	**65**

Apuleius from Madaurus in N. Africa, philosopher-rhetorician, one of the leading Latin writers of the literary flowering of the 2nd century AD called the 'Second Sophistic'. The *Apologia* (*c.* AD 155) is a defence against a charge of having used magic to induce a rich widow called Pudentilla to marry him; the *Metamorphoses* (commonly called *The Golden Ass*) is a romance about a man who turns into an ass but is then saved by the goddess Isis.
Tr.: *Apology*: (French) P. Vallette (Budé, 1960); *The Golden Ass*: R. Graves (PC, 1950).

Apol. 17	**81**
Apol. 47	**96**
Apol. 93	**93**
Metam. 9, 12	**191**

Aristophanes, greatest Athenian writer of comedies; the eleven surviving plays date between 427 and 388 BC; *Acharnians* performed 425; *Wealth* (*Ploutos*) 388; fragments of lost plays were collected and edited by Koerte. *Scholia* are explanatory notes, mainly compiled by late Roman and Byzantine schoolteachers to elucidate obscurities in the text.
Tr.: *Wealth* & *Acharnians*: A.H. Sommerstein (PC, 1973 & 1978).

Ploutos 510–526 & Scholia	**101**
Horae = Fg. 567 Koerte	**223**
Scholia on *Acharnians* 54	**160**

Aristotle (Aristotelēs), 384–322 BC; Greek philosopher with particular interests in the natural sciences and sociology, founder of 'Peripatetic' school. His general political theory as expressed in the *Politics* was based on empirical studies of particular communities: A. and his pupils wrote up the constitutions of 158 Greek states, of which that of Athens (*Athenaiōn Politeia*) survives. Among other works ascribed to Aristotle's school are two books entitled *Oikonomikos*: 1 (translated here as 'The Householder') is a systematic account of household management, 2 ('Finance Management') is a list of methods open to governments to obtain money.
Tr.; *Politics*: J.A. Sinclair (PC, 1962); *Ath. Pol.*: H. Rackham (Loeb, 1935); *Oec.*: (French tr.) B.A. van Groningen & A. Wartelle (Budé, 1968).

Pol. 1253b1 = 1, 2.1–23	**2**
Pol. 1267b14 = 2, 4.13	**159**
Pol. 1299a20 = 4, 12.3	**158**

Athenaeus, c. AD 200, wrote an encyclopaedia called *The Banqueting Sophists* (*Deipnosophistōn*); in the surviving 15 books, experts on various fields discuss a number of scholarly topics, quoting earlier Greek writers whose works are otherwise lost.
Tr.: G.B. Gulick (Loeb, 7 vols., 1927–41).

Augustine, St. (Aurelius Augustinus), AD 354–430, from Thagaste in N. Africa, a philosopher-rhetor converted in AD 386 to a neo-Platonic Christianity; later became bishop of Hippo. As a result of his voluminous scriptural commentaries, sermons and letters, he came to be the main authority of medieval Catholicism.
Text: *PL* vols. 32–47; see Altaner, *Patrology* (Eng. tr. 1960), §88.

Augustus, first Roman Emperor (63 BC–AD 14), left an account of his military and political activities ('res gestae') to be submitted to the Roman Senate after his death; much of the text survives, inscribed on the wall of a Roman temple, now a mosque, at Ankara in Turkey.
Ed. & Tr.: P.A. Brunt & J. M. Moore (Oxford, 1967).

Marcus Porcius *Cato* Censorius, 234–149 BC, Censor in 184 BC; attempted to preserve social stability by asserting traditional values against the effects of increasing wealth and of Greek culture. He thus became a symbol of old-fashioned Italian virtues.
Tr.: W.D. Hooper (Loeb, 1934).

Marcus Tullius *Cicero*, 106–43 BC, the greatest Roman orator; famous for his prosecution of the governor of Sicily, Caius Verres, in 70 BC (*Verrines*) and his attacks on Mark Antony in 44–43BC (*Philippics*). Many other speeches, rhetorical and philosophical treatises and letters survive. The *De Officiis* (*On Duties*) is a guide to proper behaviour addressed to his son.
Tr.: W. Miller (*De Officiis*, Loeb, 1913); L.H.G. Greenwood (*Verr.*, Loeb, 2 vols., 1928–35); C.A. Ker (*Phil.*, Loeb, 1938).

Collatio Legum Mosaicarum et Romanarum, a fourth-century AD essay comparing the Old Testament Jewish and Roman legal codes.

    Coll. 2, 5.5   **188**

Lucius Junius Moderatus *Columella*, *c.* AD 60—5, originally from Gades (Cadiz) in Spain, wrote a systematic treatise on agriculture in twelve books, plus a thirteenth book on trees.

Tr.: H.B. Ash, E.S. Forster & E.H. Heffner (Loeb, 3 vols., 1941—54).

    1, 7.1—7   **147**

    1, 8   **149**

    12, 3.6—9   **157**

Constantine VII Porphyrogenitus, AD 905—59, Byzantine Emperor, excerpted passages from classical writers relevant to good kingship, including Diodorus Siculus.   **229**

Crates (Kratēs), fifth-century BC Athenian dramatist (ed. Edmonds, *Fragments of Attic Comedy*, 1, p. 158).   **80**, 267ef

Cratinus (Kratinos), fifth-century BC Athenian dramatist (ed. Edmonds, *Fragments of Attic Comedy*, 1, p. 74).   **80**, 267e

Demosthenes, 384—322 BC, Athenian orator and politician, opposing Macedonian hegemony over Greece; also wrote many 'private' orations on behalf of others.

Tr.: A.T. Murray (*Private Orations*, Loeb, 1936—).

    21: *In Meid.* 47   **183**

    27: *In Aphob.* 9ff.   **86**

    59: *In Neaer.* 29—32   **22**

Dieukhidas from Megara, (lost) fourth-century BC historian.

    Jacoby, *FGrHist.* 485 F7   **80**, 262e—263a

Digest, collection of authoritative statements on Roman law by earlier jurists, edited at the instigation of the Emperor Justinian and promulgated in AD 533.

Ed. Th. Mommsen (Berlin, 1889).

    1, 5.4 (Florentinus)   **1**

    1, 5.5 (Marcianus)   **4**

    1, 14.3 (Ulpian)   **67**

    5, 3.27 (Ulpian)   **124**

    11, 3.1(4)f. — 2 (Ulpian & Paulus)   **11**

    11, 4.1 (Ulpian)   **212**

    14, 5.8 (Paulus)   **137**

    18, 1.42 (Marcianus)   **185**

    21, 1.31(21) (Ulpian)   **104**

Dio Cassius Cocceianus, Roman Senator of Bithynian origin; consul for the second time in AD 229; wrote a comprehensive history of Rome, in Greek.
Tr.: E. Cary (9 vols., Loeb, 1914–27).

Dio Chrysostom, *c.* AD 40–111, orator from Prusa in Bithynia, in later life influenced by Stoic philosophy.
Tr.: J.W. Cohoon & H.L. Crosby (5 vols., Loeb, 1932–51).

Diodorus Siculus, first century BC, from Agyrion in Sicily, wrote a universal history in Greek, influenced by Stoic ideas; the sources he copies (often verbatim) include Polybius and Posidonius.
Tr.: C.H. Oldfather and others (Loeb, 12 vols., 1933–67).

Diogenes Laertius, late third century AD, wrote ten books containing biographical and anecdotal material about Greek philosophers.
Tr.: R.D. Hicks (2 vols., Loeb, 1925).

5, 13 & 72   **95**

Dionysius of Halicarnassus, Greek teacher of rhetoric at Rome, 30–8 BC; wrote a history of Rome down to the First Punic War, stressing that Rome had always been part of the 'civilised', Greek world.
Tr.: E. Cary (7 vols., Loeb, 1937–50).
    4, 24.4–6   **69**

Ephorus, fourth century BC, wrote a (lost) history of Greece down to 340 BC.
    Jacoby, *FGrHist*. 70 F29   **80**, 263f.

Epicrates, fourth century BC, from Ambracia, dramatist (Middle Comedy); (ed. Edmonds, *Fragments of Attic Comedy*, 2, p. 350).
                                                      80, 262d

Euphorion, third-century BC Hellenistic poet and scholar; in charge of the library at Antioch in Syria.   **80**, 263e

Euripides, Athenian tragedian †406 BC; 18 surviving plays include the *Suppliants* (Hiketidai).
Tr. of *Suppliants*: *Orestes and other Plays*, P. Vellacott (PC, 1972).
    Suppl. 267ff.   **222**
    Phrixus = Fg. 827 Nauck   **80**, 264c

Festus Sextus Pompeius, second century AD Grammarian, probably from Narbonne, produced an edition of an earlier glossary by Verrius Flaccus.
Text: W.M. Lindsay (Leipzig, 1913).
    p. 159 L   **28**

Florentinus, Roman jurist, probably late second century AD.
    Instit. 9 (= D 1, 5.4)   **1**

Sextus Julius *Frontinus*, Consul AD 98 & 100, curator of Rome's aqueducts AD 97; wrote books on military subjects, the water supply and land-surveying.
Tr.: C.E. Bennett (Loeb, 1925).
    De aquis 2, 96; 98; 116–118   **167**

Gaius, possibly late second century AD; otherwise unknown Roman jurist, wrote the most influential introductory handbook for law students, as well as various commentaries on particular legal subjects.
Edn. and tr.: F. de Zulueta (Oxford, 1946–53).
    Instit. 1, 1.8–55   **5**
    Instit. 2, 86–93   **8**
    Ed. Prov. 14 (= D 38, 1.19)   **43**

Text: W.M. Lindsay (OCT, 1911).

9, 3.38	**58**

Isocrates, Athenian orator and educational theorist, 436—338 BC; in the *Panathenaicus* (*c.* 342—339 BC), he compares Athens and Sparta, to the advantage of the former.
Tr.: G.B. Norlin-L. van Hook (Loeb, 1928—45).

Pan. 181	**182**

Justinian, (Eastern) Roman Emperor AD 527—65; apart from building the Church of Hagia Sophia at Constantinople and attempting to reconquer the western Mediterranean, he was also responsible for the definitive codification of Roman law called the *Corpus Juris Civilis*, undertaken under the chairmanship of the lawyer Tribonian, and consisting of the *Codex Justinianus* (imperial legislation), the *Digest* (jurists' opinions) and the *Institutes* (an officially prescribed course for law schools).
Codex and *Institutes*: ed. P. Krueger (Berlin, 1888).

C 3, 36.5	**199**
7, 8.6 & 10.6	**9**
7, 9.1	**166**
7, 12.2	**10**
I 1, 8.2	**226**

Livy (Titus Livius), *c.* 59 BC—AD 17, wrote a patriotic history of Rome from its foundation down to 9 BC; 35 of the original 142 books survive, together with summaries (*Periochae*) of the others.
Tr.: B.O. Foster and others (Loeb, 14 vols., 1919—59); most of the surviving books in PC (tr. H. Bettenson; A. de Selincourt).

6, 12.4f	**143**
6, 27.8	**18**
8, 28.1—9	**19**
26, 27.1—9	**76**
32, 26.4—18	**227**
39, 29.8	**228**
Per. 77	**77**

Lysias, teacher of rhetoric and professional speechwriter; resident alien at Athens (Metic) between 412 and *c.* 380 BC.
Tr.: W.R.M. Lamb (Loeb, 1930).

4, 12—17	**177**
5, 3—5	**74**
12, 19	**90**
24, 5f.	**85**

2 Maccabees, one of the books of the Greek version of the Old Testament (*Septuagint*); a summary of a five-volume history of the successful revolt of the Hasmonean family against the Seleucids (175—161 BC), written in the late second century BC by Jason of Cyrene.

4, 35.6   **107**
5, 21.10   **110**

Caius *Petronius*, Arbiter, author of a Latin romance satirising the Greek genre of the romantic novel. Only sections of the original 16 books remain; one of the best-known is an account of a dinner given by a wealthy freedman (*Cena Trimalchionis*).
Tr.: J. Sullivan (PC 1965).

53   **82**
57   **79**
75–6   **47**
103   **218**

Pherecrates, fifth-century BC Athenian dramatist (ed. Edmonds, *Fragments of Attic Comedy*, 1, p. 208).   **80**, 263b

Pseudo-*Phocylides*: hexameter poem with 230 lines of moralising apophthegms, many based on Old Testament teaching; probably compiled by a Hellenistic Jew (first or second century AD?), but ascribed to the sixth century BC Milesian gnomic writer Phocylides.
Text: Teubner *Theognis* (ed. Young, 1961, pp. 95–112).
223–7   **207**

Photius, c. 820–93, Patriarch of Constantinople; resisted Papal claims to supremacy and tried to foster Greek culture, e.g. by compiling a *Bibliotheca* ('library') of excerpts from 280 Greek prose writers whose full texts are now lost, including Diodorus Siculus.
                                                 229, 230

Phylarchus, from Naucratis in Egypt, third century BC; author of (lost) history of the period 272–220 BC.
Jacoby, *FGrHist*. 81 F43   **80**, 271ef

Plato, 427–347 BC, the Athenian philosopher.
Laws tr. P.J. Saunders (PC 1970).
Leg. 776b–778a   **80**, 264d–265b

Pliny the Elder (Gaius Plinius Secundus), c. AD 23–79, Roman officer and administrative official; apart from lost historical works, he wrote a Natural History in 37 books, the basis of much 'scientific' knowledge throughout the Middle Ages.
Tr.: H. Rackham, W.H.S. Jones & D.E. Eichholz (10 vols., Loeb, 1938–62).

7, 12.56   **98**
7, 39.128   **99**
12, 5.12   **169**
12, 32.62   **131**
14, 5.47f.   **46**

Pliny the Younger (Caius Plinius Caecilius Secundus), *c.* 61 to after AD 112; as consul in AD 100, he thanked the Emperor Trajan for his appointment in a surviving panegyric; also published a collection of ten books of *Letters*, of which the last is a dossier of his official correspondence with Trajan when he was governor of Bithynia in AD 110—12. Tr.: B. Radice (2 vols., Loeb, 1969); *Letters* only (PC, 1963).

Plutarch (Ploutarkhos) from Chaeronea in Boeotia, *c.* AD 45—120; writer of popular philosophical essays, including a series of moralising biographies comparing figures from Roman and Greek history. Tr.: (*Lives*) B. Perrin (11 vols., Loeb, 1914—26); *Crassus* is in *The Fall of the Roman Republic*, tr. R. Warner (PC, 1958); *Cato* in *Makers of Rome*, tr. I. Scott-Kilvert (PC, 1965).

Polybius, *c.* 200—120 BC, Hellenistic historian, wrote an account of the period 220—167 BC in order to explain to his fellow-Greeks how the Romans had been able to conquer the Mediterranean world. Tr.: W.R. Paton (Loeb, 6 vols., 1922—27); I. Scott-Kilvert (PC, 1979).

Pomponius, Roman jurist of the mid-second century AD.

Posidonius, *c.* 135—51 BC, Stoic philosopher from Apamea in Syria, largely responsible for the reception of Stoicism by the Romans; wrote a (lost) history of the period 144—85 BC, used by Strabo and

Diodorus Siculus (see **192, 229, 230**).

Publilius Syrus, mid-first century BC writer of mimes for performance at Rome (see No. **108**); a collection of moral apophthegms (*Sententiae*) occurring in his mimes was made after his death.
Tr.: J.W. & A.M. Duff (Loeb, *Minor Latin Poets*, 1934).

Quintilian (Marcus Fabius Quintilianus), *c.* AD 35–100, most famous Roman teacher of rhetoric.
Tr.: H.W. Butler (Loeb, 4 vols., 1920–2).

Salvian, *c.* AD 400–70, Christian writer from Gaul: presbyter at Marseilles; the theme of his eight books *The Governance of God* (*de Gubernatione Dei*) is that God has allowed the Germanic barbarians to occupy the Roman Empire to punish the Romans (who as Christians ought to be morally perfect) for their sins.
Tr.: E.M. Sanford (New York, 1966); see Altaner, *Patrology* (English trans. 1960), §90.6.

Lucius Annaeus *Seneca*, *c.* 4 BC–AD 65, Stoic philosopher and political adviser to the Emperor Nero (called 'The Younger' to distinguish him from his father, a famous rhetor); wrote tragedies, essays and letters, largely on ethical themes.
Tr.: J.W. Basore, *Moral Essays* (Loeb, 3 vols., 1928–35); R. Campbell, *Letters from a Stoic* (PC, 1969).

Publius Papinius *Statius*, *c.* AD 40–96, author of epic (*Thebaid* – story of the seven against Thebes) and a collection of poems of various genres entitled *Silvae* ('Woods').
Tr.: J.H. Mozley (Loeb, 1928).

Strabo, *c.* 64/3 BC to after AD 23, from Amaseia in Pontus, historical

and geographical writer with Stoic inclinations, using earlier material (including Polybius).
Tr.: H.L. Jones (Loeb, 8 vols., 1923–32).

7, 3.12	**12**
7, 7.3	**118**
11, 2.3	**103**
14, 5.2	**106**

Gaius *Suetonius*, Tranquillus, *c*. 70 to after AD 121, State Secretary to the Emperor Hadrian, wrote short biographies of Latin poets and other literary celebrities (*de viris illustribus*), including a surviving section on grammar and rhetoric teachers (*de grammaticis et rhetoribus*), as well as longer biographies of Julius Caesar, Augustus, and his ten successors as Roman emperors.
Tr.: R. Graves *The Twelve Caesars* (PC, 1957); J.C. Rolfe (Loeb, 2 vols., 1914).

Julius 42	**142**
Augustus 21.2	**119**
Augustus 32.1	**111**
Augustus 40.3f.	**6**
Augustus 42.2	**70**
Tiberius 8	**112**
Claudius 25.1	**37**
Claudius 25.2	**203**
Gramm. 7, 11–13, 15, 23, 27	**133**
Gramm. 21	**121**

Quintus Aurelius *Symmachus*, *c*. 345–AD 402, leading representative of pagan culture in the Roman Senate, opposing attempts of the Emperor Theodosius and St Ambrose of Milan to impose Christianity; fragments of speeches as well as over 900 letters survive.
Text: ed. O. Seeck, *Monumenta Germaniae Historica*, *Auctores Antiquissimi*, vol. 6 (Berlin, 1883).

Ep. 9, 140	**215**

Publius (?) Cornelius *Tacitus*, *c*. AD 55/56–early second century AD, Roman orator, politician and historian; the *Annals* cover AD 14–68, the *Histories* 69–96. There is also a theoretical essay on rhetoric (*Dialogus de oratoribus*), a life of his father-in-law (*Agricola*) and an ethnographical essay on Germany (*Germania*).
Tr.: H. Mattingly *Germania* (PC, 1948), M. Grant *Annals* (PC, 1956).

Annals 4, 27	**233**
Annals 12, 65.1	**176**
Germ. 24.3–25.3	**20**

St *Theodoret* (Theodōrētos), bishop of Cyrrhus in Syria 423–*c*.AD 466, writer of pastoral letters, Christian apologetics, hagiography and Church history.
Text: PG 80–4; see Altaner, *Patrology* (English trans., 1960), § 73.

Comm. in I Cor. 7.21–3   **241**

Code of *Theodosius*, the first systematic collection of Roman imperial legislation (occasionally with short passages of elucidatory comment called *interpretationes*), compiled in AD 438 at the instigation of Theodosius II (reigned 408–450).
Tr.: C. Pharr (New York, 1952, reprint 1979).

3, 3.1	**123**
4, 7.1	**29**
4, 8.5 (*interp.*)	**14**
4, 12	**168**
5, 10.1	**122**
7, 13.8	**62**
7, 13.16	**63**
9, 12.1	**187**

Theopompus, late-fifth-century BC Athenian dramatist (ed. Edmonds, *Fragments of Attic Comedy* 1, p. 874).   **80**, 264a

Theopompus, c. 377–320 BC, pupil of Isocrates; wrote (lost) histories of Greece (*Hellenika*, 410–394 BC; *Philippika*, 360–336).

Jacoby, *FGrHist.* 115 F13	**80**, 272a
F122	**80**, 265bc
F171	**80**, 271cd

Thucydides (Thoukydidēs), late-fifth-century BC Athenian historian, wrote an account of the war between the Athenians and Spartans from 431 up to 410 BC.
Tr.: R. Warner (PC, 1954).

7, 27.5	**211**

Timaeus, c. 356–260 BC, from Tauromenion (Taormina), wrote (lost) history of Sicily and S. Italy.

Jacoby, *FGrHist.* 566 F5	**80**, 272b
F11	**80**, 264cd

Ulpian (Domitius Ulpianus), from Tyre in Phoenicia, Roman jurist; Praetorian Prefect in 222/3 AD; his writings, including a vast commentary on the Praetor's edict (the basic text of Roman civil law) are cited more frequently in the *Digest* than those of any other authority.

De Censu. (= D 50, 15.4(5))	**104**
Edict. 1 (= D 11, 4.1)	**212**
Edict. 15 (= D 5, 3.27)	**124**
Edict. 23 (= D 11, 3.1(4)f.–2)	**11**
Edict. 50 (= D 29, 5.1)	**180**
Edict. 57 (or 77) (= D 47, 10.15(34))	**189**
Edict. 66 (= D 37, 15.9)	**34**
Edict. Cur. Aed. (= D 21, 1.31(21))	**104**

Marcus Terentius *Varro*, 116–27 BC, Roman soldier, politican and polymath; of his voluminous writings, three books on agriculture (*rerum rusticarum*) and six on Latin philology (*de lingua latina*) survive. Tr.: *LL*, R.G. Kent (Loeb, 2 vols., 1938); *RR*, Hooper & Ash (Loeb, 1934).

Xenophon, c. 425 to after 355 BC, Athenian soldier, historian and writer on moral philosophy; his works include personal reminiscences of Socrates (*Apomnemaneumata Sokratous/Memorabilia*), essays on household management (*Oikonomikos*) and a proposal to reform the Athenian state revenues (*Poroi*). Tr.: *Mem. & Oec.*, E.C. Marchant (Loeb, 1923); *Mem.*, H. Tredennick (PC, 1970); *Poroi*, E.C. Marchant (Loeb *Scripta Minora*, 1925).

Inscriptions and Papyri

Bruns No. 132 (p. 330 = *CIL* 3.2 p. 959; No. xxv): One of a series of contracts found at Verespatak in Transylvania (Dacia) in 1855, recording purchases by Roman soldiers (4 Oct. AD 160).   **105**

Bruns No. 157 B (p. 359): Document No. 143 from the archive of Lucius Caecilius Jucundus, found at Pompeii in 1875 (10 July AD 59).
164

Bruns No. 159.3 (p. 362): Rewards for recapturing two Egyptian fugitives (146 BC).   **214**

References already included in the *Index of Passages Cited* are not repeated here.